Home Recording For Musicians For Dummies, 2nd Edition

Cheat Sheet

Producer's Glossary of Terms

W9-BZB-360

If you're going to produce your own music, you need to know how to talk like a producer (you know, muttering incoherent metaphors about colors, weather, and food to describe music). This glossary lets you in on the secret (or not-so-secret) language of the record producer. Read and be enlightened (or not)!

Air: Refers to frequencies above 12 kHz. A quality that allows the song to breathe a little. A feeling of spaciousness. Similar to shimmer.

Angular: This means nothing. If people use this term, ask them to explain themselves. They've just gone over the deep end.

Body: The frequency range of an instrument where it produces its richest tone, often around 800 Hz to 1 kHz.

Boomy: Too much low-frequency energy. To get rid of boominess, cut frequencies below 120 Hz.

Boxy: Too much 400-Hz to 600-Hz energy.

Bright: Lots of high end, usually referring to frequencies above 8 kHz.

Brown: A term for the sound that Eddie Van Halen used to get from his guitar amp. Brown usually refers to a low midrange quality (200 to 400 Hz) — not to be confused with muddy, however.

Cold: Lacking warmth. Often used as a derogatory term to describe digital recordings. It could also mean too much high end in a recording. In this case, reduce frequencies above 10 kHz slightly.

Crisp: See bright.

Dark: Lacking high-frequency brightness. Could also be dull.

Depth: Full-bodied sound. Often the result of enhancing frequencies just above and below the main body of the instrument.

Dry: An instrument without effects applied to it.

Dull: See dark.

Edgy: An extreme of punchy, bordering on uncomfortable, depending on the music.

Grainy: Poor digital resolution.

Harsh: Another derogatory term for digital recordings. This could also refer to frequencies in the 5-kHz to 8-kHz range that are too pronounced. Reduce harsh frequencies to suit your taste.

Muddy: Lack of definition in a sound, often as a result of too much low-mid (400- to 800-Hz) energy.

Nasally: Too much midrange energy, around 1 to 2 kHz in some instruments.

Orange: Get this guy out of your studio; he's just making stuff up!

Plosives: The result of saying or singing p sounds.

Presence: A nice balance between an instrument's attack and its main tone. Usually attained by adding 2- to 5-kHz frequencies.

Punchy: A nice attack and sense of presence. A punchy sound can come from your performance, your instrument, or the effective use of compression (or all three). To create punch with a compressor, set the threshold to compress just a couple of decibels (dB), set the attack long enough so that the initial transient passes through uncompressed, and set the release so that it doesn't remain longer than the instrument and so that it isn't short enough to pump the compressor.

Round: Sometimes refers to sounds that have a pronounced midrange quality. When a sound is round, bass and treble are slightly reduced.

Shimmer: Frequencies above 12 kHz. Similar to air.

Sibilance: Pronounced s sounds.

Smooth: The opposite of punchy. Smooth sounds are those that have an even level to them. The body of the sound is not overshadowed by the initial attack.

Sweet: Good or great, depending on how enthusiastically you use the word.

Warm: Lacking harshness or coldness. This is a catch-all term used to describe anything from analog equipment to a pleasing quality that can't be put into words. Use this term around nonrecording people whenever you want to sound like you know what you're talking about. When someone else uses this term repeatedly, take his or her recording advice with a grain of salt (a large one).

Wet: An instrument with effects applied to it.

Home Recording For Musicians For Dummies, 2nd Edition

Cheat Sheet

Effects Parameters

Every effect (signal processor) that you use in your studio has certain settings, called parameters, that you can adjust to tailor the sound to your liking. This part of the cheat sheet outlines the parameters for the two most common signal processors: the reverb and the compressor.

Reverb

Reverb is a natural part of every sound and represents the way a room sounds as a sound bounces around it.

- ✔ **Room size/type:** Whether you use a reverb patch within your DAW (Digital Audio Workstation) or a separate outboard reverb unit, you can choose the type of reverb that you want to use. You have the option of a room, hall, or plate (a type of reverb that uses a metal plate to create the sound). As well, you can choose the size of the room in either meters or feet.
- ✔ **Decay:** The decay is the length of time that the reverb lasts. Larger or more reflective rooms produce a longer decay.
- ✔ **Predelay:** The predelay is the amount of time from the sound's beginning to the start of the reverb (described in milliseconds). Predelay helps to define the initial sound signal by separating it from the reverb. This parameter is essential in making your reverb sound natural.
- ✔ **Density:** The density parameter controls the level of the early reflections (the first few milliseconds of the reverb sound). This parameter enables you to simulate different sizes of rooms because, in a larger room, the main section of a reverb takes longer to reach you.
- ✔ **Diffusion:** Diffusion affects the density of the reflections in the main section of the reverb sound. A higher diffusion setting results in a thicker sound.

Compressor

The compressor is used to compress the dynamic range of your signal and is used in all the stages of recording: tracking, mixing, and mastering.

- ✔ **Threshold:** The threshold setting dictates the level at which the compressor starts to act on the signal. This is listed in dB (decibels).
- ✔ **Ratio:** The ratio is the amount that the compressor affects the signal. For example, a ratio of 2:1 means that if a signal goes 1dB over the threshold setting, its output from the compressor is only ½ dB louder.
- ✔ **Attack:** The attack knob controls how soon the compressor kicks in. The attack is defined in milliseconds (ms); the lower the number, the faster the attack.
- ✔ **Release:** The release parameter controls how long the compressor continues affecting the signal after it has started. Like the attack, the release is defined in milliseconds.
- ✔ **Gain:** You use the gain knob to adjust the level of the signal going out of the compressor. This is listed in decibels. Because adding compression generally reduces the overall level of the sound, you use this control to raise the level back to where it was going in.

For Dummies: Bestselling Book Series for Beginners

Home Recording
For Musicians

FOR

DUMMIES®

2ND EDITION

Home Recording For Musicians

FOR DUMMIES®

2ND EDITION

by Jeff Strong

Wiley Publishing, Inc.

Home Recording For Musicians For Dummies®, 2nd Edition

Published by
Wiley Publishing, Inc.
111 River Street
Hoboken, NJ 07030-5774

www.wiley.com

Copyright © 2005 by Wiley Publishing, Inc., Indianapolis, Indiana

Published by Wiley Publishing, Inc., Indianapolis, Indiana

Published simultaneously in Canada

For general information on our other products and services, please contact our Customer Care Department within the U.S. at 800-762-2974, outside the U.S. at 317-572-3993, or fax 317-572-4002.

For technical support, please visit www.wiley.com/techsupport.

Wiley also publishes its books in a variety of electronic formats. Some content that appears in print may not be available in electronic books.

Library of Congress Control Number: 2005924600

ISBN-13: 978-0-7645-8884-6

ISBN-10: 0-7645-8884-2

Manufactured in the United States of America

10 9 8 7 6 5 4 3 2

2O/RZ/QX/QV/IN

WILEY

About the Author

Jeff Strong is the author of seven books including *Pro Tools All-in-One Desk Reference For Dummies* and *PC Recording Studios For Dummies*. Jeff is also the Director of the REI Institute, a MusicMedicine research organization and therapy provider. Jeff graduated from the Percussion Institute of Technology at the Musician's Institute in Los Angeles in 1983 and has either worked in or owned a recording studio since 1985. Every week, he records dozens of custom client CDs using the equipment and techniques found in the pages of this book. He has also released ten commercially available CDs, four of which can be found at www.reiinstitute.com.

Author's Acknowledgments

I owe a hearty thanks to Senior Acquisitions Editor Steve Hayes and my agent Carol Susan Roth for getting behind the first edition of this book and making this second edition possible. Also my gratitude goes out to project editor Kim Darosett and copy editor John Edwards who helped make an already great book even better. Thanks, as well, goes to technical editor Erik Scull for keeping me on track and up-to-date on the many technical aspects of this subject.

As always, I'm grateful to my family (Beth and Tovah) and my many friends (you know who you are) who indulge me in my obsession with recording and recording gear.

Publisher's Acknowledgments

We're proud of this book; please send us your comments through our online registration form located at www.dummies.com/register/.

Some of the people who helped bring this book to market include the following:

Acquisitions, Editorial, and Media Development

Project Editor: Kim Darosett

Senior Acquisitions Editor: Steven Hayes

Copy Editor: John Edwards

Technical Editor: Erik Scull

Editorial Manager: Leah Cameron

Media Development Manager: Laura VanWinkle

Media Development Supervisor: Richard Graves

Editorial Assistant: Amanda Foxworth

Cartoons: Rich Tennant (www.the5thwave.com)

Composition Services

Project Coordinator: Nancee Reeves

Layout and Graphics: Carl Byers, Andrea Dahl, Joyce Haughey, Lynsey Osborn, Heather Ryan

Proofreaders: Laura Albert, Leeann Harney, Jessica Kramer, Carl William Pierce, TECHBOOKS Production Services

Indexer: TECHBOOKS Production Services

Publishing and Editorial for Technology Dummies

Richard Swadley, Vice President and Executive Group Publisher

Andy Cummings, Vice President and Publisher

Mary Bednarek, Executive Acquisitions Director

Mary C. Corder, Editorial Director

Publishing for Consumer Dummies

Diane Graves Steele, Vice President and Publisher

Joyce Pepple, Acquisitions Director

Composition Services

Gerry Fahey, Vice President of Production Services

Debbie Stailey, Director of Composition Services

Contents at a Glance

Table of Contents

Introduction

· ·

*I*f you're like most musicians, you've been noodling around on your instrument for a while and have finally decided to take the plunge and get serious about recording your ideas. You may just want to throw a few ideas down onto tape (or hard drive) or capture those magic moments that you have with your band. Or you may want to compose, record, produce, and release the next great platinum album. Either way, you'll find that having a home studio can give you hours of satisfaction.

Well, you've chosen a great time to get involved in audio recording. Not long ago, you needed to go to a commercial recording studio and spend thousands of dollars if you wanted to make a decent-sounding recording. Now you can set up a first-class recording studio in your garage or spare bedroom and create CDs that sound as good as those coming out of top-notch studios (that is, if you know how to use the gear).

Home Recording For Musicians For Dummies, 2nd Edition, is a great place to start exploring the gear and techniques you need to create great CDs (if I do say so myself). This book introduces you to home recording and helps you to get your creative ideas out into the world.

About This Book

Home Recording For Musicians For Dummies not only introduces you to the technology of home recording but also presents basic multitrack recording techniques. In the pages to follow, you find out about the many types of digital recording systems that are available, including computer-based systems, all-in-one recorder/mixer systems (called *studio-in-a-box systems*), and stand-alone recorders that require separate mixers and effects processors.

You get acquainted with the basic skills that you need to make high-quality recordings. These skills can save you countless hours of experimenting and searching through owner's manuals. Some of these skills are as follows:

✔ You discover the ins and outs of using the various pieces of equipment in your studio.

✔ You explore tried-and-true engineering techniques, such as microphone choice and placement.

   ✔ You discover the concepts of multitracking, mixing, and mastering.

   ✔ You find out how to turn all your music into complete songs and discover how to assemble and release an album.

Home Recording For Musicians For Dummies puts you on the fast track toward creating great-sounding CDs because it concentrates on showing you skills that you can use right away and doesn't bother you with tons of technical jargon or useless facts.

Not-So-Foolish Assumptions

I have to admit that when I wrote this book, I made a couple of assumptions about you, the reader (and you know what happens when you ASSume anything). First, I assume that you're interested in recording your music (or someone else's) in your home and not interested in reading about underwater basket weaving (a fascinating subject, I'm sure, but not appropriate for a book entitled *Home Recording For Musicians For Dummies*).

I assume that you'll most likely record your music using a digital hard-drive recording system because these are the most common types of systems available. I also assume that you're relatively new to the recording game and not a seasoned professional. (Although if you were, you would find that this book is a great reference for many audio engineering fundamentals.) Oh, and I assume that you play a musical instrument or are at least familiar with how instruments function and how sound is produced.

Other than these things, I don't assume that you play a certain type of music or that you ever intend to try to "make it" in the music business (or even that you want to treat it as a business at all).

How This Book Is Organized

Home Recording For Musicians For Dummies is organized so that you can find the information that you want quickly and easily. Each section contains chapters that cover a specific part of the home recording process. In Part I, you discover the tools of your auditory craft and get them up and running, while Part II introduces you to general recording practices. Part III helps you get the best sound that you can from your instruments, and Part IV digs into the multitrack recording process. Part V shows you how to turn it all into music and helps you share your music with others, and Part VI gives you tips and resources to keep your music growing.

Part I: Home Recording Studio Basics

Part I introduces you to the basics of home recording. Chapter 1 introduces you to the process of home recording and explains the basic gear that you need to get started. Chapter 2 opens a huge can of worms and explores the many types of digital recording systems available to help you find the best system for your needs. This part ends with Chapter 3, which shows you how to set up a system so that it is easy to work with and sounds good. You also find out how to get your room to work well for you.

Part II: Recording 101

Part II gets into more gear talk — this time giving you a hands-on experience. Chapter 4 acquaints you with the role of signal flow in audio recording and shows you how this flow works in a variety of different systems. Chapter 5 demystifies MIDI (Musical Instrument Digital Interface) and gives you practical advice on how to use this powerful communication tool to enhance your music. Chapter 6 allows you to get inside the world of microphones. You find out what kinds of mics are available, how they work, and which ones work best for different situations.

Part III: Getting Ready to Record

Part III helps you dot your *T*s and cross your *I*s (er, you know what I mean) when getting your instrument's sound into your system. Chapter 7 shows you how to set the best levels for all your instruments, whether they are plugged directly into your system or miked. Chapter 8 introduces you to the art of microphone placement and how it relates to the sound you get from your instrument, and Chapter 9 gets down and dirty with some suggestions for miking a bunch of common instruments.

Part IV: Laying Track: Starting to Record

Part IV gets into the meat of recording music. Chapter 10 explains the purpose of multitrack recording and shows you how to do it to get the best sound possible. Chapter 11 helps you start recording audio tracks. This chapter gives you the specifics on every aspect of recording, including doing overdubs and replacing missed-notes (or musical) sections using a punch procedure. Chapter 12 takes you into the world of MIDI sequencing, where you can record MIDI performance data and tweak the sound (and the performance later). It also guides you through the process of editing data — moving, fixing, deleting, and so on. This process can be done in two ways (visually or aurally), and you explore both in this chapter.

Part V: Turning Your Tracks into a Finished Song

Part V helps you to take all your individual tracks and blend them together to create a finished song. Chapter 13 helps you clean up your tracks with editing. Both audio and MIDI editing are covered in detail. Chapter 14 shows you how to get your tracks to fit and sound good as a unit through the process of mixing. Chapter 15 explores how you can use effects, not only to make your music sound as natural as possible but also to help you create special effects that can add interest for your listeners. Chapter 16 demystifies the mastering process. You discover what mastering is and how to use it to make your music sound like the CDs at the music store. Chapter 17 helps you break out of your cocoon so that you can share your finished music with others by showing you how to make copies of your CD, format your music for Internet distribution, and promote your music to gain listeners.

Part VI: The Part of Tens

A staple of every *For Dummies* book, this Part of Tens contains some information that you can use every day. From ten great home recording resources (Chapter 18) to invaluable home recording tips (Chapter 19), this Part of Tens has it all (well, almost).

Icons Used in This Book

As with all *For Dummies* books, I use a few icons to help you along your way. These icons are as follows.

Certain techniques are very important and bear repeating. This icon gives you those gentle nudges to keep you on track.

Throughout the book, I include some technical background on a subject. This icon shows up in those instances so that you know to brace yourself for some dense information.

This icon highlights expert advice and ideas that can help you to produce better recordings.

This icon lets you know about those instances when you could damage your equipment, your ears, or your song.

Where to Go from Here

This book is set up so that you can read it from cover to cover and progressively build on your knowledge or you can jump around and read only those parts that interest you at the time. For instance, if you are getting ready to record your band and need some ideas on how to get the best sound out of your microphones, go straight to Chapter 8. If you're new to this whole home recording thing and want to know what kind of gear to buy, check out Chapters 1 and 2.

For the most part, starting at Chapter 1 gets you up to speed on my way of thinking and can help you understand some of what I discuss in later chapters.

Part I
Home Recording Studio Basics

The 5th Wave   By Rich Tennant

I thought you were bringing your synthesizer.

In this part . . .

*P*art I introduces you to the basics of home recording and helps you get your studio up and running.
Chapter 1 offers an overview of what you need to build
your studio and how the home recording process works.
Chapter 2 introduces you to the many types of digital
recording systems and helps you choose the best system
for your needs and goals. Chapter 3 guides you through
the process of setting up your studio so that it sounds
good and is easy to work in.

Chapter 1

Understanding Home Recording

*A*udio recording is a fun and exciting activity. Being able to put down your musical ideas and craft them into an album is nearly every musician's dream. The only problem is the learning curve that comes with being able to record your music at home; most musicians would rather spend their time and energy making music.

In this chapter, I help you get a handle on the basics of home recording and show you what's involved in the process. You discover the basic components of a recording studio and get some ideas about the gear you need to get first. In addition, you explore the multitracking process and find out what's involved in mixing your tracks. You move on to explore mastering and find out ways to get your music to your listeners.

Examining the Anatomy of a Home Studio

Whether it's a $100 portastudio or a million-dollar commercial facility, all recording studios contain the same basic components. This is an area where many people get lost and one about which I receive the most e-mails. As you glimpse into the recording world, you'll inevitably think that this will cost way too much and be way too complicated. Well, it can be. But it can also be pretty simple and cost efficient. In the following sections, I present a list of the essentials of audio recording and offer some insight into cost-saving and efficient systems that you can find in the market.

Exploring the recording essentials

To take the mystery out of recording gear, here are the essentials that you need to know:

- ✔ **Sound source:** The sound source is your voice, your guitar, your ukulele, or any other of the many sound makers that are out there. As a musician, you probably have at least one of these at your disposal right now.

- ✔ **Input device:** Input devices are what you use to convert your sound into an electrical impulse that can then be recorded. Here are the three basic types of input devices:

  - **Instruments:** Your electric guitar, bass, synthesizer, and drum machines are typical instruments that you plug into the mixer. These instruments constitute most of the input devices that you use in your studio. The synthesizer and drum machine can plug directly into your mixer or recorder, whereas your electric guitar and bass need a *direct box* (or its equivalent, such as a Hi-Z input in your mixer) to plug into first. A direct box is an intermediary device that allows you to plug your guitar directly into the mixer. Chapter 7 explores instruments and their connections to your system.

  - **Microphone:** A microphone (mic) enables you to record the sound of a voice or an acoustic instrument that you can't plug directly into the recorder. A microphone converts sound waves into electrical energy that can be understood by the recorder. I detail several types of microphones in Chapter 6.

  - **Sound module:** Sound modules are special kinds of synthesizers and/or drum machines. What makes a sound module different from a regular synthesizer or drum machine is that a sound module contains no triggers or keys that you can play. Instead, sound modules are controlled externally by another synthesizer's keyboard or by a *Musical Instrument Digital Interface (MIDI) controller* (a specialized box designed to control MIDI instruments). Sound modules — with the exception of *soft-synths* — have MIDI ports (MIDI jacks) that enable you to connect them to other equipment. (Soft-synths are software programs that don't need hardware MIDI connections because the sound modules are stored on your computer's hard drive.) Chapter 5 digs into the details about sound modules.

Depending on what your sound source is, it may also be an input device. For example, an electric guitar has pickups that allow you to plug it directly into a mixer input without having to use a microphone. On the other hand, your voice can't accept a cord, so you need to use a mic to turn your singing into an electrical impulse that can be picked up by your mixer or equivalent device. You can find out more about input devices in Chapter 7.

✔ **Mixer:** A mixer is used to get your input device into your recorder and to route signals in a variety of ways. Traditionally, a mixer serves the following two purposes:

- **To route your signals into your recorder:** This allows you to set the proper level for each input device so that it's recorded with the best possible sound. Chapter 4 explores the different mixer-type devices for this purpose.

- **To blend (mix) your individual tracks into a stereo pair (the left and right tracks of your stereo mix):** This role of the mixer is where your vision as a music producer takes center stage and where you can turn raw tracks into a polished piece of music. Chapter 14 explores this use of a mixer.

✔ **Recorder:** The recorder is where your audio data is stored. For most home recordists, this is a digital recorder. You can find out more about the different types of recorders in the next section of this chapter.

✔ **Signal processors:** Most of the time, you have to tweak your recorded tracks. Signal processors give you the power to do this. Signal processors can be divided into the following three basic categories:

- **Equalizers:** Equalizers let you adjust the frequency balance of your tracks. This is important for making your instruments sound as clear as possible and for getting all your tracks to blend well.

- **Dynamics processors:** Dynamics processors are used to control the balance between the softest and loudest parts of your tracks. They have many uses in the studio to help you make your tracks sit well together and to keep from overloading your system. Chapters 7, 15, and 16 explore ways to use dynamics processors in your music.

- **Effects processors:** Effects processors allow you to change your tracks in a variety of ways, to create either a more realistic sound or unusual effects. Typical effects processors include reverb, delay, chorus, and pitch shifting. You can find out more about these processors in Chapter 15.

✔ **Monitors:** It's impossible to know the quality of your recording and mixing without proper monitors, such as quality headphones or speakers. Monitors come in two basic designs:

- **Passive:** Passive monitors are like your stereo speakers in that you also need some sort of amplifier to run them. A ton of options are available with prices from around $100. Just remember that if you go this route, you need to budget in money for an amp. This can run a few hundred or more dollars.

- **Active:** Active monitors have an integrated amplifier in each speaker cabinet. Having a built-in amp has its advantages, including just the right amount of power for the speakers and short runs of wire from the amp itself to the speakers (this is kind of a tweaky area that some people claim produces a better sound). You can find quite a few active monitors on the market starting at just a couple hundred dollars.

Checking out recording system types

With the long list of equipment that I present in the previous section, you may think that you need to spend a ton money to get everything you need. Fortunately, a lot of home recording systems are available that contain many of the components you need without having to buy everything separately. I go into detail about these systems in Chapter 2, but here's a basic overview:

- **Studio-in-a-box (SIAB) systems:** These are all-in-one units that have everything in them except for the sound source, input device, and monitors. For very little money (starting well under $1,000), you get almost everything you need to get started recording. These types of systems are also easy to get started with and are great for musicians that don't want to spend a ton of energy tweaking their setup.

- **Computer-based systems:** These systems use the processing power of your computer to record, mix, and process your music. Computer-based systems, like the studio-in-a-box system, perform many of the typical recording functions at once. When you have one of these systems, you only need your sound source, your input devices, and your monitors.

- **Stand-alone systems:** These systems are reminiscent of traditional recording studios in that all the pieces of gear are separate. The downside is that you have to buy all your components separately, which can cost you more than buying one of the more inclusive systems (for example, the SIAB and computer-based systems). For people who already have a bunch of gear, such as a mixer and signal processors, this can be a decent option because you're buying only what you need at the time.

Getting a Glimpse into the Recording Process

It's easy to focus on all the gear that's used in audio recording and think that the process must be pretty complicated. Well, it can be if you want it to, but it doesn't need to be. The heart of recording over the last 30 years or so has been an approach called *multitracking*. At its core, multitracking involves recording all the instruments on separate tracks so that you can mix them later almost any way you want. You can multitrack by recording everything — or at least most of the instruments — at one time, just like a live performance, or you can go to the other extreme and record each instrument separately. Either way, you need a bunch of tracks to be able to record to, and you need to understand how to get all these separate pieces to blend into something musical.

Setting up a song

The first step in recording your music is to set up your system to record. Because you're probably using some sort of digital system, you need to configure your song. This usually involves setting the file type, bit depth, and sample rate. This process is one that you'll get very good at in no time. To get the lowdown on setting up songs in various systems, check out Chapter 10.

Getting a great sound

Getting your sound source to sound great in your system is the most important aspect of recording quality music (well, aside from the song and the performances). This is also an area where you'll constantly be growing and learning. I've been recording professionally for almost 20 years, but I still discover something new every time I set up a mic or plug in an electronic instrument. The great thing here is that any time you spend tweaking your mic placement or recording chain setup (configuration and levels) is time well spent and is often rewarded with added clarity or at least a more interesting sound. To help you get up to speed on all the intricacies of getting high-quality source sounds, check out Part III of this book.

Recording

After you have everything set up, the actual process of recording your music properly is pretty straightforward: You enable your track and press the Record button. This is easier said than done when the clock is ticking and you know that every mistake that you make is being documented. Luckily, digital recording makes it easy to redo a track without costing you anything in audio fidelity. (It will cost you time though, but because you record at home, you may have more time to get it right). Check out Chapter 11 for the specifics on recording using a variety of digital systems.

Overdubbing

With one track recorded, you're ready to dig into one of the most invigorating parts of the multitracking process: overdubbing. *Overdubbing* is the process of adding new tracks to your existing ones. This feature allows you to be the one-man band or to bring in other musicians to spice up your music. Overdubbing is easily done with digital multitrack recorders, and to get you going quickly, I cover the details in Chapter 11.

Making Sense of Mixing

For most recordists, the process of mixing is what turns their mish-mash of musical tracks into a song. Mixing involves the following steps:

- Cleaning up your tracks by getting rid of unwanted noise and performance glitches
- Equalizing each track so that it blends well with all the others
- Adding signal processing to enhance each track
- Setting levels for each track to tell the story you want to tell with your song

The following sections offer an overview of these steps.

Cleaning up tracks using editing

When you record, you want the best possible sound and performance for each instrument that you can get, but try as you might, sometimes you run into problems. These can include picking up unwanted sounds, such as chair squeaks, coughs, or other instruments, and can include (and often does) mistakes on the part of musician that need to be cut out. In the olden days of tape recording, this editing process took time and skill to physically cut out the bad parts of the tape with a razor blade. Today, you can do the necessary editing using the editing functions that are available in digital systems. This is nice, but it can also tempt you into doing more editing than is necessary to your tracks and, as a result, can suck the life out of them. To help you understand what you can do with digital recording systems and to help keep you on track with your editing, check out Chapter 13.

Equalizing your tracks

When you start mixing a bunch of instruments, you often need to adjust the frequencies present in each instrument so that they all blend without creating mush (a highly technical term). By adjusting the frequencies of each instrument in the mix, you can make sure that each can be heard. This process is simple, but it can be time consuming. To make it easier for you, I cover equalization in detail in Chapter 14.

Processing your signal

In the world of multitracking and small, acoustically untreated recording rooms (most home recordists use a spare bedroom or basement to record in and don't have a ton of money to make the room sound great), it is almost essential to process the sound with effects or dynamics processors. Doing so is usually intended to add some of the live feel of a concert to the recording, although many people also use signal processing to create interesting effects. Because the possibilities for processing your track using a digital system are almost limitless, this is an area where most beginners overdo it. Because this ability to alter your tracks can be used and abused, I cover some of the basics of processing in Chapter 15 to help you keep the abuse to a minimum.

Blending your tracks

This is also a process in which most new recordists run into problems. Properly mixing your tracks means keeping levels from getting out of hand, placing things where you want them in the sound field (left to right and front to back), adjusting EQ to blend all your instruments in a pleasing way, and using signal processors, such as compression and reverb, to make the most of each track. This process is a circular one and takes some skill and patience to get right. Cutting corners always results in an end product that falls short of its potential. To help you make this process easier, I cover mixing in detail in Chapters 14 and 15.

Adding the Final Touches

After your songs are recorded and mixed, all that's left to do is add the finishing touches. These include mastering your songs, putting them all on CD, and getting them out into the world through promotion.

Mastering your mixes

Mastering is an often-misunderstood (and even unknown to many) part of the music production process that can make or break a CD (well, not literally). Mastering consists of several important steps that are intended to polish your songs so that they make up a complete collection on a CD, commonly referred to as an album. Here are the steps for mastering your songs:

1. **Optimize the dynamics.**

   The goal here is to get the dynamic levels within and between each song to their best. It also means making your music *smooth* (no sharp edge to the music) or *punchy* (a pronounced attack) — or something in between. Unfortunately, most people are only concerned with getting their CD as loud as possible when performing this part of mastering. This isn't a good idea, as you find out in Chapter 14.

2. **Adjust the overall tonal balance.**

   The point of this part of the mastering process is to create some tonal continuity among all the songs on your CD. Because you probably recorded and mixed all your tunes over a period of months, they each can have slightly different tonal characteristics. This part of mastering is where you make all your songs consistent so that they sound like part of an album and not a bunch of disjointed tunes thrown together haphazardly.

3. **Match the song-to-song volume.**

   When your listeners put on your CD, you don't want them to have to adjust the volume of each song as it plays (unless they absolutely love a particular tune and want to turn it up, of course). The goal with this part of mastering is to get the volume of all the songs on a CD at pretty much the same level. This keeps one song from barely being heard while another threatens to blow the speakers.

4. **Set the song sequence.**

   How your songs are arranged on your CD helps tell your story. To make the most compelling musical statement, give some serious thought to the order of each song on your album. This part of the mastering process involves not only deciding what order everything should be in but also the steps you take to make it happen.

Putting your music on CD

Recording your finished and mastered songs to a CD for distribution and sales is one of the most exciting parts of the recording process. At last you have a product, a complete musical statement that you can share with (or sell to) others. Like a lot of audio recording and production, the act of making CDs is more involved than simply clicking the Burn button in your CD recording program (at least if you want to make more than one copy). You can either duplicate or replicate your CDs to make copies to give or sell to your fans. Here's a quick rundown on the differences between these two approaches (Chapter 16 explains them in detail):

- ✔ **Duplication:** Duplication consists of burning multiple CD-Rs from an audio file. Duplication requires very little setup, so it doesn't cost much to make smaller quantities, such as 50–200 CDs.

- ✔ **Replication:** The replication process starts with producing a glass master from your finished CD-R. This master CD is then used to create CDs using special CD presses, just like the major-label releases. Replication costs a bit more for setup, but the cost to create larger quantities of CDs is lower than that for duplication. This is a good choice for quantities of 500 or more.

Promoting your music

The final and most grueling step of recording and putting out a CD is the promotion process. This is where you either make it or break it as an independent artist. To help you along, I offer some ideas and insights in Chapter 17.

Chapter 2

Getting the Right Gear

. . . .

In This Chapter

▶ Understanding your home recording needs

▶ Taking a look at digital recorders

▶ Understanding analog studio equipment

▶ Exploring a few different recording systems

. . . .

*F*or many people, building a home studio is a gradual thing. You may start out with a synthesizer and a cassette recorder and add a microphone. Then you may decide to buy a multitrack recorder. Then you trade in your stereo speakers for real studio monitors. And before you know it, you've invested thousands of dollars in a first-rate home studio.

When setting up your home studio, you can go a couple of routes. You can walk into your local musical instrument store or pro audio shop without any forethought, get the pieces of gear that catch your eye, and then figure out where you may use them in your studio. (Hey, don't laugh; I've done this.) Or, you can determine your goals ahead of time and research each piece of equipment before you buy it to make sure that it is the best possible solution for you at the best price point. I recommend the latter approach because you end up with only the equipment that you need and not a bunch of useless gear that may only look good sitting in your studio.

The process of choosing the right equipment doesn't have to be difficult. All it takes is a little self-assessment and some basic knowledge about the different equipment options. This chapter helps you discover these things. Here, you get a chance to explore a few different system configurations and begin to understand what can work for your situation. You also get a chance to familiarize yourself with some of the many analog extras that so many people who favor digital recording want today.

Digital recording technology is evolving at an incredible rate. As soon as the ink dries on this paper, the next best thing in recording gear may surpass much of the technology that I write about in this chapter. It's tempting to always look to the next great innovation before you decide on a recording system, but I caution you against this wait-and-see attitude. Digital recording technology is now at the point that what you can record in your meager home studio can sound as fat, as clean, or as (insert your favorite recording adjective here) as the best recordings that have been released in the last 20 years.

Don't be afraid to just jump in and start recording. The way to great-sounding recordings is through hours of recording experience (not to mention having great songs with which to work).

Some of the equipment that I describe in this chapter isn't on the top of the list for most home recordists. I discuss this equipment, though, because you'll likely be taken over by a disease that runs rampant in the audio recording world. Yes, I'm sorry to inform you that you're almost assuredly going to get a chronic case of GAS *(gear acquisition syndrome)*. Don't worry; it's not terminal (unless, of course, you don't run your future purchases by your family first), but it can be uncomfortable. Nothing much is worse than having your eye on a piece of gear you just can't afford. "Let's see, food for a month or that new compressor I've just gotta have? . . . Oh well, I needed to go on a diet anyway."

The good news is that you'll never run out of new equipment to drool over and you'll never be alone in your suffering — everyone who owns a recording studio (private or commercial) suffers from GAS to some extent. The best way to keep GAS at bay is to decide on a system and buy it. Then stop looking at gear and get to work making some music. After all, that's why you bought the stuff in the first place.

Determining Your Home Studio Needs

Home studios can vary tremendously. A home studio can be simple, like a cassette deck and an inexpensive microphone set up in the corner of your bedroom. Or you can opt for something elaborate, like a multitrack digital recorder with thousands of dollars in outboard gear and expensive instruments residing in an acoustically treated addition to your house (whew!).

Whatever your budget, your first step in choosing what type of home recording system to buy is to determine your recording goals. Use the following questions to help you uncover what you truly need (and want) in your home studio. As you answer these questions, remember that most recording studios aren't built all at once — pieces of equipment are added slowly over time (a mic here, a preamp there). When getting your first home studio system, start with only those pieces of gear that you *really* need and then add on slowly when you get to know your equipment.

For most home recordists, the weakest link in their recording system is their engineering know-how. A $2,000 mic is useless until you gain an understanding of the subtleties of mic placement, for instance. (Check out Chapter 8 for more on such subtleties.) I recommend that you wait to buy that next piece of gear until you completely outgrow your present piece of equipment.

To get an understanding of what kind of home studio is best for you, ask yourself the following questions:

✔ **How much money can I spend on equipment?** For most people, money is the ultimate determining factor in choosing their studio components. Set a budget and try to stay within it. The sky's the limit on what you could spend on recording equipment for your home studio, but you don't need to spend a ton of money. If you know your goals and do your research, you can create top-quality recordings without having the best of everything.

In fact, your skill as a recording engineer has a much greater effect on the overall quality of your sound than whether you have a $3,000 preamp. With the techniques that you discover in this book and tricks that you uncover as you get to know your equipment, you can make recordings good enough to compete in the marketplace.

Digital recording technology has improved tremendously over the last few years and will continue to improve in the years to come. Don't get sucked into the belief that you have to have the latest, greatest thing to make great music. After all, great albums and #1 hits throughout history were recorded on lesser equipment than you can find in most home studios today. Focus on the song and the arrangement, practicing solid recording techniques, and you can get by with any of the pro or semipro recording systems available.

✔ **Is this studio just for me, or do I intend to hire it out to record others?** Your answer to this question may help you decide how elaborate a system you need. For example, if you eventually want to hire yourself and your studio out to record other people, you need to think about the compatibility of your system with other commercial studios. Your clients need to be able to take the music that they record at your studio and mix or master it somewhere else. You also may have to buy specific gear that clients want to use, which often means spending more money for equipment from sought-after manufacturers that may sound the same as lesser-name stuff. If you're interested in going the commercial studio route, check out other commercial studios in your area and find out what they use and what type of equipment their clients ask for.

If this studio is just for your use, you can focus on getting the best bang for the buck on gear without worrying about compatibility or marketability issues. (Check out my Web site (`www.jeffstrong.com`) for a list of "biggest bang for the least bucks" finds.)

✔ **Will I be recording everything directly into the mixing board, or will I be miking most of the instruments?** Your answer to this question is going to dictate your choice in how much of your budget goes toward equipment and acoustical treatments for your room. If you intend to plug your instruments directly into the mixer and you only need a microphone for the occasional vocal, you have more money to spend on synthesizers or plug-ins for your DAW (Digital Audio Workstation) — or you just won't have to spend as much. (DAWs are covered in detail in the section "Computer-Based DAW Systems," later in this chapter.)

Conversely, if you plan to record a band live, you must allocate enough money for those pieces of gear to allow you to do that effectively, such as having enough mics and inputs, sound isolation, and available tracks of simultaneous recording.

✔ **How many tracks do I need?** Recorders come with 4, 8, 16, 24, and sometimes more available tracks. The answer to this question has more importance if you're considering a stand-alone recorder or a studio-in-a-box (SIAB) system because they aren't as easily expandable. (For the lowdown on these systems, see the section "Studio-in-a-Box Systems," later in this chapter.)

Having more tracks is not necessarily a better thing. The more tracks you have, the more you think that you need to fill them for every song. This can make for cluttered arrangements and hard-to-mix songs. No matter how many tracks you end up with, use only those that you need to make your recording the best that it can be.

With digital recorders, you can create submixes and bounce several tracks into one or two without losing sound quality, reducing the need for more tracks. (Find out more about bouncing in Chapter 11.) Remember that some great albums were made using just 4 or 8 tracks.

✔ **Will I be sequencing the parts or playing the instruments live?** If you plan on *sequencing* all your music (that is, programming your part into a computer or sequencer and having it play your part for you), make sure that you get a good MIDI controller. You can also consider having less capability for audio tracks. But if you plan to play and record all the instruments live, make sure that your recorder has enough tracks for you to put each instrument on its own track.

Detailing Your Digital Options

Even with the fast pace of today's technology, one thing is for sure in the home recording world: Digital is here to stay. Digital recording has become the standard for home recordists and most commercial studios. And the format of choice is hard drive because it has many advantages over the other forms of digital recording. Not only does hard-drive recording create a great sound, but it's also relatively inexpensive, especially compared with an equivalent-sounding studio from 10 to 15 years ago.

In the sections that follow, I examine the main types of digital home studios: computer-based DAWs (Digital Audio Workstations), the all-in-one SIAB (studio-in-a-box) systems (such as the Roland V-Studios), and stand-alone recorders (like the Tascam MX2424). Each has its advantages. What's right for one person may not be the best choice for another. (Isn't it great to have choices?)

Regardless of the type of digital recording system that you like, consider the following things before buying:

✔ **Editing capabilities:** Some systems allow very fine editing of audio data, while others offer less. If you want so much control that you can edit down to the waveform — which basically means being able to edit out a single note or even just a part of a note — look for a system with that capability. If such control is less important to you, take a pass on such systems.

Along with the actual editing capabilities, find out how this editing is done. Is it on a tiny LCD screen or can it be done on a large computer monitor? Of course, if you won't be doing a lot of editing, this feature may not be important to you. If this is the case, you may be able to buy a system for less money that sounds as good as the one with full editing capability. It doesn't make sense to pay for something that you won't use.

✔ **Compatibility:** Compatibility between the various parts of your system (the recorder and sequencer or the software and sound card, for instance) or between your studio and other studios (your friend's or a commercial studio) is an important issue for many people and one that may come back to bite you if you don't consider it before you buy a system. For example, some plug-ins don't work with certain software programs. If you just have to have a certain soft-synth (software synthe-sizer) or amp simulator plug-in, make sure that you buy a system that allows you to use it. (*Plug-ins* are extra sounds, samples, and effects that you can "plug in" to your computer-based DAW's software program to increase its capabilities.) Likewise, some sound cards don't work well with certain software programs.

✔ **Number of simultaneous tracks:** Even though a recorder may say it has 16 tracks, it may not be able to actually record that number of tracks at one time. Most studio-in-a-box recorders, for example, record fewer tracks than they can play back at once. This usually isn't a problem because you will likely record only a few tracks at a time and overdub the rest. This would be a problem if you need to record all 16 tracks of a 16-track recorder, such as recording a band playing live at a club.

✔ **Realistic track count:** If you end up considering a computer-based system, the number of tracks that a computer software program is advertised to record and how many tracks you can actually record with your computer are often two very different things. Find out beforehand what a realistic track count is with the CPU (processor) and RAM (memory) that you have so that you're not disappointed after you've forked over your hard-earned money. The best way to do this is to go to online forums (such as the ones described in Chapter 18) or talk to other users in your area to see what their real-world experiences are.

✔ **Sample rate and bit depth:** The sample rate and the bit depth of the system determine how good a sound you can get from it. (The *bit depth* is the size of the audio sample in binary digits, and the *sample rate* is how often the sample is taken per second — notated as kHz.) Most semi-pro and pro systems have a 24-bit resolution and the ability to record at several bandwidths — 32, 44.1, 48, 88.2, and 96 kHz, for instance. The number of tracks may vary depending on what bandwidth setting you choose.

Although most pros still record at 44.1 kHz (the standard for CD audio), more people now want to record at 96 kHz (the standard for DVD audio). Even with the most expensive recorder, you have to live with having about half as many tracks at your disposal when recording at 96 kHz instead of 44.1 kHz because of the additional processing power it takes to record at the higher resolution.

✔ **Expandability:** As you learn and grow as a musician and recording engineer, your needs can also grow. Knowing this, your best bet is to plan ahead and choose a system that can grow with you. Can you add more tracks by synching another machine or increasing available RAM? Can you easily synchronize the system with other machines? For example, if you want to record 24 tracks now and you use a stand-alone recorder, can you add another recorder and have it synch properly? Or, if you buy an SIAB and you want to add more inputs later, can the system you're looking at do that? Some can and some can't, so do your research and think about your future needs.

You'll find that almost all the new semipro and pro systems available are expandable, but explore these questions carefully if you look at purchasing used gear.

Computer-Based DAW Systems

Computer-based digital recording systems are hardware and software options that you can connect to your computer. These systems can be pretty straightforward, such as simple 2-track recording freeware that you install on your home computer using a stock sound card. Or, you can go for a sophisticated system, like built-from-the-ground-up computers optimized to do one thing and one thing only: record, mix, and play back audio. (Okay, that's three things, but you get my point.)

To set up a computer-based DAW, you need the following things:

✔ A computer (preferably with a speedy processor)

✔ A bunch of memory and dual hard drives

✔ A sound card

✔ An audio interface (the interface between the computer and the outside world, usually housing the converters and sometimes the preamps)

✔ The software

Mac or PC?

Whether to buy a Mac or PC is a hotly debated topic among home recordists. Most professional studios used to favor Macintosh computers for recording audio. PCs were thought to have too many bugs to work well for audio. Even if this were true in the past, it's not true anymore. Your decision between a Mac- or PC-based recording system should be based more on your personal preferences in computer platforms and the particular software that you intend to use than which one is more stable. Either platform may or may not be stable, depending on what you're trying to do.

Choose the software that you want to use, and buy the computer that has the best track record

for running that software. Most software was originally developed on either a Mac or PC; accordingly, such software generally runs better on that platform. Pro Tools, for instance, was developed and written for the Mac. Pro Tools Free for PC software is just not as good — yet. In time, it most likely will be. But unless you want to be an unpaid test subject for a piece of software, your best bet is to research the software and decide whether you can deal with any complications that may arise from using it.

If you already have a computer or if you prefer one platform over another (PC or Mac), be sure to determine how well a program works on that platform before you buy it.

Finding the right computer setup

No matter which computer platform you choose (see the sidebar "Mac or PC?"), the stuff that you find inside your computer plays a major role in determining how smoothly (or how less-than-smoothly) your Digital Audio Workstation runs. The following list clues you in on the various pieces of hardware that you find in your computer:

- ✔ **CPU:** The CPU (processor) is the heart of your computer studio. The speed of your CPU ultimately dictates how well a program runs on it. As a general rule, for audio, get the fastest processor that you can afford. For most audio software, you need at least a Pentium IV for the PC or a G4 for the Mac. If you can, get a computer that you can dedicate for recording audio only because running other types of applications (home finance software, word processors, or video games) can cause problems with your audio applications and reduce the stability of your system.

- ✔ **Memory:** Computer-based audio programs and all the associated plug-ins are RAM (random-access memory) hogs. Here's my advice: Get a lot of RAM. Okay, that's not very specific, but how much you really need depends on your recording style. If you record a lot of audio tracks and want reverb or some effect on each track, you need more RAM (and a faster processor). If you record mainly MIDI tracks with instruments that already have the effects that you want, you can get by with less RAM (and a slower processor).

For most software programs, the recommended minimum amount of RAM is 256MB (256 megabytes), although most programs run much more smoothly with 512MB or more. RAM is relatively inexpensive, so get as much as you can.

Regardless of the platform that you choose (PC or Mac), keep in mind that you can never have a processor that's too fast or have too much memory.

✔ **Hard drives:** To record audio, make sure that you get the right type of hard drives. Notice that I said hard *drives* (plural). Yep, you should get more than one if you want to record more than a few tracks of audio. You need one hard drive for all the software and the operating system and another drive for the audio data. Having this setup greatly increases the likelihood that your system remains stable and doesn't crash, especially if you try to run 16 or more tracks.

As for the size of the hard drive, bigger is better, at least in the drive where you store your music. For the core system drive, you can get by with a 10GB (10-gigabyte) drive; for the audio drive, having even 20GB is pretty conservative because audio data can take up a ton of space. For example, a 5-minute song with 16 tracks recorded at 24 bits and a 44.1-kHz sample rate takes up about 600MB of hard-drive space (that's about 7.5MB per track minute).

Choose your hard drives wisely. For the software hard drive, you can get by with a stock drive (usually the one that comes with your computer). But for the audio side, you need a drive that can handle the demands of transferring audio data. Here are the main things to look for in an audio drive:

- **Spindle speed:** Also called rotational speed, this is the rate at which the hard drive spins. For the most part, a 7,200-rpm drive works well for recording and playing back audio.

- **Seek time:** This is the amount of time that it takes the drive to find the data that's stored on it. You want an average seek time of less than 10 milliseconds.

- **Buffer size:** Often called a *cache buffer,* buffers are memory units that store data as it's being transferred. According to the audio-recording software manufacturers, you need a buffer size of at least 512K (512 kilobytes), but I recommend that you get a drive with at least a 2MB buffer.

The track count that you get out of your system is directly related to the speed of your hard drive — the faster the drive, the more tracks you can record and play back at once. (Of course, the type of drive you get determines how large a role your processor plays.) My current choice is a Maxtor 7200-rpm ATA IDE hard drive with an 8.5-ms seek time and a 2MB cache buffer. A 120GB drive currently costs about $120.

Getting the sound in and out

After you have a computer with enough speed and muscle (see the previous section in this chapter), you need the appropriate hardware to get the sound into and out of it. This requires a device called an *audio interface*. Audio interfaces are available with three types of connection methods: PCI, FireWire, and USB. Here's a quick rundown on the three types (the details are spelled out in the following sections):

- **PCI:** PCI interfaces are inserted into one of the PCI slots located inside your computer's case.

- **FireWire:** FireWire interfaces connect to one of the FireWire ports in your computer.

- **USB:** USB interfaces connect to your computer — you guessed it — through one of the USB ports in your computer.

PCI interfaces

PCI is the old standard for getting audio into and out of a computer and has an advantage over the other interface types because of the fast transfer speed of PCI technology. This type of interface isn't without its problems, which are as follows:

- Many computers (for example, laptops and all Macs except the Power Mac) don't have a PCI slot.

- Because PCI technology is changing, all cards don't fit in all computers, so make sure that the PCI interface that you're considering can fit into your computer.

The advantage of PCI interfaces is that the PCI (the river in which the data flows) is the fastest of the currently available ways to get audio into and out of your computer. This means that less delay (called *latency*) occurs between the origin of the sound (when you hit a drum, for example) and the time that the sound gets into the computer and then back out to your monitors. This is why many pros still prefer PCI to FireWire or USB interfaces.

This doesn't mean that the delay you can get with FireWire or USB has to be noticeable or can't be dealt with. I discuss how to deal with it in the next two sections of this chapter. The latency issue, therefore, isn't the reason to go with PCI. Your decision is going to come down to what interface you like.

PCI interfaces come in the following varieties:

- **Separate sound card with no analog inputs and outputs:** In this case, you need to buy separate preamps, direct boxes, and AD (analog-to-digital) and DA (digital-to-analog) converters. For most home recordists, the separate-sound-card route isn't the best solution. In fact, even for the pros, this isn't the most popular choice — so much so that this option is quickly falling from the marketplace. Figure 2-1 shows examples of PCI sound cards.

Figure 2-1:
A PCI sound card doesn't contain analog inputs or outputs, so you need to buy separate components to use this type of card for audio recording.

✔ **Analog inputs and outputs within the card:** Having the analog connection located in the card used to cause interference with the other components in the computer's housing (such as fans and hard drives), which caused low-level hums in the recorded audio. (Not a sound you would want, I can assure you.) This is generally no longer the case unless you buy a really inexpensive card, but the bad rap led buyers to shy away from this approach and it has become uncommon as a result. You can find some less expensive audio interfaces configured this way, but the higher end of the market has generally abandoned it. Figure 2-2 shows an example of a PCI card with analog connections.

✔ **Analog inputs and outputs housed in a separate box:** This box is called a *breakout box*. Because of the low-level hum problems in the early interfaces, most manufacturers of PCI-based audio interfaces put their analog circuitry in a separate box with a cord attached to the PCI card. One advantage to this — besides eliminating the hum in early models — is that you can tweak the input and output levels without having to use a software menu. The dials for the levels are placed on the breakout box within easy reach, as shown in Figure 2-3.

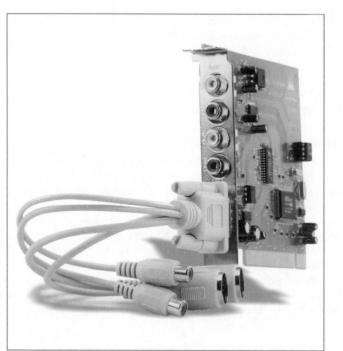

Figure 2-2:
PCI
interfaces
often come
with analog
connectors
run from the
computer.

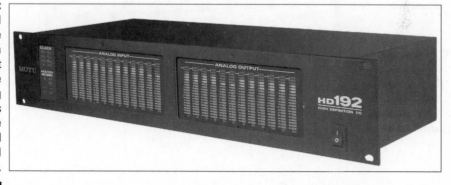

Figure 2-3:
A PCI
interface
with a
breakout
box for the
analog
components
is the
preferred
form of PCI
interface.

If you have a laptop computer but can't use a PCI-based system and you want the high transfer speed of PCI, you can buy an audio-interface card that uses the laptop's PCMCIA card slot. Of course, this only works if you have a laptop that's equipped with a PCMCIA slot.

If you want to go the PCI route, make sure that your computer has PCI slots that are compatible with the PCI interface that you're considering. For example, the Digidesign 001 doesn't work with the PCI slots that you find in the Mac G5 computers.

Quite a few PCI-based audio interfaces are available, and they cost from a couple hundred dollars to a couple thousand dollars.

FireWire interfaces

FireWire interfaces connect to the FireWire port in your computer. (Figure 2-4 shows a typical FireWire interface.) FireWire ports are inexpensive and are available on laptop computers as well as desktops, which makes FireWire interfaces more versatile than PCI-based systems. For example, you can easily move the interface from computer to computer. If you have a laptop and a desktop computer, using a FireWire interface allows you to switch between the two computers by simply moving the FireWire cable from one computer to the other. If you want to do some location recording, this is a big plus because you can take your interface and laptop to a great recording room, record the drums, for example, and then bring the audio back home for mixing and editing in your studio.

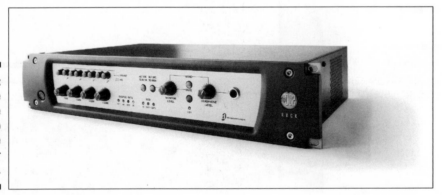

Figure 2-4:
A FireWire interface connects to the FireWire port in your computer.

Even though PCI-based systems have a faster pathway for sending and receiving audio data, FireWire is fast enough for most users. With FireWire, the latency that you can expect is only marginally more than what you would get with PCI-based systems.

FireWire interfaces generally come with eight to ten inputs and outputs and cost from about $500 to $1,500.

When using a FireWire interface — and if you want a lot of inputs and/or outputs — a problem can arise if you also have a FireWire hard drive to which you want to record audio. Basically, having the FireWire interface and the FireWire hard drive on the same FireWire bus is asking for trouble, because you're sure to reach the data-transfer limit of FireWire. So make sure that the two FireWire devices are on different buses (data channels).

USB interfaces

USB interfaces (see Figure 2-5) are handy because most computers have at least one USB port. These interfaces also represent a low-cost solution for people who need only a couple of inputs and outputs. The only problem with USB for recording audio is the relatively slow transfer speed. This slower speed translates into higher latencies than those found with either FireWire or PCI interfaces. The latency is significant enough that you're likely to hear it when you record.

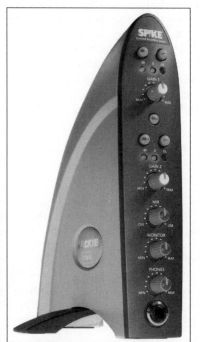

Figure 2-5:
A USB
interface
connects
to your
computer's
USB port.

To get around this deficit, most USB-interface manufacturers have incorporated some sort of "no latency" monitoring option. With such an option, you can record without hearing a delay between the tracks that you've already recorded and the one you're currently recording. The problem is that with such an option, your newly recorded track gets placed out of synch with the previously recorded tracks. To correct the synchronization, you must move your overdubbed tracks within your song file. Admittedly, this process is pretty easy, but it takes time. (I explain how to correct synchronization in detail in Chapter 11.) If you don't want to deal with the latency in USB interface–based systems, you should use a PCI, FireWire, or USB 2.0 interface.

At the time of this writing, USB 2.0 interfaces are just becoming available. USB 2.0 features a much faster transfer speed than the original USB standard, so the latency issue is, well, a nonissue.

USB interfaces can be found for under $200, and USB 2.0 interfaces currently cost about $700.

Choosing the right software

When setting up a recording system, I always recommend that you start by exploring the software that you want to use. Whatever program you decide on will work better on one type of computer compared to another. By choosing the software first, you can use the software manufacturer's guidelines to help you set up your computer. Most software is written for either a Mac or a PC and will have been tested with a variety of hardware configurations. Unless you're very computer savvy, I recommend starting with a system that's been tested to run smoothly with the program that you're interested in.

For the most part, audio-production software falls into the following two categories:

✔ **Audio-recording programs:** These programs allow you to record numerous tracks (the number depends on the program) and let you edit, equalize, and mix those tracks as well as add effects.

✔ **MIDI-sequencing programs:** These programs allow you to record MIDI performance data (without the sounds) and edit and mix the data. The difference between audio and MIDI recording is covered in detail in Chapter 5.

Many entry-level programs allow you to either record audio or do MIDI sequencing, but not both. Higher-end programs offer both audio and MIDI recording and generally do a good job of both (and they're getting better all the time). Choose the program based on its features and whether it fits with your working style.

Researching a program you're interested in

If you already own a computer and you want to get some audio recording or sequencing software to go with it, do the following research on the software you're interested in:

✔ **Find out the product's compatibility with your system:** Visit the software manufacturer's Web site for information about whether your system will work with that program as well as what additional hardware you may need to get the software up and running.

✔ **Find out what other users are saying:** On the Internet, you can find an online discussion board for each of the major audio-recording software programs. Before you buy a program, go to the sites of the choices that interest you and see what people are saying about the program. Ask questions and explore the issues that other people are having with the program. Doing so can save you lots of time dealing with bugs in your system and allow you to record a lot more music. You can find these sites by using the product name as the keyword in your favorite search engine or by checking out the Internet forums that I list in Chapter 18.

One great way to see whether a particular program is right for you is to find out what people who play your type of music are using. For instance, a lot of people who compose with synthesizers and MIDI use Logic Audio because using MIDI and software synthesizers is quick and easy in this program. It also keeps them from needing a bunch of hardware synthesizers to get the sounds they want, which saves space in their studio and money in being able to bypass the hardware to get their synthesizer sounds.

Checking out some popular programs

You can choose from numerous music-production software programs, including the ones in the following list:

✔ **Apple (www.apple.com):** Makes Logic Pro Audio and Logic Express. These programs run on both PC and Mac systems. Logic Pro Audio has been around for a while and is one of the top programs available. The downside is that it's for Macs only. Like all the programs, Logic has its way of working — some people like it while others have a hard time grasping the way the user interface functions. (I love it.)

✔ **Cakewalk (www.cakewalk.com):** Makes SONAR, SONAR XL, and Metro 5, among other programs. These are designed to run on a PC. SONAR is a redesigned version of Cakewalk Pro Audio (some would say a completely new program). SONAR does a great job of recording (and editing and mixing) both audio and MIDI.

✔ **Digidesign (www.digidesign.com):** Makes Pro Tools and Pro Tools LE. These programs work on both Mac and PC systems. Digidesign's Pro Tools Mix systems (the company offers several versions) are arguably the standard for digital audio in pro studios, although more pro studios are using any one (or more) of the other programs that I list in this section. Pro Tools is great for recording and editing audio tracks but has been a little behind the rest of the programs for MIDI. If MIDI is important to you, you may want to wait for future upgrades or try a different program.

- ✔ **Mark of the Unicorn (`www.motu.com`):** Makes Digital Performer. This program requires a Mac to run. Digital Performer is a powerful program that does MIDI and audio equally well. One advantage of this program is that MOTU makes very good audio interfaces that are designed to work well with its software. You end up with a better chance of having a system that is stable.

- ✔ **Sony Media Software (`mediasoftware.sonypictures.com`):** Makes Sound Forge, Vegas Audio, and Acid. These programs only run on Windows (PCs). Acid is a very popular program that is strong in loop-based recording. As a result, a lot of hip-hop and techno artists use this program.

- ✔ **Steinberg (`www.steinberg.net`):** Makes Nuendo, Cubase, WaveLab, and Cubasis. These programs run on both Mac and PC platforms. Nuendo is Steinberg's best program, and it is excellent for recording audio. (Nuendo is one of the best-sounding programs available; it is made to compete with Pro-Tool's top-of-the-line offering.) It's not very strong in MIDI sequencing, though, so if this feature is important to you, this may not be the best program to use. In that case, if you like the Steinberg line, you may want to try Cubase, which is a great program that's on par with SONAR, Logic, and the others and is stronger in MIDI sequencing than Nuendo.

Most of these manufacturers offer program demos that you can download for free to see whether you like them. These demos work just like the full versions except that you generally can't save or print your work.

Some of these manufacturers also make audio-interface/sound-card hardware optimized for their systems; this hardware can generally work on other systems (check with the manufacturer to make sure). You may find an easy and great-sounding solution by choosing a software and hardware setup from a single manufacturer. If you do, you are likely to have fewer compatibility problems.

Studio-in-a-Box Systems

Integrated mixers/recorders/effects processors have become quite common. Cassette port-a-studios, first introduced in the 1970s, enabled the home recordist to compose music at home without spending a fortune on equipment. But it wasn't until the Roland VS-880 came out in 1997 that great-quality recordings could be made at home using a single piece of equipment. Okay, you still needed an instrument and microphone to plug into it, but everything else fit into this one little box, which is now referred to as a *studio-in-a-box system*.

Taking a look at the benefits

One of the biggest advantages of using a studio-in-a-box (SIAB) system is that you don't need to be computer literate — just turn it on and start to record. SIAB systems are also portable — you can take them almost anywhere to record, so you're not limited to just your studio room. (You can get a view of an SIAB system in Figure 2-6.) Think about this for a second: If you want a big drum sound and all you have is a small converted bedroom for a studio, you can load up your SIAB system, a few microphones, and your drummer's drum set (don't forget the drummer) and go to an empty warehouse, gymnasium, church, or anywhere you want. In fact, if you're inventive, you don't even need to have electricity to do this. Most of these recorders draw very little power and can be hooked up to a solar panel or battery. (You have to figure out how to do this, but a quick search on the Internet should give you some ideas.)

Figure 2-6: A studio-in-a-box system contains everything that you need to make great recordings.

I love these SIAB contraptions. The only real drawback is expandability, although this is changing. Early versions of SIAB systems were somewhat limited in what they offered and weren't very friendly when it came to adding more effects (although they're easy to synch). The new generation of SIAB systems is being designed to accept third-party effects — for example, the Yamaha AW machines accept an effect card made by Waves — and other options, such as additional input and output cards — again available on the Yamaha SIAB systems. They can also save audio files in formats that you can open on other manufacturers' recorders, freeing you to transfer files between different systems.

Examining some popular SIAB systems

Many of the major recording manufacturers make SIAB systems. Check out these companies and compare the specifications of each unit:

- **Akai (www.akaipro.com):** Akai was one of the original makers of stand-alone hard-drive recorders. (The DR-4, DR-8, and DR-16 were excellent machines.) Akai has dropped the stand-alone line and is focusing on an SIAB system called the DPS-24. This is a high-end 24-track unit with 24-bit recording at a variety of sample rates, motorized faders, and internal expansion slots for future upgrades and third-party products.

- **Boss (www.bossus.com):** Boss is the entry-level line made by Roland (read more about Roland later in this section). Boss makes several basic all-in-one recorders, such as the 8-track BR864 or the 16-track BR1600, which are inexpensive and easy to use. These units record in 16 bits at a 44.1-kHz sample rate.

- **Fostex (www.fostex.com):** Fostex has been in the hard-drive recording business for a while — although not as long as Akai — and Fostex has released several SIAB devices in the last few years. Currently, its top-of-the-line SIAB system is the VF-160 16-track recorder. The Fostex units have a lot of features, but they are limited to recording at 16 bits — a real drawback for serious recording. Still, for their prices, these units are a good value.

- **Korg (www.korg.com):** Korg has quite a few recorders, from basic units such as the D-1200 12-track unit to the full-featured D32XD 32-track recorder. The Korg units sound good — they all record in 24 bits — and are easy to use.

- **Roland (www.rolandus.com):** Roland defined the SIAB recorder with its VS-880 in 1997. The company currently offers several SIAB systems, including the new flagship VS-2480 24-track recorder. Roland has the largest user base of all the SIAB systems, so if user support is important to you, you can't go wrong with one of Roland's machines. These units record at 24 bits but use a compression scheme that reduces the file sizes.

- **TASCAM (www.tascam.com):** TASCAM has been in the home recording market for a long time, first with cassette port-a-studios and now with digital systems. You can find two units — the DP-01FX 8-track recorder, which records at 16 bits, and the 2488 24-track recorder, which records in 24 bits.

✔ **Yamaha (`www.yamaha.com`):** Yamaha currently has two SIAB systems: the AW4416 and the AW2816. Both are 16-track recorders that have excellent sound quality. The AW4416 has a 44-channel mixer, motorized faders, and two expansion slots for expandability, while the AW2816 has a 28-channel mixer and only one expansion slot. Yamaha is the first SIAB system manufacturer to develop a third-party card for its expansion slots. The AW4416 records in 24 bits, whereas the AW2816 records in 16 bits.

Stand-alone Recorders

The first affordable stand-alone digital recorder to hit the market was the Alesis ADAT (which stands for Alesis Digital Audio Tape) in 1992. This machine revolutionized home recording, making it possible for the home recordist to make some pretty high-quality recordings without having to spend a fortune. Many commercial studios used ADATs as well. In fact, a lot of hit records from the last decade were recorded on ADATs. The ADAT uses digital tape cartridges, which look much like VHS videotapes, and they function much like analog tapes. And like analog tapes, the digital tape cartridges have limited editing capabilities. (For more details on editing, see Chapter 13.)

Stand-alone digital recorders are the least common type of home studio recorder because they require a separate mixer and other outboard gear, such as external effects units or preamps. This makes the cost of this type of system higher than a comparable number of tracks that you get in a studio-in-a-box or computer-based system. The advantage is that you can swap out these recorders as newer models come out without having to update your whole system. This is one reason why stand-alone recorders are so popular in commercial studios. Figure 2-7 shows a typical stand-alone recorder.

Figure 2-7:
A stand-alone recorder can easily be added to an existing system.

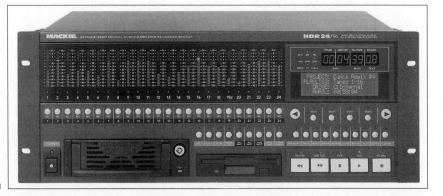

The following major manufacturers produce stand-alone hard-drive recorders:

- ✔ **Alesis** (`www.alesis.com`): Alesis makes the 24-track HD24 hard-drive recorder. This unit is the company's follow-up to the hugely popular ADAT recorders of the nineties.

- ✔ **Mackie** (`www.mackie.com`): Mackie makes the HDR-2496 and MDR-2496 recorders. They are both 24-track machines, but the HDR has many more editing capabilities and an output for a video monitor. (This makes editing much easier.)

These stand-alone units cost from about $1,500 to $2,000 or more dollars. You also have to buy other necessary gear, such as mixers, and signal processors, separately, which raises the overall cost of these systems considerably.

Because these companies' product offerings are constantly changing, your best bet is to check out each of these manufacturers' Web sites and compare their specifications with one another. The next step would be to try a demo of each product that has the features that you want to see whether you like the way that they sound. Also, be sure to check out the compatibility of the system with other systems, if that's important to you.

Analyzing Analog

Analog recording has definitely taken a backseat to digital. This is mainly a bang-for-the-buck thing. For just slightly more money than you would pay for a cassette 4-track recorder, you can get a digital 4-track unit that produces a far superior sound. And for a lot less than the cost of a full-blown pro analog setup, you can achieve the same-quality product using a digital system. (Of course, you still need great songs, top-notch engineering skills, and pricey outboard gear.) In spite of this, you may as well know what your options are for analog recording.

Cassette port-a-studio

For the budding songwriter who is just starting out, a 4-track cassette port-a-studio can be a good choice: You don't need to be technologically proficient to use one. For little money, you can be laying down tracks and putting your ideas onto tape — you can find a basic 4-track for about $100. Another bene-fit of the cassette 4-track units is that they provide a great introduction to the world of multitrack recording without having to invest a lot of time or money. If you use one of these and find that you like the process of creating your own music, you can easily move on to another system.

Open-reel multitracks

The standard for multitrack recording 20 years ago was the open-reel (reel-to-reel) tape deck. These recorders came in 4-, 8-, 16-, and 24-track configurations. They produced varying levels of sound quality, depending on the width of the tape. Semipro recorders used narrower tape (half-inch and 1-inch for 16 tracks), which have more background noise such as hiss, whereas pro recorders used a wider 2-inch tape that, in the hands of a good engineer, created a world-class sound.

The semipro reel-to-reel multitrack recorders have mostly been superseded by digital hard-drive recorders because the digital recorder is less expensive and better sounding. The wide-format (2-inch) reel-to-reel recorders, on the other hand, are still in use in many top-notch commercial studios. In fact, many great albums are still being recorded using these systems. The downside to the wide-format-tape multitrack units is that they're prohibitively expensive to buy and maintain for the home recordist.

Oh, how I yearn for that analog sound

An interesting trend in digital recording is the quest for analog sound. In the marketplace, you find new pieces of gear being marketed as having *warmth* or a *vintage sound.* What exactly is this sound?

This sound is . . . (wait for it) . . . distortion. Yep, good ol' noise and distortion. Why would someone want to duplicate that now?

When the mild distortion that's inherent in good analog recordings was eliminated in digital recordings, we missed it (sigh). In analog recording, you find a technique that's used to add something wonderful and beautifully pleasing to a recording: *tape saturation.* This is caused by recording the sound onto a tape recorder at a high enough level that the tape becomes saturated (hence the term *tape saturation*), and certain aspects of the sound change.

For the most part, tape saturation adds *even harmonics* to the sound. Not to get too technical, but these are the tones present in the music but, for the most part, hidden behind the main tone. Tape saturation brings those tones out just a little, and we find them pleasing to listen to. Tape saturation also mellows out the high frequencies by *smearing* them together a little. Without this sound, many listeners (certainly not all) find digital recordings somewhat *harsh* or *cold.* In case you didn't know, these are highly technical terms meaning, "I don't hear that thing I'm used to hearing in an analog recording."

Digital recording can't duplicate this sound. In fact, if you try to use the tape-saturation technique with a digital recorder (by overriding the input levels), all you get is more harshness and a horrible clipping sound. (The sound is clipped off by the digital converters, and you hear crackles and clicks.)

If you're in the market for a used narrow-format multitrack recorder because you just gotta have analog (see the sidebar "Oh, how I yearn for that analog sound"), know that you not only need to be proficient in good engineering practices, but you also need to be able to maintain the recorder — align and clean the heads, for instance, and perform other housecleaning chores. If you can't do this yourself, you need to have the bucks to hire someone to do it for you. Also, finding analog tape is getting more difficult. In fact, anything but ¼-inch, ½-inch (both for mastering decks) and 2-inch tapes are nearly impossible to find new, and even these sizes (¼-inch, ½-inch, and 2-inch) are getting hard to find.

Analog goodies

So you find that you gotta have that analog sound, too, but you don't want to (or can't) deal with the expense of a complete analog system. Well, you're in luck! Do I have a deal for you! You, too, can add some of the warmth to your digital recordings if you're willing to shell out the green. Yep, come on down and I'll set you up!

Seriously, you can buy some analog extras to help you add a little of that analog distortion to your music. Don't get me wrong; many of these products are great and have a place in a home studio. Just don't get so hooked by the need to have warmth in your recordings that you go out and buy everything that you can to add mild distortion. This warmth is just distortion, after all.

Most of the time people use tube gear on their instruments to get them to sound warmer. (Sounds like California surfer lingo, dude.) In sound recording, *tube gear* refers to components that still use the ancient technology of vacuum tubes to get them up and running — and up and running with all that distortion that some listeners describe as warm. Tube microphones, preamps, compressors, and equalizers are only a few of the types of products available to add some semblance of the much-sought-after analog sound.

If you want to go tubeless, look for special tape-saturation emulators on the market to give you that analog edge. See the section "Tape-saturation emulators," later in this chapter, for more info.

The tube stuff

Vacuum-tube microphones, preamps, compressors, and equalizers have been around for decades. In fact, before solid-state (transistor) technology was developed, everything electronic had vacuum tubes in it — both good-quality and bad-quality audio gear. Vacuum-tube equipment definitely had a sound to it, and tube technology definitely had its limitations — the main one being the coloration that was added to the music. This coloration is highly sought after in today's world of digital recording (see the sidebar "Oh, how I yearn for that analog sound"), so the tube stuff has become increasingly popular.

To get the pleasing analog distortion that's so popular today, you don't need to buy gear with vacuum-tube circuitry. Some top-quality solid-state gear can get you the same sound as the vintage tube stuff. In fact, some of the most sought-after vintage preamps, equalizers, and compressors — particularly those bearing the "Neve" name — are solid state, and they still have a beautifully *colored* (distorted) sound. So, when you go in search of the tube sound for your studio, remember that you can get the sound you're after without having to buy actual vacuum-tube gear.

Not all "tube" gear produces a pleasing sound. Sometimes the distortion that a piece of gear adds to your music creates more noise and *mud* (lack of clarity in the sound) than it adds warmth. Be sure to listen to the equipment that you're interested in before you buy it. Make your purchase decision based on how you like the way the equipment sounds for your particular music. Do your homework before adding any tube gear — or any new equipment that you spend your hard-earned money on. Read reviews and specifications, talk to people, and above all, listen to the equipment before you buy.

Many audio-recording retailers allow you a certain amount of time after you buy a piece of equipment to return it if you don't like it. Of course, you have to pay for it before you leave the store, but you usually get some time in which you can return it. Ask your music retailer to be sure of its return policy before you buy.

Tape-saturation emulators

The new great thing in audio recording is the *analog tape emulator,* also known as a *tape-saturation emulator.* These are designed to add the characteristics that you get from recording high levels onto tape, such as the mild distortion that analog aficionados love (see the sidebar "Oh, how I yearn for that analog sound"). You can find both stand-alone analog emulators and plug-ins for your computer-based system. These can be expensive (over $2,000 in some cases), but many pros swear by them. As I write this book, this technology is in its infancy, so expect the prices to drop dramatically and the choices to expand exponentially over the next few years.

Since the first edition of this book was published a few years ago, one really decent tape-saturation plug-in for computer-based systems has appeared. This emulator, called the Vintage Warmer (www.pspaudioware.com), can add some pleasing distortion to your tracks for about $150. If you use it, be careful not to overdo it. It is easy to use too much saturation and ruin an otherwise good track.

Reality check

Do you need any tube or analog emulator gear in your studio? The short answer is: No, you don't. You can make great recordings without any of this stuff. All you need is an instrument, a microphone, a mixer, a recorder, and some monitors — oh, and some good, solid engineering skills.

What really counts is your music. People who listen to music don't care whether you use (insert gotta-have gear here) to record your masterpiece. All they care about is whether they like the music. So don't make yourself nuts (or go broke) over any of this stuff.

Exploring Sample Setups

In this section, I help you get some ideas about the best system configuration for your needs. Whether you're an electronic musician who only needs a sequencer, some MIDI instruments, and a 2-track recorder or you're a purist who wants 16 tracks of simultaneous recording and needs dozens of microphones to record your whole band live, I help you figure it out in this section.

Because I don't know what type of recording you want to do, I outline three basic systems to give you an idea of what may work for you. You can see a system that works well for both live recording and MIDI sequencing, a system for MIDI sequencing and the occasional instrument or vocal overdub, and a live rig that contains little or no MIDI instrumentation. This is only a starting point, but as you shop around for a system, you'll be able to find a setup that best meets your needs.

You can configure your home recording system in almost unlimited ways. Part of what will influence your decisions is your initial budget and how you like to work. Look around and talk to other people who have a home studio. Join an Internet forum and discover the different ways that people are recording — find out what works for them and what doesn't. (Check out Chapter 18 for some great resources on the Internet.) Then jump in and don't look back. The most important component in your studio is you!

Live and MIDI studio

The live and MIDI studio is your best choice if you want to incorporate both MIDI-sequenced parts and live instruments (such as guitar, electric bass, and drums). For this type of system, you need a recorder, a mixer, and a MIDI controller. You also need a few microphones and any instruments that you plan to record — generally at least one synthesizer or sound module, an electric guitar and bass, and a drum machine or real drum set. Figure 2-8 illustrates a setup that's centered around an SIAB recorder with a computer for sequencing. Of course, you could use a stand-alone recorder instead (you need a separate mixer), or you could incorporate the whole system into a computer if you choose.

You want a system with a fair amount of tracks (at least 8) that allows you to record at least 2 tracks of MIDI instruments as well as several tracks of guitar, bass, drums, and vocals.

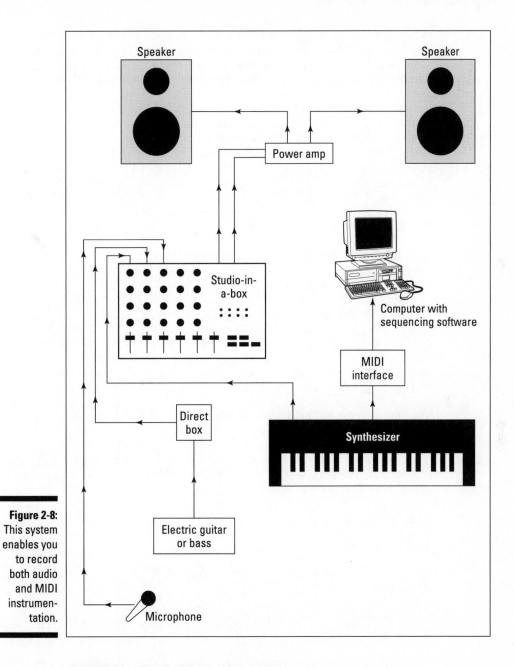

Figure 2-8:
This system
enables you
to record
both audio
and MIDI
instrumen-
tation.

MIDI-intensive studio

Are you a one-man band? Do you prefer to program a performance rather than to play it? If so, you may want to have a MIDI-intensive studio. The advantage of the MIDI studio is that one person can "play" many instruments at the same time. A disadvantage is that the music can sound somewhat stiff. (See Chapter 12 for advice on how to overcome this.) And you may lose touch with what it feels like to play with other musicians, which is not always a bad thing, especially if you're into that whole reclusive artist thing.

Because MIDI instruments can be programmed to play the part perfectly, with all the dynamic variations that you want, you can spend your time working on the parts (composing, setting levels, and creating effects) without actually having to record them. As a result, you can get by with fewer audio tracks in your system, but you need to have more MIDI tracks available. An advantage to this approach is that MIDI tracks take less CPU power and RAM to run compared to the same number of audio tracks. So, you can get by with a less expensive computer (or use the one you already have) and save your bucks for more synthesizers or plug-ins.

For a MIDI-intensive studio, such as the one shown in Figure 2-9, you need a *sequencer* (a device that allows you to record and play back MIDI performance information) and at least one sound source. This could be a keyboard synthesizer, sound module, sampler, or computer equipped with sounds, called *soft-synths*. You also need a drum machine or drum sounds in your computer if you intend to make any music other than ambient or classical-type music. In addition, you need a MIDI controller to, well, control these sound sources. This, too, could be part of the computer software, or it could be the synthesizer. Check out Chapter 5 for more on MIDI controllers. If you end up using a computer-based sequencer, you'll also need a MIDI interface.

In addition to the MIDI stuff, you need some sort of recorder. Again, this could be included in your computer setup. If you plan to sequence all the parts and don't want to include any vocals, you could get by with a decent 2-track recorder. On the other hand, if you see yourself including vocals or any non-MIDI instruments — such as an electric guitar, for example — you need a microphone (for the vocals) and the ability to record more tracks.

Live studio

Thirty years ago, when a band wanted to record, the members all went into a studio together, set up their gear in one large room (with maybe a few dividers between them), and played as if they were at a concert. Then they would overdub a guitar solo, backup vocals, and maybe a few percussion instruments.

The beauty of this type of recording for a band is that you have a better chance of capturing the magic of a live performance. The disadvantage is that it takes a little more recording skill to get a good sound. (Of course, you discover many of these skills in this book.)

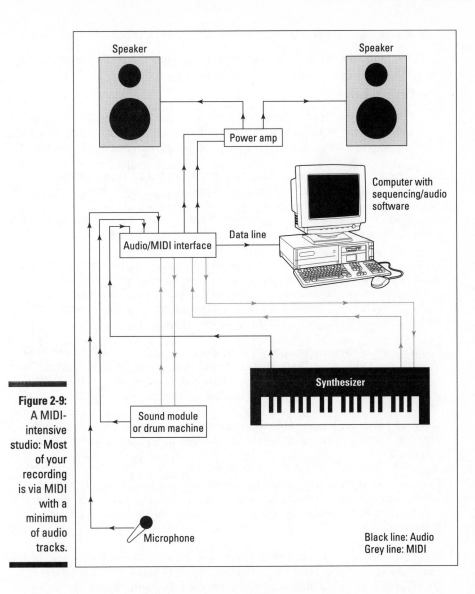

Figure 2-9:
A MIDI-
intensive
studio: Most
of your
recording
is via MIDI
with a
minimum
of audio
tracks.

For the live studio, you need a recorder with at least as many available simultaneous tracks as you think you need for your band. Eight tracks are usually enough for most bands. The tracks would break down as follows:

- **Rhythm guitar:** 1 track
- **Bass guitar:** 1 track
- **Piano, organ, or synthesizer:** 1 or 2 tracks

> ✔ **Rough vocals:** 1 track
>
> You generally record this track over again after the rest are done to get a cleaner track.
>
> ✔ **Drums:** 2–4 tracks
>
> The number of tracks varies depending on the type of sound that you want. You may need a separate mixer to create a submix of the drums if you're only using 2 tracks. (For more on submixes, check out Chapter 14.)

Aside from the simultaneous track count, you probably want some extra tracks available to record a guitar solo, some background vocals, and maybe some percussion instruments. In this case, a 16-track recorder is a great solution. If you want more flexibility in getting your band's sound, you could get a recorder that can record as many as 16 simultaneous tracks.

Figure 2-10 shows a system that can work well for live recording. This setup is illustrated using a stand-alone recorder. The reason for this is that most stand-alone recorders can record all their available tracks simultaneously. With this system, you need a separate mixer and all the cords to connect them. (Check out Chapter 3 for more details on cords.)

If you're one of those many people who like to record 1 or 2 tracks at a time but still want to play all the instruments live (with no MIDI sequencing), your need for lots of simultaneous tracks is reduced. An SIAB system is probably your best solution because it costs less and takes up less space.

You could also use a computer-based system to record all the instruments live. Just make sure that you have both the inputs and available tracks that you need.

If you record all the instruments live (all at once or one at a time), you also need to get enough microphones and mic stands. And you have to contend with making your room conducive to recording live instruments (I discuss this more in Chapter 3).

With the many ways to configure a home recording system, you'll probably lean more toward one type of system than another (computer-based, SIAB, or stand-alone). Then it's just a matter of weeding through the options until you find one that resonates with you (and your budget).

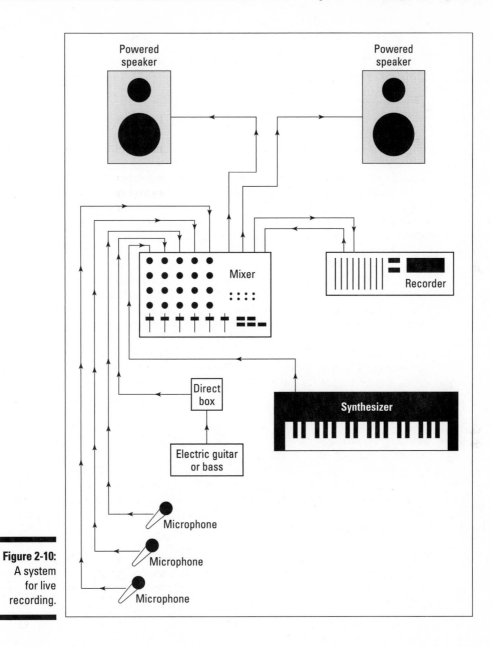

Figure 2-10:
A system
for live
recording.

Chapter 3

Getting Connected: Setting Up Your Studio

In This Chapter

▶ Getting to know the various types of connectors

▶ Plugging in your equipment

▶ Creating an efficient workstation

▶ Making your room sound great (or at least decent)

*O*kay, so you're ready to turn that spare bedroom or basement into a recording studio. You need to unpack all your shiny new gear and get it plugged in properly, and you need to get your room to work for you. This involves creating an efficient place to work, but above all it means getting your room to sound good. This can be tricky; after all, pro studios spend tons of time and money getting their studios to sound great. You're going to need to do the same. You may not need to spend a ton of money (as if you could), but you do need to spend some time.

After you decide on a space for your home recording system, the next steps involve setting up the system and getting your space to work for you. In this chapter, I help you make sense of all those analog or digital connectors and help you get them all plugged in properly. You probably have experience with analog connectors and cords, such as the ones on your stereo system. But you may have never come in contact with digital connectors, unless you've plugged a DVD player into your TV or had a chance to go into a recording studio using digital gear.

This chapter also shows you how to find the best way for you to work in your environment, with a fair measure of tips and tricks thrown in to make your room sound as good as possible.

Understanding Analog Connections

You've probably had a chance to see and use a variety of analog connectors. If you play a guitar or keyboard (synthesizer), for example, you're familiar with a ¼-inch analog plug. Some microphones use an XLR analog plug. Keeping all these connectors straight can be a little confusing: Why do you have to use one plug for one thing and another for something else? And what's a TRS plug, anyway?

Read on to discover the most common analog connectors: ¼-inch (mono/TS and stereo/TRS), XLR, and RCA.

The ¼-inch analog plug

The ¼-inch plug is the most common audio connector and one of the most versatile. These plugs come in two varieties: mono/TS and stereo/TRS.

Mono/TS

The plug on a cord that you use for your guitar or synthesizer is an example of a mono ¼-inch plug. The *mono* part of the name refers to the fact that you have only one channel with which to send the signal. This type of plug is also referred to as a *TS* plug (short for Tip/Sleeve). The tip is the end of the plug, and the sleeve is the rest of the metal part. A plastic divider separates these two sections. Check out Figure 3-1 to see this familiar plug.

Figure 3-1:
A typical ¼-inch plug used for guitar and other electric instruments.

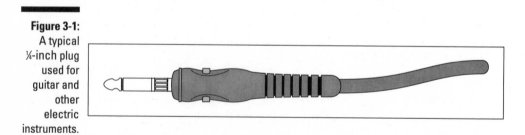

TS plugs are used for a variety of purposes — to go from your guitar to your guitar amp, from your synthesizer to your mixer, from your mixer to your power amplifier (amp), and from your power amp to your speakers. You would expect that one cord could work for all these applications. After all, a TS plug is a TS plug, right? Well, not really. The same plug can be wired differently, and it can carry different levels of power. For example, here are the differences between instrument and speaker cords:

✔ **Instrument cord (the one you use for your synthesizer or guitar):** This cord contains one wire and a shield — the wire is connected to the tip, and the shield is connected to the sleeve. You need the instrument cable's shield to minimize noise. If you use a speaker cord (discussed next) for your instrument, you may end up with some noise (that is, you may hear a hiss or a buzz — or even a radio station — coming out of your amp or coming from where you've plugged in your instrument).

Instrument cords are often called *unbalanced lines* because of the way that they're wired. An unbalanced cord has one wire surrounded by a braided shield; the wire is connected to the tip of the TS plug, and the shield is connected to the sleeve. The signal is sent through the wire, and the shield is used for the ground. (It keeps the noise down.) You can also find balanced lines, which I explain in the next section of this chapter.

✔ **A speaker cord:** This cord contains two wires and no shield — one wire is connected to the tip and the other to the sleeve. The speaker cord carries a lot more current (power) than the instrument cable. This is the reason that it doesn't have a shield. The signal level covers noise that's present in the cord. Because you have much less current present in an instrument, you don't want to use a speaker cord for your instrument.

When buying cords with TS plugs, first be sure to look at (or ask about) what purpose the cord is designed for. Then, when you get the cord home, be sure to make a note of what type it is so that you use it correctly. You can mark your cord in a number of ways: You can put colored tape on it (red for speaker or blue for instrument, for example), put a tag on it, or — gasp — dot it with nail polish.

You generally don't need to worry about which end of the cord you plug into your instrument — the signal can travel equally well in either direction. However, you can buy cords that are designed to send the current in one direction. (This cord has an arrow on it, designating in which direction the signal should flow.) I call these *designer cords,* and two of the most common brands are Monster and Planet Waves. The theory behind these cords is that they do a better job of preserving the sound qualities of the instrument for which they're designed. These cords are specifically designed for almost every instrument and application known to man.

Stereo/TRS

A stereo/TRS (short for Tip/Ring/Sleeve) ¼-inch plug looks like a stereo head-phone plug (take a look at Figure 3-2). The tip is the end of the plug, the ring is the small middle section located between the two plastic dividers, and the sleeve is the rest of the metal part of the plug. A TRS plug can be used for the following three types of cords:

✔ **Stereo cord:** A stereo cord is used for signals that contain two separate portions: one for the right channel and the other for the left channel. This type of cord is generally wired with the left-channel signal attached to the tip, the right-channel signal connected to the ring, and the shield wired to the sleeve. This type of cord is typically used for headphones.

Figure 3-2:
Use a
balanced
(TRS) plug
to connect
professional
audio gear.

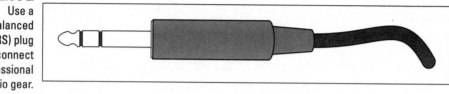

✔ **Balanced cord:** A *balanced cord* is used on professional audio gear to join the various pieces of equipment (to connect the mixer to the recorder, for example). The advantage with a balanced cord is that you can have longer cord runs without creating noise.

Why are balanced cords so conveniently noise free? The balanced cord has two wires and a shield inside and has the same signal running through both wires. One signal is 180 degrees out of phase with the other (that is, their waveforms are opposite one another), and when the signals get to the mixer (or whatever they're plugged into), one of the signals is flipped and added to the other. When this happens, any noise that built up in the signal is cancelled out.

✔ **Y cord:** A *Y cord* consists of a TRS plug on one end and two TS plugs on the other, forming — you guessed it — a nice representation of the letter *Y*. This cord allows you to insert an effect processor — a compressor or equalizer, for example — in the line of a mixer (more specifically, into the insert jack of the mixer). Check out Chapter 4 for details on mixers. The TRS plug both sends and receives a signal. This cord is wired so that the tip sends the signal and the ring receives it (see Figure 3-3). The sleeve is connected to the shield of each cable.

XLR

The XLR connector is used for microphones and some line connections between professional gear. This cable has a female and a male end (see Figure 3-4). The cord is wired much like a TRS connector and is balanced to minimize noise. The XLR microphone cable is also called a *low Z cable* because it carries a low-impedance signal.

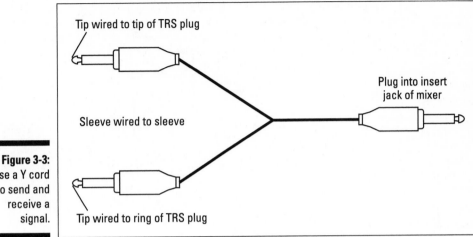

Tip wired to tip of TRS plug

Plug into insert jack of mixer

Sleeve wired to sleeve

Figure 3-3:
Use a Y cord
to send and
receive a
signal.

Tip wired to ring of TRS plug

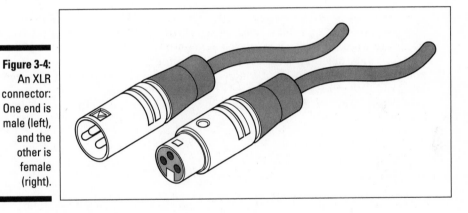

Figure 3-4:
An XLR
connector:
One end is
male (left),
and the
other is
female
(right).

RCA

RCA plugs — named for good old RCA and also called phono plugs — are common on home stereos and on some semipro audio gear (see Figure 3-5). They function much like a TS plug but aren't very common in professional audio equipment. However, you find them on some mixers so that you can connect a tape deck. They are also used for digital S/PDIF signals (see the next section for more details on these babies).

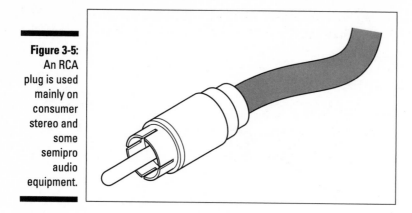

Figure 3-5: An RCA plug is used mainly on consumer stereo and some semipro audio equipment.

Delving into Digital Connections

If you're going to record using a digital recorder or mixer, you're going to run into digital connectors (plugs and cables/cords). Digital audio equipment is a recent invention, and as such, no one standard has emerged. Because of this lack of standardization, a variety of digital connection methods are on the market, only a few (or one) of which may be on the equipment that you own or intend to purchase. Regardless, knowing about the most common types of connectors and their purposes can help you decide what equipment is right for you.

MIDI

MIDI, short for Musical Instrument Digital Interface, is a handy communication protocol that allows musical information to pass from one device to another. To allow the free passage of such information, MIDI jacks are located on a whole host of electronic instruments — synthesizers, drum machines, sound modules, and even some guitars have MIDI jacks. And, to connect all these instruments, you need some MIDI cables. The MIDI connector contains five pins (male) that plug into the female MIDI jack (port) on the instrument or device (see Figure 3-6).

AES/EBU

AES/EBU (Audio Engineering Society/European Broadcasting Union) cables are much like S/PDIF cables (described in the next section). The AES/EBU standards require these cables to transmit two channels of data at a time. They differ from S/PDIF cables in that they consist of XLR plugs and use balanced cables. (Figure 3-7 shows what the inputs look like on the recording equipment.)

AES/EBU was developed to be used with professional audio components; hence the use of balanced cords — the kinds used in professional-level equipment.

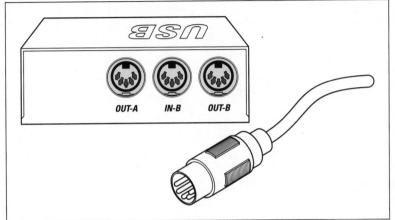

Figure 3-6: MIDI connectors have two male ends. The device contains the female jack.

S/PDIF

S/PDIF (short for Sony/Phillips Digital Interface Format) cables consist of an unbalanced coaxial cable (one wire and a shield) and RCA plugs. (Figure 3-7 shows what the inputs look like on the machine.) These cables can also be made from fiber-optic cable and a Toslink connector. The S/PDIF format can transmit two channels of digital data at one time. S/PDIF protocols are similar to AES/EBU standards, except S/PDIF was originally designed for the consumer market — which explains why unbalanced cords are used. In spite of being developed for the consumer market, S/PDIF connectors are found on a lot of pro recording gear along with (or instead of) AES/EBU.

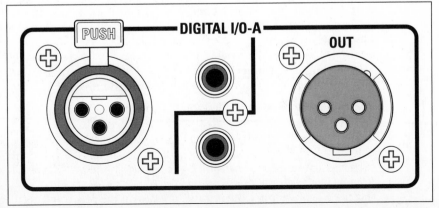

Figure 3-7: S/PDIF and AES/EBU connectors look the same as analog RCA (S/PDIF) and XLR (AES/EBU) but are marked as digital on the machine.

If you want to use cords that are longer than 3–4 feet when using an S/PDIF connector — or about 15 feet for AES/EBU connectors — your best bet is to use video or digital audio cables. Regular audio cables degrade the sound at longer distances because they can't transmit the type of signal that digital produces without affecting the quality of the sound. If you use audio cables for longer distances, you lose some of the sound's definition. Some people describe this sound as "grainy."

ADAT Lightpipe

The ADAT (Alesis Digital Audio Tape) Lightpipe format allows eight tracks of digital audio to be sent at once. Developed by Alesis, ADAT Lightpipe (or simply Lightpipe for short) has become a standard among digital audio products. It consists of a fiber-optic cable that uses a special connector developed by Alesis.

TDIF

TDIF (Teac Digital Interface Format) is Teac's return volley to the ADAT Lightpipe format. TDIF uses a standard computer cable with a 25-pin connector. Like the ADAT Lightpipe, TDIF cables can transmit eight channels of digital data at a time. TDIF isn't nearly as common as ADAT Lightpipe because Alesis made its Lightpipe technology available to other companies to use for free. Alesis encouraged these companies to adopt it as a "standard" because the Alesis ADAT recorders were so common.

USB

USB, which stands for Universal Serial Bus, is a common component in nearly all modern computers. In fact, your computer probably has more than one USB port. In case it's been a while since you've had to use your USB connection, take a look at Figure 3-8. As you can see, USB has the following different plugs that fit different jacks:

- **Rectangular connector:** This is called the "A" connector and is for any receiving device, such as your PC or a USB hub.
- **Square connector:** Called the "B" connector, this is used for a sending device, such as your USB audio interface or printer.

Figure 3-8:
USB uses
two types of
connectors:
the "A"
connector
(left) and
the "B"
connector
(right).

Aside from having two different types of jacks and plugs, USB also has two different standards, as follows:

✔ **USB 1.1:** This, the original, standard can handle a data rate of up to 12 Mbps (megabits per second).

✔ **USB 2.0:** This standard can handle 40 times the data flow of the earlier standard — 480 Mbps.

Currently, USB interfaces primarily use the USB 1.1 standard and, because of the relatively slow transfer speed, have limited input and output options. USB 2.0 has considerably faster transfer rates, so expect more audio interfaces to use this approach in the future. (Chapter 2 has more details on audio interfaces.)

FireWire

Developed by Apple Computer, FireWire (also known as IEEE 1394 or iLink) is a high-speed connection that is used by many audio interfaces, hard drives, digital cameras, and other devices. Even though FireWire was developed by Apple, you can find FireWire ports on devices from many manufacturers. FireWire cables, unlike USB cables (see the preceding section), have the same connector (see Figure 3-9) on both ends.

Figure 3-9:
FireWire is a
high-speed
data-
transfer
protocol.

Like USB, FireWire comes in two flavors, which are described as follows:

- **FireWire 400:** This standard supports data-transfer speeds of up to 400 Mbps. Many audio interfaces currently use FireWire 400 as a way to connect with your computer. These interfaces can handle quite a few inputs and outputs.

- **FireWire 800:** Yep, you guessed it — this standard can handle data-transfer rates of 800 Mbps. You should see interfaces supported by FireWire 800 in the not-too-distant future. (I admit that this isn't exactly a risky assumption.)

Sampling Some Studio Setups

Everyone's studio setup is a little different. Because I can't come into your home to help you set yours up, in this section I show you some typical setups that you can use to configure your system.

I outline these three systems in the sections that follow:

✔ **Audio with some MIDI:** This system is designed to record audio tracks and run MIDI tracks simultaneously using stand-alone components.

✔ **MIDI-intensive setup:** This setup relies heavily on MIDI, using a computer to run audio and MIDI.

✔ **Live audio:** This setup optimizes live-instrument recording with no MIDI devices, which consists of a studio-in-a-box (SIAB) system.

Whenever you connect or disconnect cables within your system, make sure that the power to the equipment is turned off or that the volume on the device is turned all the way down.

Audio with some MIDI

The most common home studio setup includes one or two MIDI devices connected to a digital recorder and one or two microphones plugged in to record vocals or an instrument. Figure 3-10 shows this typical setup. Here, the guitar and bass may be either miked from the amp or plugged directly into the mixer using one of the following three techniques:

✔ Use a direct box, a device that changes the impedance level of your guitar so that the mixer can process the signal.

✔ Plug your guitar into your amp and run a cord from the line output of the amp to the mixer's channel input.

✔ Use the Hi Z input of your mixer, if this input is available.

The setup in Figure 3-10 consists of a stand-alone recorder, a separate mixer, and a computer running MIDI sequencing software. Here's how you connect the equipment in this scenario:

✔ **Plug all your instruments into the channel inputs of the mixer.** For example, insert a TS plug into a ¼-inch jack and an XLR plug into an XLR jack.

✔ **To connect the synthesizer to the MIDI controller (computer), run a MIDI cable from the MIDI-output jack of the MIDI interface to the MIDI-input jack of the synthesizer.**

The connection between the MIDI interface and computer depends on your MIDI interface. This connection is usually made using a USB port, but you can find MIDI ports in many audio interfaces. In this case, the connection type depends on the type of interface you use. Chapter 2 has more details on audio interface connection types.

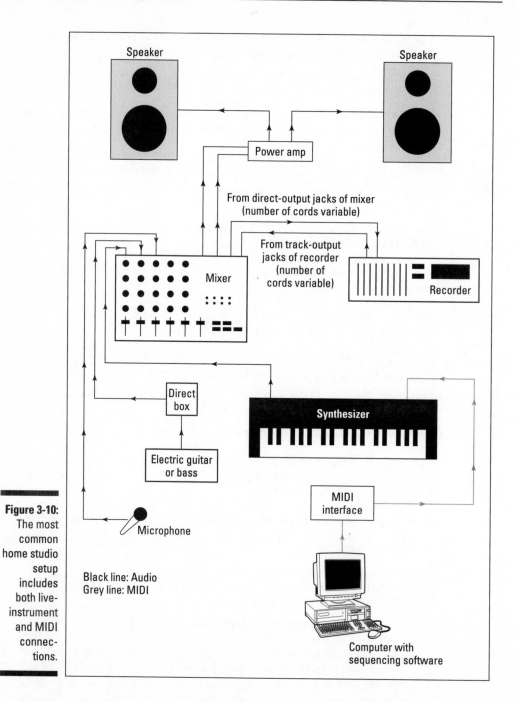

Figure 3-10:
The most common home studio setup includes both live-instrument and MIDI connections.

Speaker

Speaker

Power amp

From direct-output jacks of mixer (number of cords variable)

From track-output jacks of recorder (number of cords variable)

Mixer

Recorder

Direct box

Synthesizer

Electric guitar or bass

MIDI interface

Microphone

Black line: Audio
Grey line: MIDI

Computer with sequencing software

✔ **To connect the mixer to the recorder, run ¼-inch line cords from the direct-output jacks of the individual channels to the line (track)–input jacks of the recorder.**

Figure 3-10 shows only one cord running from the mixer to the recorder (and one running from the recorder back to the mixer), but you can have as many cords as you have direct-output jacks in your mixer or line-input jacks in your recorder. For example, if you have an 8-track recorder, you have cords running from channels 1–8 of your mixer into the track-input jacks 1–8 of your recorder. Of course, if your system consists of a studio-in-a-box or a computer-based system, you don't need to run these cords because the connections are made within the box (see the section "Live audio," later in this chapter).

✔ **To monitor the tracks of the recorder, run cords from the individual line-output jacks of the recorder back to the mixer.** You would generally plug these cords into channel inputs 9–16. Again, if you have a studio-in-a-box or a computer-based system, you don't need to do this.

If you connect your recorder and mixer as I just outlined, you have channels 1–8 on your mixer controlling all the inputs and channels 9–16 controlling the recorded tracks. If you don't have that many channels in your mixer, you need to jockey some cords around. The routing possibilities are almost endless with a mixer. Check your owner's manual for some recommended setups and routing suggestions.

As an example, suppose that you have a 12-channel mixer and an 8-track recorder. If you don't intend to record more than 4 tracks at a time, you can use tracks 1–4 for your channel inputs from your instruments and tracks 5–12 for the track inputs from your recorder.

If you need more inputs and don't want or need to listen to the tracks as you record, you can allocate fewer channels for track monitoring and more for instrument inputs.

✔ **Run line cords from the main left and right output jacks of the mixer to your power amp (or powered speakers).**

✔ **Run speaker cords from the power amp to the speakers.** (You obviously don't need these if you have powered speakers because the connection is internally wired.)

MIDI-intensive setup

The MIDI-intensive setup has numerous MIDI devices hooked up to a mixer and a microphone occasionally plugged in to record vocals. The system shown in Figure 3-11 features a computer running audio and sequencing software as well as an audio and MIDI interface. The mixer is housed within the software program. All your instrument and microphone audio outputs are plugged into the audio inputs of the interface, and the MIDI connections are made using the MIDI input and output jacks.

The diagram shows both MIDI input and output connections on all the sound modules and synthesizers. This allows two-way communication between the MIDI controller (located in the computer) and the instruments, which gives you more flexibility with sequencing.

Because all routing is done within the computer, you don't need as many cords as you would with a stand-alone system.

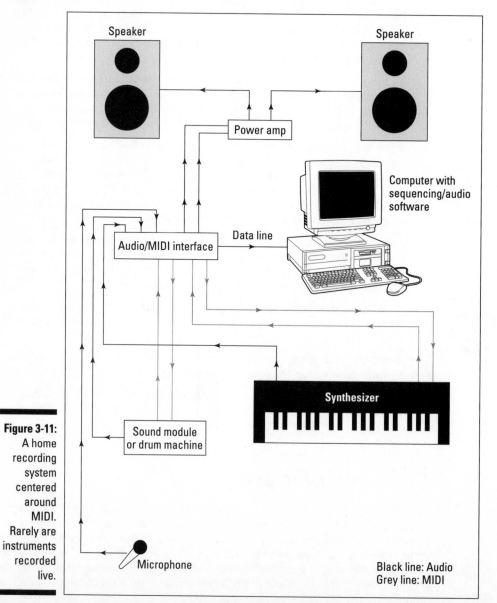

Figure 3-11:
A home recording system centered around MIDI. Rarely are instruments recorded live.

Live audio

If you intend to record a live band, you are likely to use this setup. The live audio setup requires more microphone connections and rarely has MIDI devices running into it. Figure 3-12 shows how you would make the connections for this type of application.

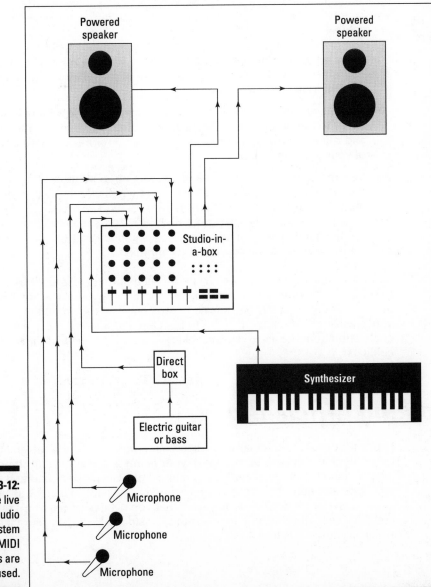

Figure 3-12: The live audio system setup. MIDI devices are rarely used.

The setup in Figure 3-12 consists of a studio-in-a-box (SIAB) system (a Roland VS-1880, for instance). Because all the routing takes place within the box, your setup is simple. All your instruments and microphones plug directly into the SIAB (most units even have one Hi-Z input for a guitar or bass). If you want to plug both the electric guitar and bass in at the same time, you still need one direct box or line output from your amp.

If you plan to use more than two microphones at once, make sure that you have enough inputs because most SIAB systems only have two XLR jacks. If you want to plug in more mics than you have XLR jacks, you have the following options:

✔ **Use a separate analog mixer for plugging in extra mics.** Then run an instrument cord from the channel output of the mixer to the channel's line input on your SIAB system.

✔ **Use one or more external preamps to convert the low-impedance mic cords to high-impedance TS cords.** Just plug your mic into the preamp and run an instrument cord from the preamp to the channel's line input of your SIAB system.

✔ **Use line converters, such as a direct box or an adapter.** Plug your mic cord into the direct box or adapter and then plug into the channels' line input of your SIAB system's mixer. (You can find an adapter at Radio Shack for about $12 — part no. 910-0913.) This is the least expensive option, but it costs you more in terms of sound quality — it doesn't sound as good as the previous two options.

All that's left is to run line cords from the main outputs of your SIAB system to the inputs of your powered speakers. In this case, you use ¼-inch instrument cords (T/S) rather than speaker cords because the input on your powered speakers is actually the input to the amplifier and not the speakers. The connection from the amp to the speakers is made internally in the speaker cabinets.

Working Efficiently

I hope that you'll spend many hours in your studio creating some great music (possibly to the dismay of the rest of your family). One important thing to keep in mind is that you need to be comfortable. Get a good chair and set up your workstation to be as easy to get around as possible. Figure 3-13 shows a classic *L* setup. Notice how everything that you need is within arm's reach. If you have enough room, you may want to consider a U-shaped setup instead, which is shown in Figure 3-14.

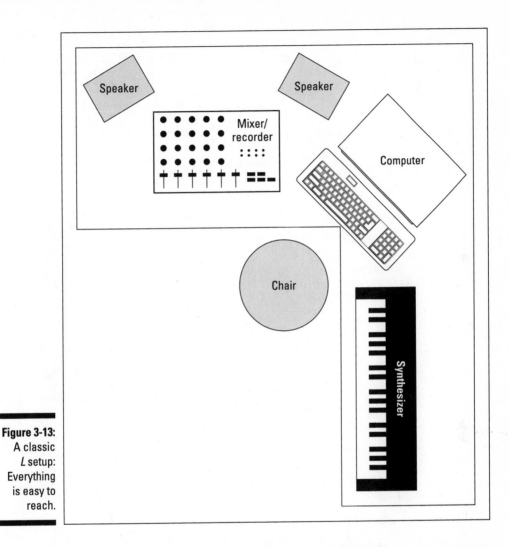

Figure 3-13:
A classic
L setup:
Everything
is easy to
reach.

If you use a lot of outboard gear — such as preamps or effects processors —
and you think that you need to plug and unplug a lot, invest in a good patch
bay (see Figure 3-15) so that you don't have to strain to get at the cords that
are tucked away behind your mixer. A *patch bay* is a device that has a bunch
of inputs and outputs in it that allows you to route your gear in (and out) in
an almost infinite variety of ways. If you're going to do much plugging and
unplugging, you'll quickly find out that a patch bay is an indispensable item.
It can save your back — and your cords (repeated plugging and unplugging
wears them out quickly and produces buzzes that can be hard to locate).

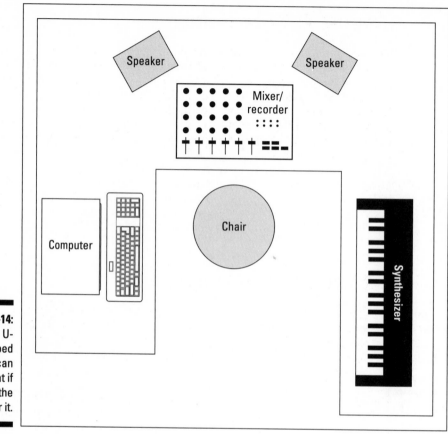

Figure 3-14:
The U-shaped setup can work great if you have the room for it.

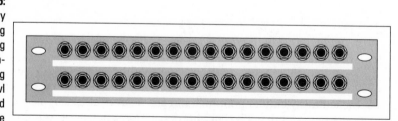

Figure 3-15:
A patch bay lets you plug and unplug gear without having to crawl behind each piece of gear.

Taming heat and dust

The number one enemy of electronic equipment is heat. Dust is a close second. Try to set up your studio in a room that you can keep cool and fairly dust free. Air conditioning is a must for most studios. Be careful with a window air conditioner, though, because it can make a lot of noise, requiring you to shut it off when you record. Depending on where you live, this could quickly warm your room. Regarding dust, try to cover your equipment when you're not using it, especially your microphones. A plastic bag placed over the top of a mic on a stand works well.

You could also just put your mics away when you're not using them. However, if you use a particular mic a lot, you're better off leaving it on a stand rather than constantly handling it — some types of mics are pretty fragile. (You can find more details on caring for your mics in Chapter 6.)

Monitoring your monitors

If you have a set of near-field monitors (speakers) — the kind that are designed to be placed close to you — they should be set up so that they are the same distance from each other and from you, forming an equilateral triangle (see, high school math has some real-world applications). The monitors should also be placed at about the height of your ears.

Figure 3-16 illustrates the best placement for your monitors. Placing your monitors this way ensures that you hear the best possible sound from them and that you can accurately hear the stereo field. (For more on the stereo field, see Chapter 14.)

Optimizing Your Room

Your studio probably occupies a corner in your living room, a spare bedroom, or a section of your basement or garage. All of these are less-than-ideal recording environments. Even if you intend to record mostly by plugging your instrument or sound module directly into the mixer, how your room sounds has a big effect on how good your music turns out.

As a home recordist, you probably can't create a top-notch sound room. Professional studios spend serious cash — up to seven figures — to make their rooms sound, well, professional. Fortunately, you don't need to spend near that much money to get great-sounding recordings. All it takes is a little understanding of the way sound travels, some ingenuity, and a little bit of work.

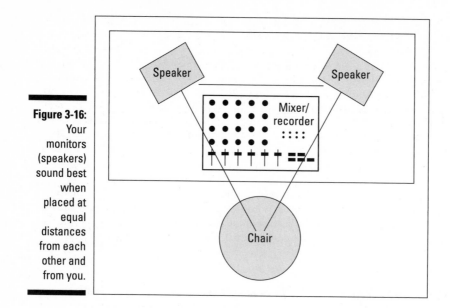

Figure 3-16:
Your
monitors
(speakers)
sound best
when
placed at
equal
distances
from each
other and
from you.

Isolating sound

One of the concerns that you (and your neighbors) are probably going to have when you start recording in your home is the amount of sound that gets into and out of your room. Sound waves are nasty little buggers. They get through almost any surface, and you can't do a lot to stop that from happening.

You've probably noticed this phenomenon when somebody with a massive subwoofer in his car drives by your house blasting some obnoxious music. (Ever notice how someone else's music is obnoxious whereas your music never is, no matter how loud you play it?) Your windows rattle, your walls shake, and your favorite mug flies off the shelf and breaks into a thousand pieces. Well, this is one of the problems with sound.

The best (and classic) way to isolate your studio room from everything around it is to build a room within a room. I don't have the space to go into detail here, but you can visit my Web site (www.jeffstrong.com) to find some resources to get you started. If you don't have the money or space to build a room within a room, the best thing you can do is to try to understand what noises are getting in and getting out and deal with those noises. For example, if you live in a house or apartment with neighbors close by, don't record live drums at night. You could also consider using a drum machine or electronic drum set instead.

Another idea is to choose a room in your house or apartment that is the farthest away from outside noise (an interior room, for instance). Basements also work well because they're underground, and most of the sound gets absorbed by the ground. Placing a little fiberglass bat insulation in the ceiling — the typical house insulation that you can find at your local home center — can isolate you pretty well from your neighbors. Detached garages are generally farther away from other buildings, so sound has a chance to dissipate before it reaches your neighbors (or before your neighbors' noise reaches your garage).

Also, keep the following points in mind when trying to isolate your studio:

- **Dead air and mass are your friends.** The whole concept of a room within a room is to create mass and dead air space so that the sound gets trapped. When you work on isolating your room, try to design in some space that can trap air (dead air) — such as a suspended ceiling or big upholstered furniture — or use double layers of drywall on your walls (mass).

- **Don't expect acoustical foam or carpet to reduce the noise.** Using these items helps reduce the amount of sound that bounces around inside the room, but acoustical foam or carpet does little toward keeping the sound in or out of the room.

- **Isolate the instrument instead of the room.** Isolating the sound of your guitar amp can be much less expensive than trying to soundproof your whole room. Most commercial studios have one or more isolation booths that they use for recording vocals and other acoustic instruments. You can use that concept to create your own mini-isolation booths.

One idea for a truly mini–isolation booth is to make an insulated box for your guitar (or bass) amp. If you just *have* to crank your amp to get the sound that you want, you can reduce the amount of noise that it makes by placing it inside an insulated box. Check out Figure 3-17 to see what I mean.

You can also create an isolated space in a closet by insulating it and closing the door when you record, or you can put your guitar amp (or drums) in another room and run a long cord from there to your recorder. If you do this, remember that for long cord runs, you need to use balanced cords; otherwise, you may get a bunch of noise and your signal may be too low to record well.

Controlling sound

After you create a room that's as isolated from the outside world as possible, you need to deal with the way sound acts within your room.

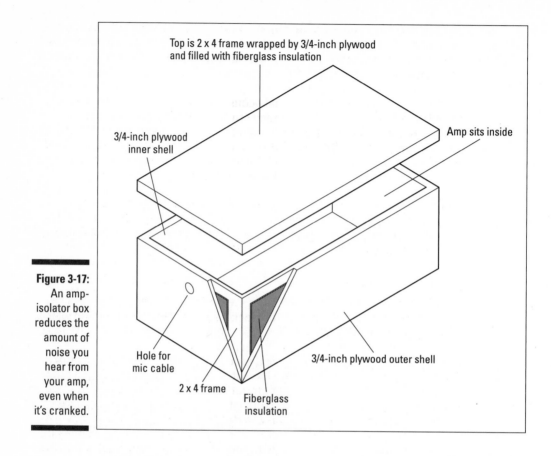

Top is 2 x 4 frame wrapped by 3/4-inch plywood and filled with fiberglass insulation

3/4-inch plywood inner shell

Amp sits inside

Figure 3-17:
An amp-isolator box reduces the amount of noise you hear from your amp, even when it's cranked.

Hole for mic cable

2 x 4 frame

Fiberglass insulation

3/4-inch plywood outer shell

Sound travels through the air in the form of waves. These waves bounce around the room and cause *reflections* (reverberations or echoes). One of the problems with most home studios is that they're small. And because sound travels very fast (about 1,130 feet per second — the exact speed depends on the humidity in the environment), when you sit at your monitors and listen, you hear the reflected sound as well as the original sound that comes out of your speakers. With big rooms, you can hear the original sound and reflections as separate sounds, meaning that the reflections themselves become less of a problem. For a good home studio, you need to tame these reflections so that they don't interfere with your ability to clearly hear the speakers.

How all these reflections bounce around your room can get pretty complicated. Read up on acoustics (the way sound behaves) to discover more about different room modes: *axial* (one dimension), *tangential* (two dimensions), and *oblique* (three dimensions). Each relates to the way that sound waves interact as they bounce around a room. Knowing your room's modes can help you come up with an acoustical treatment strategy, but very complicated formulas are used to figure out your room's modes, especially those dastardly tangential and oblique modes.

You can find out more on room modes, as well as discover some room mode calculators, by using your favorite Internet search engine and searching for *room modes*. I recommend that you research these modes; this topic alone could fill an entire book.

At the risk of offending professional acoustical engineers, I'm going to share some tricks that I've been using in my studios. My main goal has been to create a room with a sound I like that gives me some measure of control over the reflections within the room. Because I (and most home recordists) both record and mix in one room, it's helpful to be able to make minor adjustments to the acoustics to get the sound I want.

Sound control plays a major role in two aspects of recording — tracking and mixing — and each requires different approaches for you to get the best possible sound from your recordings. I cover both of these aspects in the sections that follow.

Sound control during tracking

Tracking is what you're doing when you're recording. Two things that can make a room a bad environment for tracking are not enough sound reflection and too much sound reflection.

When tracking, your goal is to have a room that's not so dead (in terms of sound reflection) that it sucks the life out of your instrument and not so alive that it overcolors the sound. The determining factors in how much reflection you need in your room are the instrument that you record and the way it sounds in the room. If your room is too dead (with not enough sound reflection), you want to add some reflective surfaces to liven things up (the room, that is). If your room is too alive (with too much sound reflection), you need to add some absorptive materials to tame those reflections.

You could buy a bunch of foam panels to catch the reflections or install a wood floor or attach some paneling to the walls to add some life, but then you would be stuck with the room sounding only one way. It may end up sounding good for recording drums or an acoustic guitar, but it would probably be too alive for getting a great vocal sound — which requires a deader space. One solution that works well is to get (or make) some portable panels that can either absorb or reflect the sound.

Figure 3-18 shows an absorber/reflector that I've used and have found to work well. (Go to my Web site, www.jeffstrong.com, for plans to build your own.) One side has an absorptive material (dense fiberglass insulation), and the other has a reflective surface (wood). They are assembled in an attractive frame and designed to stack easily. Even with minimal woodworking experience, you can crank out a set of them in a weekend for very little money (about $30 per panel). I guarantee that if you make them (or hire someone to make them for you), you'll find dozens of uses for them around your studio. (I outline a bunch of ways to use them in Chapter 8.)

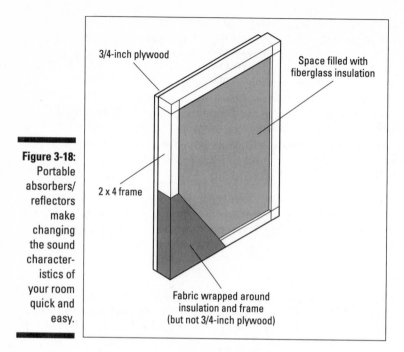

Figure 3-18: Portable absorbers/ reflectors make changing the sound character- istics of your room quick and easy.

3/4-inch plywood

Space filled with fiberglass insulation

2 x 4 frame

Fabric wrapped around insulation and frame (but not 3/4-inch plywood)

Sound control during mixing

The following sections detail the steps that can help you control the sound of your (probably less-than-perfect) room during mixing.

Get a good pair of near-field monitors

Near-field monitors are designed to be listened to up close (hence the *near* in their name) and can lessen the effects that the rest of the room has on your ability to accurately hear them and to get a good mix.

Mix at low volumes

I know; mixing at low volumes takes the fun out of it, right? Well, as fun as it may be to mix at high volumes, it rarely translates into a great mix. Great mixing engineers often listen to their mixers at very low levels. Yes, they occasionally use high levels, but only after the mixing is almost done and only for short periods of time. After all, if you damage your ears, you'll end up with a short career as a sound engineer (hey, that rhymes!). I don't want to sound like your mother, but try to resist the temptation to crank it up. Your ears will last longer, and your mixes will sound better.

Use panels to tame sound

Even with these two things (near-field monitors and low mixing levels), you still need to do something to your room to make it work better for you. The secret to getting a good mixing room is to tame the sound reflections coming out of your speakers. Dealing with high and midrange frequencies is pretty easy — just put up some foam panels or the absorptive side of the panels from Figure 3-18. (See, I told you that you would have a use for those panels.) Here's a rundown on how to place absorption panels in your studio:

✔ **Start by hanging two panels (or by putting them on a stand or table) so that they're at the level of your speakers on the wall behind you.**

✔ **Put one panel on each side wall, right where the speakers are pointed.** This positioning, shown in Figure 3-19, gets rid of the higher frequencies and eliminates much of the echo.

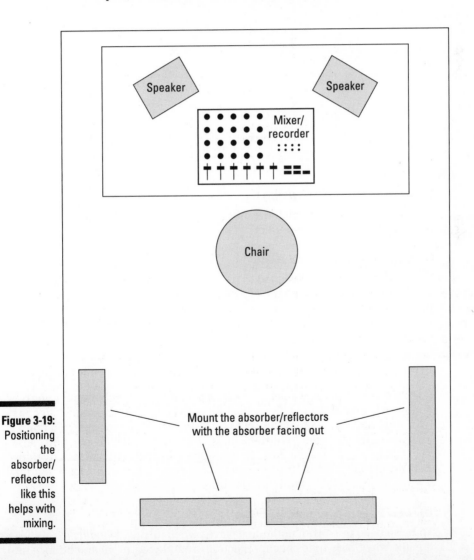

Figure 3-19: Positioning the absorber/reflectors like this helps with mixing.

✔ **You may need to put some type of panel on the ceiling right above your head.** This is especially important if you have a low (8-feet-high or less) or textured ceiling (you know, one with that popcorny stuff that gets sprayed on).

You may not want to mount one of the absorber panels over your head because they're fairly heavy. A couple of 2-x-4-foot dense fiberglass panels (the same ones that you used in the absorber/reflectors) wrapped with fabric would work perfectly. In fact, you can easily make some overhead diffusers like the ones shown in Figure 3-20. (The plans for these are also on my Web site — www.jeffstrong.com.)

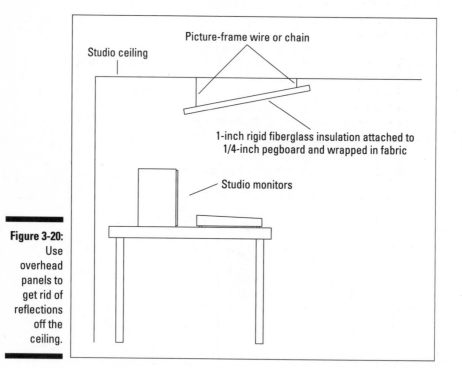

Figure 3-20: Use overhead panels to get rid of reflections off the ceiling.

Studio ceiling

Picture-frame wire or chain

1-inch rigid fiberglass insulation attached to 1/4-inch pegboard and wrapped in fabric

Studio monitors

✔ **You can also place a set of fiberglass panels in the corners of your room behind the speakers.** Just hang the panels at the same height as your speakers so that they cut off the corner of the room. If you don't have enough room to fit the panels at an angle in the corner, you can eliminate the backing from the fiberglass and bend the fabric-covered panel to fit right in the corner. Either approach absorbs sound that may bounce around behind the speakers.

Use bass traps to tame standing waves

You also need to consider standing waves when mixing. *Standing waves* are created when bass tones begin reflecting around your room and bounce into each other. Standing waves can either overaccentuate the bass from your speakers (resulting in mixes that are short on bass) or cancel out some or all of the bass coming out of your speakers (resulting in mixes with too much bass). One problem with standing waves is that they can really mess up your mixes, and you may not know that they are there.

To find out whether you have a problem with standing waves in your studio, sit in front of your monitors and carefully listen to one of your favorite CDs. Okay, now lean forward and backward a bit. Does the amount of bass that you hear change as you move? Next, get up and walk around the room. Listen for places within the room where the bass seems to be louder or softer. You may find places where the bass drops out almost completely. If either inspection proves to be true, you are the proud owner of standing waves. Don't worry, though. You can tame that standing-wave monster with a pair of bass traps.

Bass traps absorb the energy in the lower frequencies so that they don't bounce all over your room and throw off your mixes. You can buy bass traps made of foam from some music stores or (yep, you guessed it) you can make your own out of wood and insulation. Check out Figure 3-21 for a look at some homemade bass traps. (The plans to make these are located on my Web site: www.jeffstrong.com.)

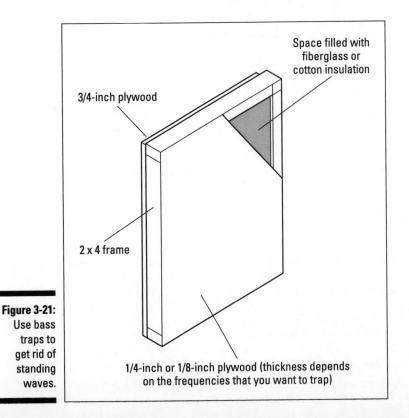

Space filled with fiberglass or cotton insulation

3/4-inch plywood

2 x 4 frame

Figure 3-21: Use bass traps to get rid of standing waves.

1/4-inch or 1/8-inch plywood (thickness depends on the frequencies that you want to trap)

The most common placement for bass traps is in the corners behind you when you're sitting at your mixer (see Figure 3-22). Placing a set of bass traps in the other corners of the room can help even more.

After you place the bass traps, do the listening test again. If you notice some areas where the bass seems to get louder or softer, try moving the bass traps around a little. With some trial and error, you can find a place where they work best.

Try not to get stressed out about the sound of your room. As important as your room's sound may be, it has a lot less impact on the quality of your recordings than good, solid engineering practices. I know, I keep saying this, but it's important to remember. So do what you can and then work with what you have.

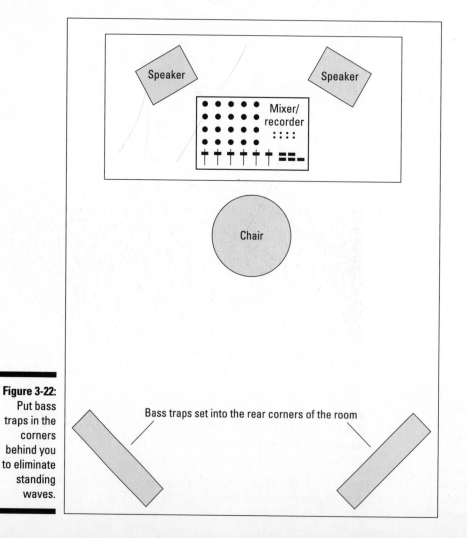

Figure 3-22:
Put bass traps in the corners behind you to eliminate standing waves.

Part II
Recording 101

"Aren't you taking this world music thing a bit too far?"

In this part . . .

Part II gets into more gear talk — this time allowing you to get a deeper understanding of the main parts of a home studio. Chapter 4 introduces you to the way the signal flows through different systems. You get a chance to understand the role of all the knobs, buttons, and connectors in recording systems. Chapter 5 explores MIDI (Musical Instrument Digital Interface) and shows you how you can harness this powerful communication tool to enhance your music. Chapter 6 takes you inside the world of microphones. You discover the three most common types of microphones for the home studio along with practical advice on which ones work best for each instrument.

Chapter 4

Meeting the Mixer

*I*f you've ever been to a recording studio and watched a great recording engineer create a mix, you've probably been entranced by the way that he or she interacted with the mixing board: a dance around the mixer, a twist of a knob here, a push of a slider there. All this works to the beat of the music. It's like watching a genius painter paint, or a great orchestra conductor conduct, or a brilliant surgeon surge . . . er, operate. I'll even bet that one of the reasons that you got interested in home recording is so that you could have a chance to play with those knobs and sliders yourself. Go ahead and admit it — you'll feel better.

Well, you get your chance in this chapter. Not only do you discover what all those knobs and sliders do, but you also begin to understand all the functions that the mixer fulfills in the studio. You discover what makes up a channel strip and how it's used. You get a chance to see how busing and routing work and even discover what these terms mean. But first you start by examining the different types of mixers that are used in home studios.

Meeting the Many Mixers

For the home recordist, mixers come in several varieties: the analog desk, the digital mixer or computer control surface with or without sliding faders and fader banks, and software mixers controlled by your computer mouse and keyboard.

Your choice of mixer mostly depends on the other equipment that you use in your studio and on your budget. Here's the lowdown for the three basic types of recording systems:

- **Studio-in-a-box (SIAB) system:** These all-in-one units come with a digital mixer — just plug in your instrument or microphone and you're ready to go. Most mixers in these units offer quite a bit of flexibility in routing your signal, so you'll likely be able to do quite a bit with little hassle. The features of the mixer in each SIAB system vary, so look at the specs of the unit you're interested in before you buy.

- **Computer-based system:** All recording software includes a digital mixer that's controlled by your keyboard and mouse. Most of these programs also allow you to connect an external bit of hardware called the *computer control surface.* This gives you real knobs and sliders to tinker with as you work.

- **Stand-alone components:** Because everything is separate in this type of system, you need to buy a mixer before you can use your recorder. Here you can choose between an analog or digital mixer, and you need to invest in the cords necessary to make the proper connections (this alone can get expensive). The type of mixer you choose will partly be based on your budget, but it will mostly be based on your working style and whether you prefer analog or digital mixing. I talk more about these mixers in the next two sections.

Analog mixer

The analog mixer, shown in Figure 4-1, enables you to route the signals within the analog domain. Analog mixers tend to have many knobs, lights, and faders — a set for each channel. If you want to change from mixing inputs (your instruments) to mixing sounds recorded on the recorder, you need to plug and unplug cords, or you need to get a mixer with twice as many channels as your recorder.

Analog mixers are quickly becoming relics of the past for most home recordists. This is because digital mixers offer more functions for the price and generally sound just as good — if not better — than their analog counterparts. That said, many commercial studios still use (and prefer) large analog desks for their mixing needs. This is because top-notch analog mixers ($100,000+ to over $1 million) have a sound that many pros prefer. They also look impressive, and many engineers are used to the workflow they get with them.

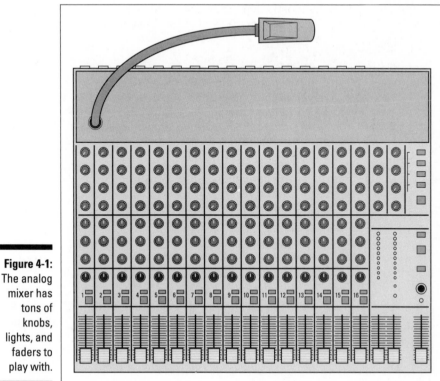

Figure 4-1:
The analog
mixer has
tons of
knobs,
lights, and
faders to
play with.

Digital mixer

The digital mixer, shown in Figure 4-2, is a great option for home studio
owners because it can perform the same functions as a conventional analog
mixer in a lot less space. Routing — the process of sending your signals to
various places within the mixer — becomes almost easy using one of these
mixers. You can switch between input and track channels without having to
change a single cord.

Digital mixers handle all the busing and routing tasks within the digital
domain. With no cords to mess with, you have a lot less possibility for noise
to enter the system. And if noise does enter the system, it's easier to find and
eliminate.

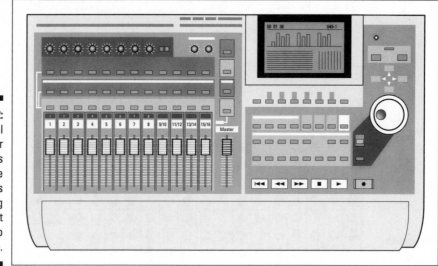

Figure 4-2:
The digital mixer performs the same functions as an analog mixer but takes up less space.

One of the great things about digital mixers is the ability to automate your mix. You can set up complex fader and effects changes to run automatically. Some digital mixers even have motorized faders, which are really fun to watch!

Software mixer

If you want the flexibility of a digital mixer and don't have an overpowering need to physically touch the faders and knobs, a software mixer (shown in Figure 4-3) may work for you. The software mixer is included with any computer audio or MIDI production software. The advantage of a software mixer is that after you have the computer and audio software that you want, you have nothing else to buy.

Software mixers work much the same way as digital mixers. Because software mixers are digital, you have an almost infinite variety of routing choices that you can make without having to patch and repatch cables. Still, some people may not be too keen on having to use a keyboard and a mouse to get mixing work done rather than working with the more traditional knobs or slide faders.

For those of you who want the best of both worlds — high-tech computer software and tactile stimulation — you can find control surfaces that allow you to control the software's mixer using real faders and knobs, as described in the next section.

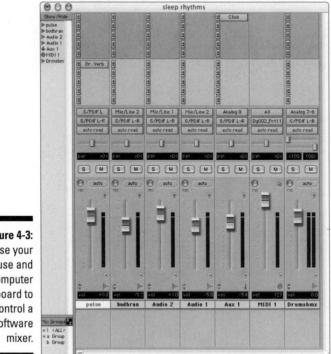

Figure 4-3:
Use your mouse and computer keyboard to control a software mixer.

Computer control surface

If you end up with a computer-based system with a software mixer, you'll have some knobs, buttons, and faders to play around with on the *computer control surface,* as shown in Figure 4-4. Aside from being able to fiddle with some knobs, you'll find that a computer control surface is a handy tool if you decide to use a computer-based Digital Audio Workstation (DAW) and want (or need) to control the virtual mixer with some hardware.

These controllers send MIDI messages — messages encoded using the Musical Instrument Digital Interface communications protocol — to the computer that tells it which parameters to change. These controllers can easily be programmed to work like a separate digital mixer.

Not all software works with each computer control surface, so check with the software or computer control surface manufacturer before you buy to make sure that the computer control surface is compatible with your system.

Figure 4-4:
A computer
control
surface acts
like a digital
mixer for a
computer-
based
system.

Understanding Mixer Basics

The mixer is an extremely versatile piece of equipment, allowing you a staggering variety of input and output configurations. And digital mixers (both hardware and software) are even more flexible than their analog counterparts. In fact, many digital mixers can be programmed to do almost anything that you can imagine. Regardless of the type of mixer that you use, some mixing aspects are universal: the inputs, the channel strip, busing (also known as routing), and the outputs. The rest of the chapter explores these functions.

Think of a mixing board as a sort of air-traffic controller for the audio world. Just as the guys (and gals) in the towers near an airport communicate with all the planes in the air, making sure that collisions are avoided and that traffic moves quickly and efficiently, the mixer routes all the incoming and outgoing signals from the instruments, effects, and recording devices so that the signals get to their desired destination without any problems.

Examining Inputs

To move your audio signal around within your mixer, you need to first get the signal into the system and then you need to adjust the signal level. You perform these steps with the input jacks and the trim control.

Inputs

You find the following three basic types of inputs, which are generally located in the back of your system:

- **Microphone:** This is the XLR input (the three-pin thingy). It's used for microphones and often also has *phantom power* as part of its connection (which generally can be turned off if you want). Phantom power is necessary for condenser mics to function. See Chapter 6 for more on phantom power.

- **Line/instrument:** This is a ¼-inch jack (generally TS but sometimes TRS-balanced) that accepts line-level signals from a synthesizer, drum machine, or the line output from your guitar amp.

- **Hi-Z:** This is a relatively new input that's designed for the home recordist. This type of input uses a mono ¼-inch (TS) jack and allows you to plug your electric guitar (or bass or fiddle — anything with an electronic pickup) directly into your system without having to mic it or run it through a direct box first.

For more on the different connector types, check out Chapter 3.

Many digital mixers, computer audio interfaces, and SIAB systems are wired to let you plug your electric guitars and similar instruments into one or more of the instrument inputs instead of having a dedicated Hi-Z input.

A *direct box* (or DI box, short for direct injection) is traditionally used to connect your guitar or bass directly to the mixer without having to run it through your amp first. A direct box's purpose is twofold:

- To change the guitar's impedance level so that the mixer can create the best sound possible (otherwise, it can sound thin or noisy)

- To change the cord from unbalanced ¼-inch to balanced XLR so that you can use a long cord without creating noise

For more on cord types and balanced versus unbalanced signals, see Chapter 3.

If you use a computer-based system, the inputs and outputs are located in your audio interface — the hardware you use to connect the analog world to the computer world. Chapter 2 has more on the various types of available interfaces.

Trim control

The Trim control is a knob that's used to adjust the level of the input signal as it enters the mixer. You usually find the Trim control at the top of the front panel of your hardware unit. On SIAB systems and analog and digital mixers, this control is generally located at the top of the mixer section for each channel, and on audio interfaces, it's often found on the front panel. The amount that you adjust the Trim control depends on the instrument that you have plugged into the channel strip. If the Trim control is set too high, you get distortion; if it's set too low, you get a signal that's too weak to record. So be sure to listen as you make your adjustments.

Most Trim controls have a switch or markings for Line or Mic(rophone) signals, with the Line level to the right and the Mic level to the left. Turn the knob all the way to the left for line sources or slowly keep turning it to the right for microphone sources until you get a nice, clean sound coming into the mixer. See Chapter 7 for more on setting input levels.

For microphone sources, you use the Trim control to adjust the level for recording. Turning the control up (turning the knob clockwise) activates an internal preamp in the mixer, which boosts the level of the signal coming from the mic. The internal preamp in pro mixers is usually fairly decent (it can sound pretty good). However, many professionals prefer to use an external preamp because it can often sound better or have a sound characteristic that they want.

If you use an external preamp, check the owner's manual of your mixer to see whether you can bypass the internal preamp. Most professional mixers enable you to do this. Sometimes just turning the Trim control all the way down (to the Line marking) disengages the preamp from the circuit.

Checking Out the Channel Strip

The mixer is composed of numerous channels through which you route your signal when you record or mix. This is called the *channel strip*. The channel strip contains a lot of information, and the visual position of the various functions often doesn't correspond with the actual flow of the signal. In the following sections, I explain both the elements of a typical digital channel strip and the path of the signal through this part of the mixer.

Viewing the channel strip layout

Figure 4-5 shows the channel strip in a typical analog mixer, and Figure 4-6 shows the channel strip for a software mixer. Even though the mixer may look confusing with all its knobs or buttons, lights, and sliders, you only need to understand the basic makeup of one channel to understand them all. The channel strip's job is to take the signal from an instrument or microphone and send it where you want it to go.

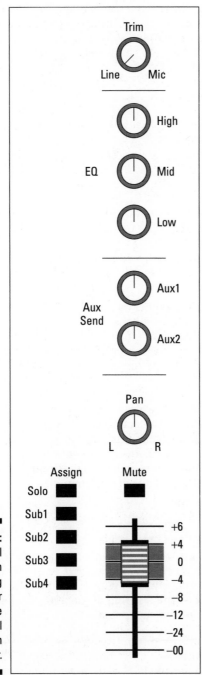

Figure 4-5:
The channel strip in an analog mixer moves the signal through your mixer.

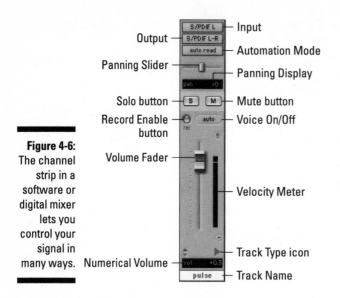

Figure 4-6:
The channel strip in a software or digital mixer lets you control your signal in many ways.

Output — Input
— Automation Mode
Panning Slider —
— Panning Display
Solo button — — Mute button
Record Enable button — — Voice On/Off
Volume Fader —
— Velocity Meter
— Track Type icon
Numerical Volume — — Track Name

Because most home recordists use a digital mixer of some sort — whether software or hardware — I explain the channel strip in Pro Tools to give you an idea of the functions of digital mixers in the channel strip window (as shown in Figure 4-6). Your mixer may have some different features (and a different layout), but the basic functions are pretty universal. These features are as follows:

✔ **Input:** This is where you choose the input that's assigned to the channel strip. In most systems, making the selection is as simple as clicking the Input button and choosing from a menu that opens on-screen. You can generally choose between a physical input from your hardware interface or a bus (an internal signal). For more on routing an input, see the section "Recognizing Mixer Routing," later in this chapter.

✔ **Output:** This button controls the output of the track — where the sound goes when it leaves the track. This can be a hardware output or any of the buses (internal signal paths) that are available in your system.

✔ **Automation Mode:** In digital systems, *automation* means having certain channel strip parameters, such as volume, panning, mute, send level, and insert level, adjust dynamically throughout the song. Using this button, you can choose among the different automation modes. These vary depending on the type of system you have.

✔ **Panning Slider:** Use this slider (or a knob in many systems) to pan your track to the left or the right in the stereo field. (For more on panning, see Chapter 14.)

✔ **Panning Display:** This display shows your track's panning position — its place to the left, right, or center in the stereo field.

✔ **Solo and Mute:** These buttons either solo or mute the track. Solo means that every other track in your song is silenced (muted). Muting means that only the selected track is silenced.

✔ **Record Enable:** Pressing the Record Enable button enables the track for recording. When enabled, this button flashes red. In digital mixers, SIAB systems, and computer control surfaces, this button is located on the physical unit and not on the screen.

✔ **Voice On/Off:** This selector lets you choose between Off, where the track does not play, or Auto, where the track plays if data is present. This feature is unique to Pro Tools. In its place on some SIAB systems, you may find a virtual track selector, where you can choose from a list of additional tracks called, logically enough, virtual tracks.

✔ **Volume Fader:** This is the control for setting the volume of the audio that's contained in this track.

✔ **Velocity/Volume Meter:** This display, located to the right of the Volume Fader, shows you the volume (Pro Tools calls this *velocity*) of the track as the music plays. If you have a color display, any notes above digital 0 usually show in red at the top of the display.

✔ **Group:** The little red *G* is present if this track is grouped with others. You can find out which group the track belongs to by clicking and holding over the icon. This feature is unique to Pro Tools as well.

✔ **Track Type:** This icon shows you the type of track. This is handy with systems that can record and play back audio and MIDI tracks.

✔ **Numerical Volume:** This display shows you the volume of the track in decibels.

✔ **Track Name:** Many digital mixers allow you to customize the name of your tracks to make it easier to remember what you have recorded on them. This is the place where the name is listed. You can change the name at any time by clicking the name and typing in a new one.

Following the flow of the signal

One of the most important things to understand when recording is how the signal moves within your system. This knowledge lets you make the most of your tracks and helps you to tailor the sound to match the music you hear in your head as you compose, engineer, or produce your masterpiece.

Using the ubiquitous Pro Tools as an example again, here's how the signal flows through the channel strip (shown from top to bottom in Figure 4-7):

✔ **Source audio or input:** This is the signal that is coming from your hardware input or that is recorded to your hard drive. The signal starts here and enters the track's channel strip.

✔ **Insert:** This function lets you insert effects into your track. This function is for effects, such as equalizers or dynamics processors, where you want to change the sound of the entire signal. Some SIAB systems, such as the Roland boxes, have separate EQ sections.

✔ **Send Prefader:** The Send function lets you route part of your signal out to an Aux bus, where you can then insert an effect such as reverb. With effects such as reverb, you don't want to use the Insert function — as you would with a compressor — because you want to be able to control how much of the effect you hear. (Compressors only enable you to affect the entire signal, not some portion of it.)

Adjust this slider or knob to *send* as much or as little of the signal to the appropriate *auxiliary* component (Aux, get it?) for effects processing, applying as much or as little of that effect to your final sound. Turning the knob to the left produces less effect, and turning it to the right gives more effect.

Along with being able to set the Effect Send level at each channel (you can send more than one channel's signal to each effect), you can also adjust the level of the affected signal that's brought back into the mixer by using the Aux bus fader (which is described in the next section).

The Aux Send function can often be set to send the track's signal either prefader or postfader. Having this option gives you more flexibility to control the affected sound. For example, you can send the dry signal of a kick drum to a reverb (with the switch in the Pre position) and then boost the bass on the dry signal. Doing this gives you some reverb on the higher frequencies without adding it to the lower ones, which would create some mud in the final mix.

The downside to this is that you can't control the level of the signal being sent to the effect using the fader. (You bypassed the fader in the Pre position.) In this case, if you raise and lower the channel fader, the amount of effect that you hear in relation to the dry signal changes as well. For example, when you lower the fader, you hear more effect because less dry signal is mixed in, and when you raise the fader, you hear less effect because the dry signal is louder and the effect level is the same.

✔ **Solo and Mute:** These buttons let you solo (silence all other tracks) and mute (silence) the output of the track.

✔ **Fader:** This function lets you control the level (volume) of your signal leaving the track and going to the output(s) you have chosen in the Output section of the channel strip.

✔ **Send Postfader:** When you have the Pre button disengaged, your Send signal is sent from your track after it passes through the track fader.

Adjusting the volume of the track also adjusts the level going through your Send function.

- **Pan:** This control lets you adjust the amount of your signal that goes to the left or right channel of your stereo output.
- **Output:** This is where your signal goes as it leaves the track's channel strip. This can be the master bus (connected to one of your physical outputs) or an aux or a submix bus, where it will later be sent to the master bus.

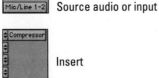

Mic/Line 1-2
Source audio or input
Compressor
Insert
Dr. Verb
m
p
Send Prefader
S
M
Mute
auto
Fader (track volume)
vol
0.0
Dr. Verb
m
p
Send Postfader
Pan
<100
100>
Analog 1-2
Output

Figure 4-7: Sound travels through the channel strip from top to bottom.

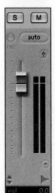

Recognizing Mixer Routing

After you have an instrument plugged into the mixer channel strip, you want to send that signal somewhere. This is referred to as *routing* or *busing*. (The place where the signal ends up is, conveniently enough, referred to as a *bus*.) Most mixers offer numerous busing possibilities, as follows:

- ✔ **Master bus:** This is where your signal goes before it leaves your system and where you mix all your tracks.
- ✔ **Submix bus:** This is where you can mix several tracks before they go to the master bus.
- ✔ **Auxiliary bus:** This is where you can add an effect to your signal and then move it along to the master bus.

In the next few sections, I introduce you to some of the most-used busing options and describe some ways to make this process easier.

Master bus

The master bus is where your music gets mixed and where you choose which of the physical outputs this stereo mix goes to. The Pan knob setting for each channel strip (how far to the left or right) dictates how much signal is sent to the left or right channels of the master bus.

The master bus has a channel strip of its own where you can insert effects such as a compressor or EQ. (I'm not a big fan of this, as you find out in Chapter 16.) The master bus channel strip looks like a, ahem, stripped-down version of a regular channel strip — it doesn't have some routing options such as an input selector, sends, or solo and mute buttons. This is because, as the final stage of your signal flow, these functions aren't necessary.

Faders for each channel control how much level is sent to the master bus and how the volume of each channel relates to the other. The master fader only determines the amount of overall volume of all channels that are routed to it (for sending out to your speakers or to the stereo mix level).

Sub (submix) bus

Sometimes you have a group of instruments (such as drums) that you want to control as a group independently of the master fader. Sending these tracks to another track and submixing them there enables you to adjust the overall volume of the drums without affecting the volume of any other instruments that aren't assigned to this channel. This is called a submix, and signals sent this way are sent (wait for it . . .) through the submix bus. When your signal exits this bus, it goes to the master bus, where it's blended with the rest of your tracks.

Software mixers, such as the one in Pro Tools, often don't have submix buses per se. Instead, you can simply route your signal to any of the internal buses, where you can adjust the level of all the signals coming to that bus using the channel strip fader associated with the bus.

Auxiliary (aux) bus

The aux bus is where you send your signal when you use one of the Send functions in your channel strip. This bus often has a channel strip of its own, where you can insert the effect you want to use. From this bus, your signal goes to the master bus, where it's mixed with the rest of your tracks.

Opting for Outputs

Most mixers have a bunch of output jacks that are located on the left side of the back of your hardware. You often find output jacks for the master bus, headphones, and monitors.

Master Out jack

The Master Out jack goes to the power amp for your speakers or goes directly to powered monitors, if you have any. This jack is generally controlled by the master fader and sends the signal that's routed through the master bus.

Phones jack

The Phones jack is for your headphones and is fed by the Phones knob on the master console. This jack carries the same signal as the master bus — only you get to control the volume separately.

Monitors jack

The monitors jack generally contains that same signal as the headphones and master outs but gives you another place to be able to plug in some speakers or headphones. Oftentimes, the Monitor Out jack is also used for "hardware monitoring" in systems that have it. Hardware monitoring is common on computer-based audio interfaces and is designed to allow you to monitor directly from the interface without having to wait until the audio signal goes into the computer and back out again before it reaches your ears. This reduces the latency that is often heard when listening to yourself as you record.

Chapter 5

MIDI and Electronic Instruments

In This Chapter

▶ Understanding MIDI (Musical Instrument Digital Interface)

▶ Getting to know MIDI ports

▶ Making sense of MIDI data

▶ Choosing the MIDI gear you need

My first job in a recording studio was in 1985. I can still remember the first time I walked into that studio. The owner was sitting, arms crossed, in a chair in front of the mixing console (it was called a console in those days because the mixer took up nearly the whole room). He looked at me and pressed a key on the Macintosh computer sitting next to him. Then all of a sudden, a synthesizer started playing, then another, and yet another. This is cool, I thought. But then I heard my nemesis — the drum machine.

Drum machines made me lose my recording gigs as a drummer and drove me to expand my career to that of a recording engineer as well. However, I eventually came to love that drum machine and the many others to follow (sigh). In fact, over the years, I became so captivated by the whole MIDI/drum machine thing that I assembled a whole series of electronic drum sets using drum machines and samplers — all controlled through MIDI.

In this chapter, you find out how MIDI enables synthesizers and computers to communicate with one another — a revolutionary thing for a musician. You get your hands dirty in the world of *sequencing* — the process of recording MIDI performance information so that you can play your performance automatically. You also peruse a variety of MIDI-capable instruments and explore the ins and outs of controlling your MIDI gear.

Like audio recording, MIDI can be a deep subject. You can go nuts trying to understand every little nuance of MIDI. (I know some guys who are not quite the same after plunging head first into this stuff.) The reality is that to use MIDI effectively, you don't need to know every little thing about it. In this chapter, I focus on what you need to know to get started.

Meeting MIDI

MIDI is a protocol that musical instruments use to communicate with one another. They do this through a cabled connection and a language that allows each one to understand the other, regardless of the manufacturer or instrument. All that's required is an instrument equipped with MIDI ports (jacks).

MIDI data is different from an audio recording because it contains no sound as such; rather, it's limited to performance information. This includes information about various performance characteristics, including the following:

- **Note-on and note-off:** What note is played and when
- **Velocity:** How hard someone presses a key
- **After-touch:** Whether the key pressure changes after the initial press
- **Vibrato and pitch bend:** Whether the pitch changes while a key is pressed

This information allows the MIDI musician to potentially create a performance that is as rich in texture as those of the world's finest players.

Digital messages that are sent from one device to another across a cable (called the MIDI cable, of course) create MIDI data. The cable connects to MIDI ports on each device, and the messages are sent in the form of binary digits. Each instrument can understand and respond to these messages.

Perusing MIDI ports

Three types of MIDI ports exist:

- The **out port** sends messages.
- The **in port** receives incoming messages.
- You use the **thru port** when you create a *daisy chain* to connect more than two devices. The thru port sends the messages that one device receives directly to the in port of another instrument. Figure 5-1 shows a daisy chain setup.

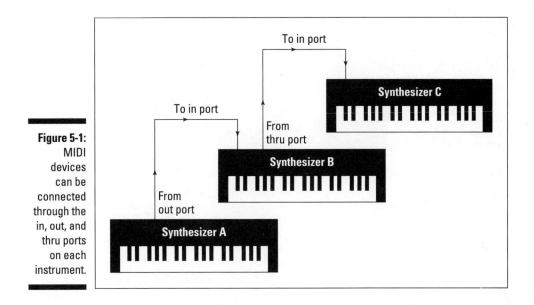

Figure 5-1:
MIDI
devices
can be
connected
through the
in, out, and
thru ports
on each
instrument.

MIDI signals travel in only one direction. Data flows from the out port of a device to an in port of another device, but not the other way around. Likewise, data going through the thru port originates from the first device in the chain and not the device whose thru port is being used. The way that data flows allows a lot of flexibility in how you can connect different devices. Here are some examples:

✔ **Example 1:** In Figure 5-1, three synthesizers are connected in a daisy chain lineup. A cable connects device A's out port to device B's in port. Another cable connects device B's thru port to device C's in port. In this scenario, device A controls devices B and C. Devices B and C can't control any other device, because neither device B nor device C has a connection from its out port.

✔ **Example 2:** Suppose you connect device B to device C by using device B's out port instead of its thru port. In this case, device A sends messages to device B but not to device C. Device B controls device C. Device C has no control over either A or B because neither one is connected to device C's out port.

✔ **Example 3:** Now take a look at Figure 5-2. In this figure, two devices (a synthesizer and a computer sequencer) have MIDI cables running from the out port of each to the in port of the other. (The MIDI interface in this figure is necessary to make MIDI connections in a computer.) This allows the communication to go both ways. For example, a master synthesizer and a computer sequencer are frequently connected this way so that you can send performance information from the synthesizer to the sequencer when you're recording your part and from the sequencer back to the synthesizer when you want to play the part back.

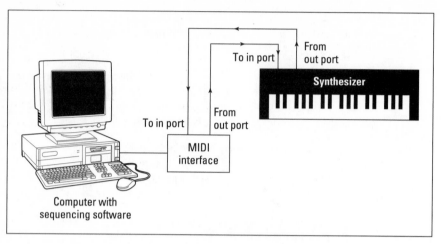

To in port

From out port

Synthesizer

To in port

From out port

MIDI interface

Figure 5-2:
Connecting
two devices
with cords
going both
ways allows
two-way
commu-
nication.

Computer with
sequencing software

A connection to a MIDI device's in port or through a device's thru port doesn't allow the device to control another device. A MIDI device can control another device only if the cable is connected from its out port to the other device's in port.

Understanding MIDI channels

Okay, so you have a daisy chain of MIDI instruments all hooked together and you want to control them from your master keyboard or sequencer program. Now you want the drum machine to play the drum part and a sound module to play the string part. This is where the MIDI channels come in handy.

The MIDI channels allow you to designate which messages go to a particular machine. You can program each machine to receive messages on one or more of the 16 MIDI channels. For instance, you can set your drum machine to receive messages on channel 10 (the default channel for drum sounds) and set the sound module with the string sounds to receive data on channel 1. (You set the MIDI channels on your instrument by using the System Parameters menu. Check your owner's manual for specific procedures.) After you assign your channels, your master keyboard sends the performance information for both the drum machine and the sound module playing the string sounds across one MIDI cable. Each receiving device responds only to the messages directed to the MIDI channel that it's assigned to receive.

In this scenario, the sound module with the string sounds receives all the data from the master keyboard, responds to the messages on channel 1, and simultaneously sends the data from the master keyboard to the drum machine (via the sound module's thru port). The drum machine receives the same messages from the master keyboard as the sound module but only responds to those sent for channel 10.

Having 16 MIDI channels allows you to have up to 16 separate instruments playing different parts at the same time. You may use 16 different devices or 16 different parts from the same device if you have a multitimbral sound generator. (For details, see the section "Synthesizer," later in this chapter.)

You would think that each MIDI channel would be sent along its own wire in the MIDI cable, but this is not the case. Inside the MIDI cable are three wires. Two wires are used for data transmission, and one is a shield. MIDI messages are sent across the two wires using a channel code, which tells the receiving device what channel the data following the code applies to. So a MIDI channel message, called a *channel voice message,* precedes each performance command.

Appreciating MIDI messages

For MIDI instruments to communicate with one another, they need to have a common vocabulary. This is where MIDI messages come in. MIDI messages contain an array of commands, including the following:

✔ **Performance data messages:** These messages consist of note-on and note-off, velocity, after-touch, vibrato, and pitch-bend messages.

MIDI performance data messages each have 128 different values. For example, each note that you play on the keyboard has a number associated with it (middle C is 60, for instance). Likewise, velocity is recorded and sent as a number between 0 and 127, 0 being the softest volume (no sound) and 127 being the loudest that you can play.

✔ **Control change messages:** These are a type of performance data message. These messages contain data about expression, including modulation, volume, and pan.

✔ **System-common messages:** These messages contain data about which channel the performance data is sent to and what sound in the sound library to play. System common messages also include information about timing data, master volume, and effects settings.

✔ **System-exclusive messages:** These messages contain information that is exclusive to the system or device. The messages can include data transfers of new sound patches, among other things.

To use MIDI effectively, you don't need to know all (or many, really) of the MIDI messages that a device can recognize. If you hook up your gear and play, your MIDI devices generate and respond to the messages for you.

Not all MIDI devices recognize all the MIDI commands. For example, a sound module generally can't send performance data messages, such as after-touch messages, because a sound module doesn't have triggering mechanisms that produce these commands.

Check your instrument's manual for a MIDI Implementation Chart. All MIDI instruments come with this chart. In it, you can find a list of all the MIDI commands that the device can send or receive. The chart also includes information on *polyphony,* which refers to how many notes the instrument can play at once, and *multitimbrality,* or how many different sounds the instrument can produce at the same time.

Managing modes

Your synthesizer, drum machine, or other MIDI module has the following four operating modes that dictate how your instrument responds to the MIDI messages it receives:

- ✔ **Mode 1 — Omni on/poly:** In omni on/poly mode, your instrument responds to all the MIDI messages coming across the wires (well, except the MIDI channel data). This means that your synthesizer or other device tries to play the parts of all the instruments hooked up to your MIDI controller. In this mode, your device also plays *polyphonically* (more than one note at a time).

  Some older MIDI devices default to omni on/poly mode (mode 1) when you turn them on. In this case, you need to reset your instrument if it's one of several in your MIDI setup because if you don't, the instrument responds to any MIDI messages sent from the controller, not just the ones directed toward it.

- ✔ **Mode 2 — Omni on/mono:** Omni on/mono allows your device to receive messages from all MIDI channels but only lets it play one note at time (monophonically). This mode is rarely, if ever, used.

- ✔ **Mode 3 — Omni off/poly:** In the omni off/poly mode, your device can play polyphonically but responds only to MIDI signals on the channels that it's set to. This is the mode you use most often when sequencing.

- ✔ **Mode 4 — Omni off/mono:** In the omni off/mono mode, your instrument responds only to the messages sent on the MIDI channel that it's set to and ignores the rest. Rather than play polyphonically, as in mode 3, your instrument plays only one note at a time. This can be advantageous if you're playing a MIDI controller from an instrument that can play only one note at a time, such as a saxophone.

Taking a look at General MIDI

If you compose music for other people to play on their MIDI instruments or if you want to use music from another composer, General MIDI is invaluable to you. General MIDI (GM) is a protocol that enables a MIDI instrument to provide a series of sounds and messages that are consistent with other MIDI instruments. With General MIDI, you can take a Standard MIDI File (SMF) of a song that was created on one sequencer program, transfer the file to another program, and use that other program to play the exact performance — sounds, timing, program changes, and everything else.

GM instruments contain numerous sound patches that the MIDI community has standardized. Not all of these sounds are exactly the same as far as sound quality goes, but their sound type and location (acoustic grand piano on patch #1, for instance) are the same on all GM-compatible machines.

Not all MIDI-capable instruments follow the GM standards. If this feature is important to you, be sure to find out whether the instrument that interests you is GM compatible before you buy.

GM standards dictate not only the particular sounds of a synthesizer but also which drum sounds are located on which keys, how many notes of polyphony the instrument has, and how many different channels the instrument can receive and send instructions on. Here are the two levels of GM compatibility:

- ✔ **GM level 1 compatibility:** Level 1 protocols were developed in 1991 and consist of a minimum of 128 instrument patches, 24 notes of polyphony, receiving and sending capability for all 16 MIDI channels, 16-part multi-timbrality, and a host of controller and performance messages.

- ✔ **GM level 2 compatibility:** Level 2 was implemented in 1999 and includes more sounds, polyphony, and features. A GM-compatible device has 32 notes of polyphony, 16-channel support, up to 16 simultaneous instrument sound patches, and a host of additional sounds (384, to be exact), including 2 channels of simultaneous percussion sounds. Also added to the GM2 standard are reverb and chorus effects.

Gearing Up for MIDI

Okay, so this MIDI thing sounds kind of interesting to you, and you want to know what you're going to need to buy to do some MIDIing yourself. Well, I'm sorry to inform you that you can't do any of this cool MIDI stuff with your vintage

Stratocaster guitar or your acoustic drum set (unless you do some fancy rigging to your gear). Here's the equipment that you need to have to record using MIDI:

- **Sound generator:** This device enables you to hear the music and may be a synthesizer, drum machine, sound module, or sampler.
- **MIDI controller:** This device controls the MIDI instruments in your studio.
- **Sequencer:** This device records and plays the MIDI performances that are programmed into it. The sequencer allows you to program your part into the synthesizer and have it play back automatically (much like the old-time player piano).
- **MIDI interface:** This interface enables your computer to send and receive MIDI data.

I know this sounds like a lot of stuff, but most of this gear performs more than one function in the MIDI studio. For example, nearly all synthesizers come with drum sounds, and some synthesizers even include a sequencer. In this case, this one synthesizer can do the job of a sound generator, drum machine, MIDI controller, and sequencer all in one.

In the following sections, I discuss the different types of sound generators. Although you may find one piece of equipment that does everything you want, in this section, I separate all the features that different equipment may have to help you understand the function of each feature and decide how to configure your studio.

Sound generators

The sound generator is the core of the MIDI studio. This is what produces the sounds that you hear. Without it, you may as well skip the rest of the stuff because, of course, you can't hear any of your work.

Sound generators can come in many different shapes and sizes: You find the fully functional keyboard synthesizer, the independent drum machine, the stand-alone sound module, samplers, software synthesizers (soft-synths), and the computer sound card. Each of these devices has its strengths and weaknesses (read on for the details).

Synthesizer

A *synthesizer,* like the one shown in Figure 5-3, consists of not only sounds but also a keyboard on which you can play these sounds. Synthesizers come in a variety of sizes and configurations. For example, some keyboards come with 61 keys (5 octaves) while others provide as many 88 keys — the size of an acoustic piano keyboard.

Figure 5-3:
A syn-
thesizer
contains a
keyboard
and a
variety of
sounds.

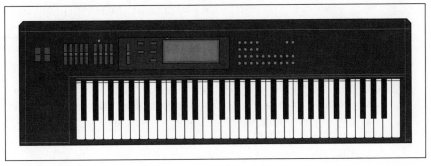

If you're in the market for a synthesizer, you need to consider the following things:

- ✔ **Polyphony:** This is the number of keys that sound at one time. Most decent modern synthesizers have at least 16 notes of polyphony, although ones with 32 notes are not uncommon.

  Each manufacturer treats polyphony differently, and the GM standards (discussed in the section "Taking a look at General MIDI," earlier in this chapter) allow some variations on the effective use of this parameter. For instance, a synth patch may use more than one sound to create the sound that you hear. The synth patch that you love so much may, in fact, consist of four different sounds layered on top of one another. In this case, you just reduced your polyphony to one-fourth with that one patch. If your synthesizer has 16-note polyphony, it's now down to 4-note polyphony because each of those 4 notes has four "sounds" associated with it. If you use this patch, you can play only 4 notes (a simple chord) at a time, not the 16 that you thought you had to work with.

  Your best bet is to buy a synthesizer (or sound module) with the highest polyphony you can afford, especially if you want to layer one sound on top of another or do multitimbral parts with your synth.

- ✔ **Multitimbrality:** Most decent keyboards allow you to play more than one sound patch at a time. This is called multitimbrality, which basically allows you to have your keyboard divided into several groups of sounds. For example, a multitimbral synth can divide a song's chords, melody, bass part, and drum-set sounds into different groups of sounds and then play all those groups at once.

  If you do any sequencing, a multitimbral synth is a must-have. Otherwise, you would need a separate synthesizer for each type of sound that you want to play. Fortunately, with the GM standards, compatible synthesizers made in the last ten years have the ability to play 16 sounds at once.

- ✔ **Keyboard feel:** Some keyboards have weighted keys and feel like real pianos, while other keyboards have a somewhat spongy action. If you're a trained piano player, a spongy keyboard may feel uncomfortable to you. On the other hand, if you have no training in piano and don't need weighted keys, you don't have to pay the extra money for that feature.

✔ **Sound quality:** This is a subjective thing. Choose the synthesizer that has the sounds that you think you'll use. I know this seems kind of obvious, but buy the synthesizer whose sounds you like even if this means waiting and saving some more money before you can buy. If you buy a synth that was a good deal but you don't love the sounds, you are wasting your money because you'll just end up buying the more expensive one later anyway.

✔ **Built-in sequencer:** Many keyboards contain a built-in sequencer, which allows you to program and play back your performance. These are usually called *keyboard workstations* or *MIDI workstations* because they contain everything you need to create a song. If you're considering buying one of these complete workstations, take a good, hard look at the sequencer and the user interface to make sure that you like the way it works. Each manufacturer treats the process of sequencing a little differently; you can probably find a sequencer that fits your style of working.

Drum machine

A *drum machine* contains not only the sounds of the drum set and other more exotic drums but also a sequencer to allow you to program rhythms. Figure 5-4 shows you a typical drum machine.

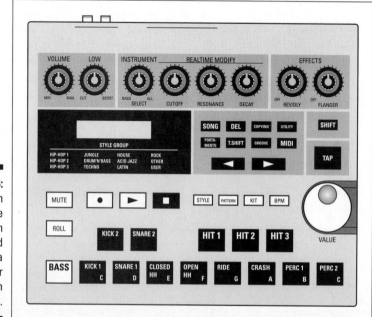

Figure 5-4: A drum machine has drum sounds and often a sequencer to program rhythms.

Most drum machines contain hundreds of drum sounds, numerous preset rhythm patches, and the ability to program dozens of songs. All stand-alone drum machines have pads on which you can play the part. The more advanced drum machines can give your rhythms a more human feel. Effects, such as reverb and delay, are also fairly common on the more advanced drum machines.

Sound module

A *sound module* is basically a stripped-down version of a synthesizer or drum machine. Sound modules don't contain triggering devices, such as the keys for the keyboard or pads for the drum machine. What they do contain is a variety of sounds (often hundreds) that a master controller or sequencer triggers. The advantage of sound modules is that they take up little space and cost considerably less than their fully endowed counterparts (the synths and drum machines, that is).

If you already have a master keyboard, adding sound modules can be a cost- and space-effective way to add more sounds to your system.

Samplers

A *sampler* is a sound module that contains short audio samples of real instruments. Most samplers come with sound libraries that contain hundreds of different types of sounds, from acoustic pianos to snare drums to sound effects. These sounds are often much more realistic than those that come in some synthesizers.

The real purpose of a sampler is to allow you to record your own sounds. For example, in the '80s, it was cool to make a drum set out of unusual percussive sounds. A snare drum could be the sound of a flushing toilet (don't laugh; I actually did this) or breaking glass. Tom-toms could be grunts set to certain pitches. You would be amazed at the strange stuff that people have turned into music — all with the help of a sampler.

Another common use of a sampler is for recording short sections of already-recorded songs. This can be a melodic or rhythmic phrase, a vocal cue, or a single drum or synth sound. Sampling other songs is common in electronic music, rap, and hip-hop (be careful of copyright issues before doing this, however). If you're into electronic music or hip-hop, you may find a sampler a necessary addition to your studio.

Soft-synths

If you've chosen a computer-based system to run your home studio on, your DAW (Digital Audio Workstation) software enables you to produce great sounds by using soft-synth plug-ins. *Soft-synths* are basically software equivalents of stand-alone synthesizers, sound modules, or samplers. As you can see in Figure 5-5, a soft-synth's graphical user interface (GUI) is often designed to look just like a piece of regular hardware, complete with buttons and knobs.

Of course, soft-synths have advantages and disadvantages, as follows:

- **Advantages:** Soft-synths cost less than stand-alone units because no hardware is involved.

- **Disadvantages:** Unlike regular synthesizers, soft-synths need a computer to run and require quite a bit of processing power to work effectively. This can slow your computer system and prevent you from recording as many audio tracks or applying as many effect patches as you would like.

Countless soft-synth plug-ins are available for most DAW programs. The best way to find the soft-synths for your DAW program is to visit an Internet news-group or message board that covers your software. Then do a search for soft-synths or ask the other members what software they use.

Sound card

Most sound cards that you can install in your computer (or that come with a computer) have General MIDI sounds in them. Depending on the quality of your sound card, the sound may be decent or border on the unbearable.

To find out whether the GM sounds in your computer's sound card are any good, play a MIDI file on your computer. First, do an Internet search for MIDI files (just type **MIDI** in your favorite search engine). Some sites require you to pay to download a song — especially for popular or familiar tunes — but many sites allow you to choose a song to listen to without downloading or paying a fee. Click a song and it should start playing automatically. You'll immediately know whether you like the sound of your sound card.

If you bought a new sound card for your computer to record audio with, you'll generally find that the sounds are pretty good. And with your audio program, you have access to soft-synth patches.

MIDI controller

A *MIDI controller* is a device that can control another MIDI device. MIDI controllers come in many different formats. In fact, a MIDI controller can be anything from a synthesizer to a drum machine or a computer to a xylophone.

When MIDI first came out, your controller choice was limited to a keyboard, but now you can choose among keyboards, wind controllers (for saxophones or other wind instruments), guitars, and drums. So even if you don't play piano, you can find a controller that resembles an instrument that you know how to play. Look around, and you may find one (or more) MIDI controllers that allow you to create music your way.

Sequencer

Although you can get stand-alone sequencers and sequencers integrated into a synthesizer, you probably want a computer-based sequencer for your home studio. The reasons for this are many, but the overriding factor is that you can have your MIDI and audio tracks in one place, and a computer-based sequencer gives you more-powerful editing capabilities than a sequencer that's contained in a box and that uses a tiny LCD screen.

Of course, if you want to do only a minimal amount of MIDI in your studio, you don't necessarily need all the power of a computer-based sequencer program.

For example, imagine that you have a drum machine and an 8-track recorder that has synchronization capabilities (your owner's manual describes whether the recorder can synchronize with other devices) and that you play guitar-based music. Being a guitar freak, you want to use six tracks for your guitars and two for your singing. With a MIDI connection from your drum machine to your recorder, you may be able to synch these two machines and wait to record your drum parts until the final mix. This effectively gives you a lot more tracks — one for each drum sound that you're using because you can adjust the volume, pan, and sound of each instrument in your drum machine. This setup is similar to recording each instrument on a separate track in your recorder.

MIDI interface

The MIDI interface allows you to send and receive MIDI information from a computer. Many sound cards have a MIDI port, but if you end up doing a lot of MIDI sequencing and use more than one sound module or external controller, you need a separate MIDI interface, such as the one shown in Figure 5-6.

Figure 5-6:
You need
a MIDI
interface to
connect
your instru-
ment to a
computer.

MIDI interfaces come in a staggering variety of configurations, so you need to consider several things when you buy a MIDI interface. The following questions can help you to determine your needs:

- **What type of computer do you own?** MIDI interfaces are usually configured to connect to your computer using either a USB port or an audio interface, and MIDI interfaces use one of three available options: PCI, FireWire, or USB. (Chapter 2 has more details on audio-interface connection types.) You determine which option to use by the type of port(s) you have in your computer. For example, new Macs only have a USB port, although you can add a serial port if you remove the internal modem. A PC has either a parallel port or a USB port (and sometimes both). PCs also have a joystick port that accepts a special MIDI joystick cable (no MIDI interface is needed).

- **How many instruments do you intend to connect?** MIDI interfaces come with a variety of input and output configurations. Models are available with two ins and two outs, four ins and four outs, and even eight ins and eight outs. You can also buy "thru" boxes, which have one or more inputs and several outputs. If you have only one or two instruments, you can get by with a smaller interface (in this case, a 2×2 interface — two ins and two outs — would work great). If you have many instruments that you want to connect, you need a larger box.

Chapter 6

Understanding Microphones

In This Chapter

▶ Discovering the various type of microphones

▶ Positioning microphones for the best sound

▶ Exploring a variety of preamps

▶ Understanding how to care for your microphones

A microphone's job is generally to try to capture, as closely as possible, the sound of an instrument. But you can also use a microphone to infuse a specific sound characteristic into a performance. Likewise, a preamp, which boosts the signal of a microphone as the signal travels to the recorder, can be used to accurately represent a sound or to add texture and dimension to it. Microphones and preamps are the center of the sound engineer's palette. Just as a painter has his paints and brushes, you have your microphones and preamps. And just as a painter can create a stunning variety of visual textures with his tools, you too can make your creative statement with the judicious use of these two pieces of equipment.

In this chapter, I explore the two most versatile tools of your auditory craft. You look at the various types of microphones and preamps, and you gain an understanding of each one's role in capturing a performance. You also discover what types of mics and preamps work for particular situations. To top it off, this chapter guides you through purchasing and caring for your precious new friends (the mics and preamps, that is). You can find out how to use your mics in Chapter 8, where I discuss specific mic placement options.

Meeting the Many Microphone Types

When you start looking at microphones, you basically find three different types of construction methods (condenser, dynamic, and ribbon) and three basic polarity patterns (omnidirectional, cardioid, and figure-8). The following sections explore these various constructions and patterns and help you make sense out of them.

Construction types

Whether a microphone is a $10 cheapie that has a cord permanently attached to it or a $15,000 pro model with gold-plated fittings, all microphones convert sound waves to electrical impulses that the preamp or mixer can read and the recorder can store. Each of the three construction types captures this auditory signal in a different way, and as such, each adds certain characteristics to the sound. Here's how the different mics affect sound:

- ✔ **Condenser:** This type tends to have a well-rounded shape to its frequency response and a fast response, allowing it to often pick up high transient material, such as the initial attack of drum, very well. These mics can sound more natural, but they can also be somewhat harsh if placed too close to a high transient source.

- ✔ **Dynamic:** Dynamic mics tend to accentuate the middle of the frequency spectrum because the thick diaphragms (relatively speaking when compared to a condenser mic) take longer to respond.

- ✔ **Ribbon:** Because the ribbon mic is relatively slow to respond to an auditory signal, it tends to soften the transients (the initial attack of an instrument) on instruments such as percussion and piano. The high end isn't as pronounced as with other construction types, so these mics tend to have a rounder, richer tone.

I detail these aspects in the following sections. In most cases, the type of construction dictates the general cost category in which the mics fit.

Condenser microphones

The condenser microphone is without a doubt the most popular style of microphone used in recording studios (home or commercial). Condenser mics are sensitive and accurate, but they can also be expensive. Recently, however, condenser mics have come down in cost, and you can buy a decent one for about $200. Very good ones start at about $500.

Phantom power

Phantom power is a term used to describe the small amount of voltage that is applied to a condenser microphone. This power enables the mic to function properly. In most cases, the phantom power comes from your mixer or preamp and is sent to the microphone through one of the wires in the XLR cable. (I cover XLR cables in Chapter 3.)

Some condenser mics have an internal battery or separate power supply that provides this power.

A switch, which is usually located on the preamp or mixer, enables you to turn the phantom power off and on. Even though dynamic microphones don't use phantom power, this small amount of voltage doesn't damage them.

The condenser microphone has an extremely thin metal (or metal-coated plastic or Mylar) diaphragm (the part that senses the signal). The diaphragm is suspended in front of a metal plate (called a *backplate*). Polarizing voltage is applied to both the diaphragm and the backplate, creating a static charge in the space between them. When the diaphragm picks up a sound, it vibrates into the field between it and the backplate. This produces a small signal that can then be amplified. Figure 6-1 shows how a condenser mic is constructed.

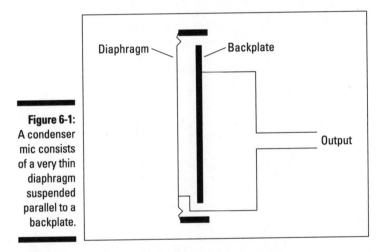

Figure 6-1: A condenser mic consists of a very thin diaphragm suspended parallel to a backplate.

Condenser mics need a small amount of voltage (from 9 to 48 volts) to function. If you use a condenser mic, make sure that either it has its own internal battery or you have a preamp or mixer equipped with *phantom power,* which is described in the nearby sidebar.

Here are a few additional decisions you need to make when selecting a condenser mic:

- ✔ **Tube or solid-state?** Condenser mics can be made with either transistors (known as solid-state) or vacuum tubes. As with all the tube or solid-state gear, base your decision on the sound characteristics that you prefer. For the most part, tube condenser mics have a softer high end and a warmer overall tone. Solid-state mics, on the other hand, are often more *transparent* — the sound is captured by them with less coloration.

- ✔ **Large- or small-diaphragm?** Condenser mics come in two broad categories: small-diaphragm and large-diaphragm (see Figure 6-2). Large-diaphragm mics are more popular than their smaller-diaphragm counterparts, partly because large-diaphragm condenser mics have a more pronounced bottom end (low frequencies). Large-diaphragm mics also possess a lower *self noise,* that is, noise created by the microphone.

Before you buy only large-diaphragm mics, consider this: Small-diaphragm condenser mics often have an even frequency response and can more accurately capture instruments with a pronounced high-frequency component (violins, for instance).

Figure 6-2:
Condenser mics can have either small or large diaphragms.

Dynamic microphones

You've probably had the chance to use a dynamic mic. The hugely popular Shure SM57 and SM58 often characterize this type of mic. Dynamic microphones have several qualities that make them unique. They can handle a lot of volume (technically known as *SPL,* meaning *sound pressure level*), which makes them perfect for extremely loud signals, such as drums, amplifiers, and some rock vocalists. Dynamic mics are also not as transparent (they don't accurately represent high frequencies) as condenser mics, so they often impart a "dirty" or gritty" sound to the signal.

The dynamic microphone uses a magnetic field to convert the sound impulse from the diaphragm into electrical energy, as shown in Figure 6-3. The diaphragm is often made of plastic or Mylar and is located in front of a coil of wire called a *voice coil.* The voice coil is suspended between two magnets.

When the diaphragm moves (the result of a sound), the voice coil moves as well. The interaction between the voice coil's movement and the magnets creates the electrical signal.

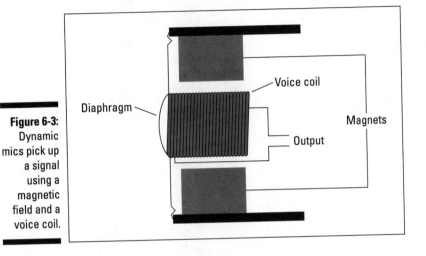

Figure 6-3: Dynamic mics pick up a signal using a magnetic field and a voice coil.

The sound of a dynamic mic can be described as somewhat boxy, meaning that these mics don't represent the highest or lowest frequencies of your hearing spectrum accurately (not necessarily a bad thing). They are also durable. Rough treatment probably won't damage them much, aside from the diaphragm, and a tough metal screen protects it. Dynamic mics are typically used for live shows. These mics are often very inexpensive to buy and maintain; you can get a good dynamic mic for about $100.

Ribbon microphones

A ribbon microphone produces its sound in much the same way as a dynamic mic. The diaphragm is suspended between two magnets. The ribbon mic differs from the dynamic mic in that it uses a thin ribbon of aluminum instead of plastic or Mylar (see Figure 6-4). Ribbon mics were popular from the 1930s through the 1960s but have, for the most part, now taken a backseat to condenser mics in today's studios. This is mainly because ribbon mics are fragile and expensive and aren't as transparent as condenser mics. In fact, a gust of wind or a strong breath blown into the diaphragm is all it takes to break an aluminum ribbon in one of these mics. (It's not the end of the world, though; ribbons aren't that expensive to replace — they generally cost $100 to $150.)

Ribbon mics are experiencing a renaissance because of the number of recording engineers who are searching for an old, vintage sound. Ribbon mics have a unique sound that is often described as silky or smooth. This essentially means that the high frequencies tend to roll off slightly (gradually reduce) and the lower frequencies smear together a bit.

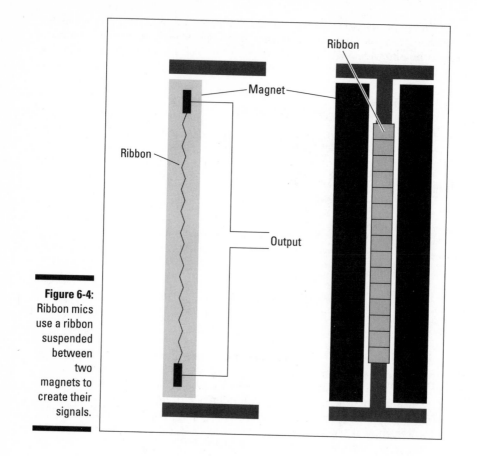

Figure 6-4:
Ribbon mics
use a ribbon
suspended
between
two
magnets to
create their
signals.

Ribbon mics used to be fairly expensive (at least $1,000), but as interest in them has increased from digital recordists, you can now find some decent ones for just a few hundred dollars.

Polarity patterns

Microphones pick up sounds in different ways, which are known as *polarity patterns.* Here's how the various patterns work:

- ✔ **Omnidirectional** mics can capture sounds all around them.
- ✔ **Cardioid** (or directional) mics pick up sounds just in front of them.
- ✔ **Figure-8** (or bidirectional) mics pick up sounds from both the front and back.

The polarity patterns on microphones are represented on a chart that often comes with the microphone (or is part of its spec sheet). This chart is often called a *polar graph,* and the graph shows how well the microphone picks up various frequencies in front of or behind it.

Omnidirectional

The omnidirectional mic can pick up sounds coming from anywhere around it. Omnidirectional mics are useful for situations where you want to capture not only the source sound but also the sound of the room that the source is coming from. You can find omnidirectional mics used in stereo pairs for drum overheads and groups of acoustic instruments, such as orchestras.

Omnidirectional mics are not generally used for *close miking* — when you place the mic less than a foot from the sound source — because they tend to catch too much background noise. You can see the pickup pattern of an omnidirectional mic in Figure 6-5. The round pattern shows that the mic picks up sound from all directions.

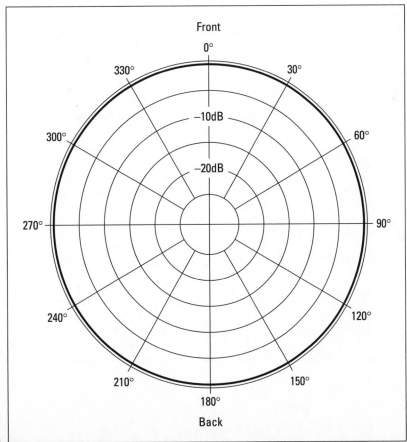

Figure 6-5: The omni-directional mic picks up sounds from all around it.

Cardioid

Cardioid microphones pick up the sound in front of them and reject sounds that come from behind. Cardioid mics are the most common types for live bands because you can control the sound that they pick up. If you have a cardioid mic on the tom-tom of a drum set, the mic picks up only the sound of that drum and not the sound from the other instruments around it.

The three types of cardioid microphones are cardioid, super-cardioid, and hyper-cardioid. The differences among the types of cardioid patterns of each mic aren't that great. Check out the graphs in Figure 6-6 to see how the polarity patterns of cardioid microphones differ.

Figure 6-6: The three types of cardioid mics have similar polarity patterns.

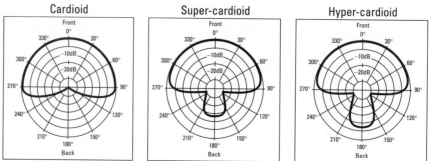

Generally, you don't need to think about the minor polarity-pattern differences among the types of cardioid mics when you buy or use a microphone. You won't notice the practical differences in the way these three types of mics work.

Cardioid mics all produce more bass when they are close to the sound source. This is called the *proximity effect.* Essentially, the closer the mic is to its source, the more bass the mic picks up. You don't find the proximity effect in omnidirectional or figure-8 mics. Many cardioid condenser mics have a bass roll-off switch that allows you to eliminate added bass that may occur from having the mic close to the source.

Figure-8

Figure-8 mics (also called bidirectional mics) pick up sound from both the front and back, but not all the way around. If you look at the graph in Figure 6-7, you can see that sound is not effectively picked up from areas on the sides of the microphone.

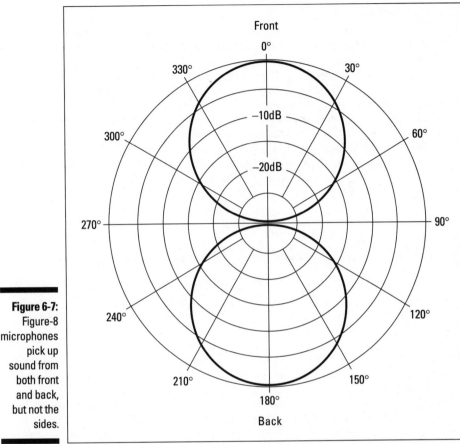

Figure 6-7:
Figure-8
microphones
pick up
sound from
both front
and back,
but not the
sides.

Figure-8 mics are often used to record two instruments simultaneously. For example, you can place the microphone between two horn players with the side of the mic perpendicular to the players. This allows you to capture both instruments while eliminating any sound in front of the musicians.

Most figure-8 condenser mics have the same frequency response for both the front and back sides, but some ribbon mics produce very different responses, depending on whether the sound is coming from the front or the back. For instance, a Royer r121 mic picks up more high frequencies from the back side of the mic than the front. You can use this to your advantage when recording an instrument. If the sound has too many low frequencies, just turn the mic around a little or a lot, depending on how many high frequencies you want to add (more on this in Chapter 9).

Multiple-pattern mics

Some condenser microphones can switch among various pickup patterns. These are generally large-diaphragm mics. These mics have a switch that allows you to choose from cardioid, omnidirectional, or figure-8 (refer to the right image in Figure 6-2). These mics can do this because they generally contain two sets of diaphragms and backplates, which are positioned back to back. You may want to have at least one of these types of microphones around to give you more variety in microphone positions.

The omnidirectional pattern in a multiple-pattern microphone works (and sounds) differently from a true omnidirectional mic. So for critical applications (recording an orchestra, for instance), the multiple-pattern mic may not be a fair substitute for an exclusively omnidirectional mic.

Assessing Your Microphone Needs

Buying microphones is, without a doubt, one of the most critical decisions that you make when setting up your home studio. Using the right microphone for the job can mean the difference between recording okay tracks and truly spectacular ones.

As recently as just a few years ago, you had to choose between inexpensive dynamic mics (what most home recordists could afford) and expensive condenser or ribbon mics (what the pro studios had). But, as luck would have it, you've entered a time in home recording where you have many more options. In fact, a whole line of project studio mics has recently emerged. This is a new market that manufacturers have found to be hugely profitable, so the choices are expanding almost daily. In some cases, a $500 project studio mic can rival a $2,000-plus pro mic — at least for the home recordist's purposes.

So the question that you're inevitably going to ask is, "What microphones should I get for my home studio?" Good question. And the answer is, "Well, it depends on what you need." So before I go into detail about what mics may be best for you, you should spend a minute assessing your needs. The following questions may help you in your assessment:

✔ **What type of music will you record?** If you play rock or pop music, you should probably start with dynamic mics because they're inexpensive and their limitations in high or low frequencies don't matter as much as if, for example, you wanted to record your string quartet. In this case, a pair of condenser mics would do the trick.

✔ **What instruments will you record?** Loud amps, drums, and screaming singers beg to be recorded with dynamic mics, whereas light percussion, vocals, and stand-up basses shine through with large-diaphragm condenser mics.

✔ **How many mics will you use at once?** If you need to record your whole band at once, budget constraints may dictate your choice between dynamic and condenser mics or a condenser or ribbon mic for vocals. If you need only a couple of mics to record the occasional vocal or instrument, you can invest more in each mic.

Deciding How Many Microphones and What Kind

You will likely build your microphone collection over time rather than buying all your mics at once. This is the best way to buy mics, because it gives you time to develop an understanding of what you can do with the microphone that you have before you plunk down your money for another one. You're better off having a few mics that best fit your situation than having a whole bunch of mics that just sorta work for you.

If you're like most people, your budget dictates how many mics you can buy and what kind they may be. In the following sections, I try to help you get the best mics for your recording needs and guide you through the process of slowly accumulating microphones.

 Before you buy a ton of mics, know this: Many digital systems have an effect called a *mic simulator.* The mic simulator allows you to use a relatively inexpensive mic and get the sound of a much more expensive one. If your system has a mic simulator program (you can find out by searching through your system's effects patches), I recommend that you get a basic dynamic mic first. You may find that you like the way the mic simulator sounds and discover that you don't need as many mics as you thought.

Getting started

A basic mic setup consists of a couple of dynamic mics for drums, guitar amps, or other loud instruments and a decent large-diaphragm condenser mic for vocals or other acoustic instruments. The next sections lay out the mics that I would consider if I were starting out on a budget.

Dynamic mics

A Shure SM57 is hands down the best choice for your first dynamic mic. This is a great dynamic mic for very little money — about $80. This mic works well for miking amps and drums and the occasional gritty vocal. Everyone should have at least one of these mics.

Large-diaphragm condenser mics

Your choice here depends on your voice and the acoustic sound that you're looking for. I would check out the following mics:

- ✔ **Studio Projects B1:** This inexpensive mic is a good choice for your first large-diaphragm condenser mic. You can find one for about $80.

- ✔ **MXL 990:** This mic has a slightly different sound than the Studio Projects B1 and costs about the same ($70 to $80). Buy the mic that sounds better to you.

- ✔ **MXL V63M:** This mic is a step up from the MXL 990 — its street price is about $100 — and you may like this one better than its less expensive brother. Again, only buy the more expensive mic if you think it sounds better.

- ✔ **Octava MK319:** This mic is a little more expensive than the previous three — about $125 — but it's still at the lower end of the price spectrum and may work better for your vocals than the others.

- ✔ **Audio Technica AT3035:** This mic is more expensive than the others I list here (about $200), but if you can afford it, check it out. Some people prefer the sound of this mic over that of the other mics.

A large-diaphragm condenser mic is the first condenser mic for most home recordists. These good all-around mics can work well for a lot of applications.

Movin' on

After you have your basic mics, you can start to add a few more. If you intend to record your band, you need to at least mic the drum set (four mics can get you around the set). In this case, you can add a couple more dynamic mics and perhaps get one or two that are designed for particular applications. For instance, mics are made to work best on the kick drum of a drum set. At this point, you can also get a second condenser mic — maybe a small-diaphragm condenser mic this time or a large-diaphragm tube condenser mic. You may want to choose one that sounds different from the one you already have, or if you love the one that you have, you can get a second one just like it to use as a stereo pair.

Dynamic mics

For additional dynamic mics, I would add one or two more SM-57s and try one of the following:

- ✔ **Sennheiser e609:** I like Sennheiser mics; this is one of my favorite (and inexpensive) amp or kick drum mics. It has a different sound than the venerable SM-57 and doesn't cost much more — a little over $100 — so adding one of these lets you cover some more bases.

✔ **Audio Technica ATM25:** This is a pretty good kick drum mic for not a lot of money — about $200 — although it is more costly than some other dynamic mics. If you record drums live, this mic is worth trying.

Large-diaphragm tube condenser mics

If you're on a budget (and who isn't?), try out the following inexpensive large-diaphragm tube condenser mics:

✔ **Rode NTK:** This is an awesome mic regardless of price, but for about $400, it's one of the best deals available. This mic is good for vocals and acoustic instruments. I've even used a pair for the overheads on a drum set.

✔ **Studio Projects T3:** This mic has an advantage over the Rode NTK because it has a variable polar pattern selector, allowing you to choose among cardioid, figure-8, and omnidirectional patterns — and patterns in between. The NTK are cardioid only. This variability gives you more options when recording and increases the versatility of the mic, making this $600 mic worth checking out.

Small-diaphragm condenser mics

Though not sexy to most recordists, small-diaphragm condenser mics can come in handy. Here are a few inexpensive ones that are worth checking out:

✔ **Octava MK012:** This mic is a great buy. It's inexpensive (under $100) and sounds good on many types of acoustic instruments — guitars, violins, cellos, double basses, drum overheads, and percussion. The only drawback to this mic is that quality control has been known to be, shall we say, variable. You need to try out each mic carefully before you buy it because some just don't sound good.

✔ **MXL 993:** I don't like this mic as much as the Octava, but if you can't find the Octava or are squeamish about testing a bunch of mics to find a good one, the MXL 993 is worth considering. At about $80, it's a pretty good-sounding mic.

Going all out

As your mic collection grows, you'll probably start looking for a vocal mic that works best for you. In this case, you may look at large-diaphragm tube condenser mics or even a ribbon mic.

Choosing a vocal mic is a personal thing. If you're a singer, audition a bunch of mics by using your voice to see what sounds best to you. If you record more than one singer and each has a different type of voice (tenor or soprano, for instance), you may need to look for more than one vocal mic.

After this, consider buying a stereo pair of small-diaphragm condenser mics for drum overheads (mics placed over the drum set) or other multi-instrument applications. You may also want to start adding some higher-quality (and more expensive) mics to your collection. The following sections detail some mics that offer a good bang for the buck.

Dynamic mics

Here are a couple of higher-end dynamic mics that I use:

- **Sennheiser MD421:** This is arguably the industry-standard tom mic. It's been used on tons of recordings over the years. If you intend to record drums with more than the basic 3- or 4-mic setup (see Chapter 9 for more details), having a couple of these tom mics is a necessity. They aren't cheap — at about $350 each — but for their purpose, they are worth every penny.

- **EV RE20:** This is a common kick drum mic that is also used for amps and some vocals. You can get this mic for about $400 to $450.

Large-diaphragm condenser mics

You can find a ton of good large-diaphragm condenser mics, and the sky's the limit on how much you can spend on them. That said, consider the following reasonably priced options:

- **Shure KSM-44:** I really like this mic. It's a multipattern mic that offers cardioid, figure-8, and omnidirectional configurations. The sound is pretty neutral by today's standards — many manufacturers like to boost the top and bottom ends of their mics to make them sound "sexy." The KSM-44 doesn't have this feature, and as a result, the mic is very versatile. I often use one for drum overheads and other acoustic sources such as big percussion instruments (like surdos, congas, and djembes) and acoustic string instruments — and even as a room mic for ensembles. This mic costs about $650.

- **AKG C414B:** This is another industry-standard mic that sounds great on a lot of sources — vocals, acoustic instruments, drums, and others. Like the KSM-44, this mic has selectable polar patterns. In this, you have five choices: omnidirectional, cardioid, wide-cardioid, hyper-cardioid, and figure-8. This mic sells for about $800.

- **Soundelux U195:** This is an awesome mic for a lot of sources, including many vocalists, percussion, and drums. (I love to use this as a room mic placed 6 to 8 feet in front of the kick drum.) This mic isn't cheap — at about $1,200 — but you'll never need to upgrade it.

Ribbon mics

Ribbon mics used to be very expensive and required a great preamp with lots of clean *gain* (volume) because they don't produce a very strong signal. This is changing. You can now find a ribbon mic for just a few hundred dollars, and if you don't have a high-gain preamp, you can find a mic that produces a stronger signal (called *active-ribbon mics*). Here are some ribbon mics that I recommend:

- ✔ **Octava ML19:** This is the least expensive ribbon mic available, and it sounds pretty good, especially for the price (roughly $400). For the budget-minded recordist who needs a ribbon mic, you can't go wrong with this one.

- ✔ **AEA R84:** This is one sexy mic. It looks gorgeous and sounds great. For classic "silky" vocals or to take the edge off instruments such as trumpets and other horns, this mic is awesome. Of course, awesome doesn't come cheap — about $1,000 plus a good high-gain preamp. Still, if you like the vocals sound that you can only get from a ribbon mic or if you record a lot of horns, you need to try this mic.

- ✔ **Royer Labs 122:** This is the first active-ribbon mic. It has electronics that boost the mic's signal, so you don't need a super high-gain preamp to get a good sound. Royer Labs ribbon mics are known as great mics, and this one costs about $1,500.

Small-diaphragm condenser mics

If your budget allows you to get a pair of great small-diaphragm condenser mics, the following two provide good value:

- ✔ **Josephson C42:** I can't recommend this mic highly enough, especially the matched pair (model no. C42mp). A pair of these mics is great for drum overheads and almost every acoustic instrument I've tried them on. I love to use a single mic on double bass, a pair on piano, and a pair on a live ensemble. These mics run about $475 each, but you would be hard-pressed to find a mic at double the price that sounds better.

- ✔ **Peluso CEMC6:** The CEMC6 mic is a nice unit, especially for under $300 each. These mics rate almost as highly as the Josephson. But if you're on a tight budget, try one or a pair of these mics.

You won't find either of these mics at the big music retailers, so if you're interested in them, you'll need to look around a bit. I suggest doing a search on Google (www.google.com) to find an Internet retailer. You can find a bunch of reputable dealers who carry them.

Finding the Right Mic for the Situation

Certain mics work better than others for particular situations. In this section, I present some typical applications to give you an idea of what types of mics are traditionally used for various purposes. (You can find more ideas about mic usage in Chapter 8, where I discuss specific miking techniques.)

When you consider a mic, think about the frequency spectrum that the instrument encompasses. If you use a dynamic mic for a symphonic orchestra performance, for example, you'll be disappointed by the results because it lacks an accurate high-frequency response. On the other hand, using a small-diaphragm condenser mic on the tom-toms of a drum set makes them sound thin and is a waste of money because you can get by with a much less expensive dynamic mic for this purpose.

Microphone choice is fairly subjective. The following list contains some basic suggestions based on what is typically used:

- ✔ **Vocals:** Most people prefer the sound of a large-diaphragm condenser mic for vocals. If you have the budget, you may also want to audition some ribbon mics for your voice. A dynamic mic is best when you're going for a dirty or raw sound (excellent for some harder rock, blues, or punk music) or if your singer insists on screaming into the mic. A small-diaphragm condenser mic is rarely the first choice for most singers, but it's not out of the question for some vocalists if you don't mind a bright, present (high-frequency) sound.

- ✔ **Electric guitar amp:** A dynamic mic or a small-diaphragm condenser mic works well on an electric guitar amp. Some people use large-diaphragm condenser mics on guitar amps and like the added low frequencies that can result. A ribbon mic can sound great, but take care in placing the mic so that you don't overload it and blow the ribbon. Move the mic back a bit or off to the side and you should be fine.

- ✔ **Electric bass amp:** Your first choice when miking an amplified electric bass is either a large-diaphragm condenser mic or a dynamic mic. Either one can capture the frequency spectrum that the bass guitar encompasses. Small-diaphragm condenser mics aren't a good choice because of their inherent high-frequency focus. I like ribbon mics for electric bass, but you need to take the same care as you would with a guitar amp.

- ✔ **Acoustic guitar and other stringed instruments:** A large- or small-diaphragm condenser mic or a ribbon mic works well in most instances. A dynamic mic has too limited a frequency response to create a natural sound (but may create an effect that you like). Choose the large- or small-diaphragm type based on the overall frequency spectrum of the instrument. For example, to capture the depth of a guitar's tone, choose a large-diaphragm mic, but for an instrument with a higher register, such as a violin or mandolin, a small-diaphragm mic works great. I'm partial to small-diaphragm condenser mics for these instruments because I can get more clarity and I don't have to fight the low-end bump that often occurs with a large-diaphragm condenser mic.

- ✔ **Horns:** I'm partial to ribbon mics for horns. These types of mics can soften the tone slightly and make the horns sound more natural, especially if you mic closely (within a couple feet or so). My second choice is a large-diaphragm condenser mic in a figure-8 or omnidirectional pattern placed off to the side of the instrument a bit. For this, you need a large-diaphragm condenser mic that has multiple patterns, such as the AKG C414B or the Shure KSM-44. Some people like a tube condenser mic, so if you're on a budget, the Studio Projects T3 is a good place to start.

- ✔ **Piano:** Both large- and small-diaphragm condenser mics are generally used for piano. Your choice depends on where you place the mics and how the room sounds. For example, a great-sounding room begs for a pair of omnidirectional small-diaphragm mics placed away from the piano a bit. I'm not a fan of ribbon or dynamic mics for this instrument.

- ✔ **Drum set:** The tom-toms, snare drum, and kick (bass) drum all sound good with dynamic mics because they don't contain high frequencies. You can also use large-diaphragm condenser mics, but be careful where you place them because if your drummer hits them, they're toast.

- ✔ **Cymbals:** For the cymbals of a drum set, a pair of small-diaphragm condenser mics works well, although some people prefer to use a large-diaphragm mic instead. A ribbon mic also sounds pretty good and can take some of the harshness of cymbals when recorded digitally. A dynamic mic would lack the high-frequency response to make the cymbals shine through in a mix.

- ✔ **Miscellaneous percussion:** Now, here's a broad category. By miscellaneous, I mean shakers, triangles, maracas, and other higher-pitched percussion toys. For these instruments, either small- or large-diaphragm condenser mics can work well. If it's a very quiet instrument, a large-diaphragm mic would be preferable because of the higher self-noise of the small-diaphragm mic.

You may choose a different type of mic, especially if you try to create a certain effect. For instance, using a ribbon mic on a metallic shaker rather than a small-diaphragm condenser mic softens the highest frequencies of the instrument and gives it a mellower sound.

If you intend to record loud instruments — drums, amplified guitars, or basses, for example — look for a mic with a high SPL (sound pressure level) rating. This is a rating of how much volume (listed in decibels) the microphone can handle before distorting. A high SPL is above 130 decibels.

Some professional condenser mics have a pad switch that allows you to reduce the sensitivity of the mic, thereby increasing its ability to handle high sound pressure levels.

Partnering Mics with Preamps

One of the most important relationships in your home studio is the one between your microphones and the *preamp* — the nice bit of hardware that boosts the mic's signal so that it can be recorded. The greatest microphone in the world run through a cheap preamp won't sound good. By the same token, a cheap mic plugged into a great preamp sounds only as good as the bad mic.

If your mixer includes XLR inputs (low-impedance microphone inputs), you already have internal preamps in the channels with the XLR jacks. For the most part, these preamps are of lesser quality than the external variety, but they may work for you. For instance, some home recordists swear by the internal preamps in the Mackie VLZ-Pro mixers.

Plug in your mic and listen to the sound that you get. If you like it, you may not need to buy external preamps right away. If not, you may have to allocate some of your gear money for an external preamp.

You can find three types of preamps in the marketplace — solid-state, vacuum tube, and hybrid — and each has its own characteristics. In the following sections, I explore some preamp styles and discuss how each relates to the sounds that are produced by the types of microphones I discuss earlier in the chapter. This can help you to understand the relationship between the microphone and preamp in your studio.

Solid-state

Solid-state preamps use transistors to boost the level of the microphone. These preamps can be designed to produce as clear and detailed a sound as possible (often referred to as "transparent") or can be designed to create a pleasing level of distortion (warmth) to your music. Solid-state preamps cost from a couple hundred to several thousand dollars.

A clean and clear solid-state preamp (such as the Earthworks or GML brands) is a great choice if you want as natural a sound as possible on your recording of an instrument or if you are using a microphone that has a sound quality that you want to hear as clearly as possible. For example, I particularly like the way that a solid-state preamp works in conjunction with a tube condenser or ribbon mic. The warmth and smoothness of these types of microphones shine through clearly with a clean solid-state preamp.

On the other hand, a more aggressive (warm or pleasingly distorted) solid-state preamp, such as those modeled after the classic Neve designs, can add just a touch of "grit" to certain instruments. These types of preamps are great with dynamic, ribbon, or condenser mics, especially when recording drums, guitar, and some vocals.

Vacuum tube

These preamps use vacuum tubes to process and amplify the microphone's signal. This generally adds some coloration to the sound of your mic (how much and what kind of coloration depends on the particular preamp). As you've undoubtedly discovered after reading any other chapter in this book, digital recording aficionados love the sound of tube gear, especially tube preamps. The advantage of a tube preamp is that it can add a warm sound to your mics. The disadvantage is that you often can't get rid of this colored sound. Professional recording engineers often have several tube preamps in their studios to give them different coloration options.

TIP

The preamps that are included in your mixer are solid-state. If you find that you want the colored sound of a tube preamp, you need to buy an external one.

Tube preamps are great for imparting a subtle low-frequency addition to the sound of the microphone signal. Tube preamps also seem to slightly soften the higher frequencies. If you're like most people, you'll like the addition of a tube preamp, especially if you intend to record rock, blues, or acoustic jazz music. The downside is that all-tube preamps are expensive, with the least expensive costing about $1,000 (the Peavey VMP-2) and most running several thousand dollars (brands like Manley Labs, for instance).

I prefer to use tube preamps with drums and any "woody" instrument (acoustic guitar, for instance). In this case, I often reach for a large-diaphragm condenser mic, and in extreme cases, I may even use a large-diaphragm *tube* condenser mic with the tube preamp (for an extra dose of "tubiness").

Hybrid

A hybrid preamp contains both solid-state and tube components to boost the mic's signal. Most of the inexpensive (under $1,000) "tube" preamps that you find in the marketplace are actually hybrids. An advantage to this design approach is that the preamp can often be adjusted to have varying degrees of that warm tube sound. The disadvantage is that these relatively inexpensive tube preamps don't have as clear a sound as a great solid-state preamp and they don't have quite the same pleasing character as an expensive all-tube preamp.

For most home recordists, this type of preamp offers a lot of flexibility and can allow you to get either the fairly clear, open sound of a solid-state preamp or the warm, colored sound characteristic of a classic tube preamp. If you can afford only one external preamp, one of these hybrid versions may be right for you.

The countless hybrid preamps on the market vary widely. (In fact, most of the hybrid preamps are marketed as tube preamps.) Your best bet in choosing a hybrid — or any preamp for that matter — is to do some research. Talk to people, read reviews, visit Internet forums, and then audition the two or three that stand out to you. Choose the one that you think sounds best for your needs.

Considering Compressors

A compressor enables you to alter the dynamic range (that is, the difference between the softest and loudest sound) of an instrument. Along with the microphone and preamp, the compressor is often added to the signal chain before it goes to the mixer. The advantage of using a compressor in the signal chain before it hits the mixer is that you can control the transients and have a hotter (higher) signal level going into the converters or recorder. This hotter level used to be necessary when recording at 16 bits, but with 24-bit recording, you don't need to worry as much about getting the highest signal into your system. I discuss setting optimal levels in more detail in Chapter 7.

If you record a lot of vocals or real drums, a decent external compressor may be a good idea — just go easy with it (again check out Chapter 7). You can find some great-sounding compressors for as little as $200. My favorite is the FMR Audio RNC-1773 (a really nice unit).

As long as you're looking at preamps and compressors, take a look at some *channel strip devices,* which are integrated preamp, compressor, and equalizer combos. For some people (and maybe you), a channel strip device is the way to go. It allows you to have just one unit, reducing the amount of cords, and it's designed to make the three parts function well together. Quite a few great-sounding channel strip devices are available for under $500.

Analyzing Some Microphone Accessories

Along with your new mics, you're going to need a few accessories. These include mic cords, mic stands, and pop filters.

Microphone cords

Microphone cords can cost from about $10 to several hundred dollars. You're probably asking yourself, "Is there really a difference between a $10 or $20 mic cable and one that sells for hundreds of dollars?"

My answer is, "Supposedly — but chances are, you'll never hear it." Let me qualify this answer a little. Unless you have a *very* good mixer, recorder, microphones, preamps, analog/digital and digital/analog converters, and monitors, you're wasting your money on expensive microphone cords. I know only one sound engineer (not me though — I've spent too many years behind the drums) who claims that he can hear the difference between an average mic cord and one of the expensive ones. And even he says that the difference is very subtle. (It would have to be; otherwise, I would hear the difference, too.)

Don't waste your money on an expensive mic cord (or any cord) until the cord is the weakest link in your signal chain. By then, spending a couple hundred dollars on a cord will seem trivial because you'll already have invested tens of thousands of dollars in top-quality gear.

Microphone stands

A sturdy mic stand is essential for your studio. Mic stands are relatively inexpensive, so resist the temptation to buy a flimsy one. A good mic stand has a sturdy base and can securely hold your mics.

Good mic stands cost about $30 and have either a round cast iron base (great for getting into tight spaces) or a tripod base. Either one works well.

Pop filters

A *pop filter* is a nylon screen that eliminates the "pops" (technically called *plosives*) that singers make when they sing. Plosives are the result of sudden bursts of air projected into the mic (from singing words starting with *P*s and *T*s, for example). If you record vocals, a pop filter is a must-have.

Pop filters are relatively inexpensive (starting at about $20), but if you want to make your own, use a pair of tights or pantyhose and a coat hanger. Bend the coat hanger into a circle and stretch the nylons or pantyhose over it. You can attach the coat hanger to the mic stand by using duct tape. Adjust the coat hanger so that the pop filter is 4 to 6 inches away from the microphone, and then have the vocalist sing through it. Check out Figure 6-8 to see a homemade pop filter.

Figure 6-8:
You can make a pop filter out of a coat hanger and a pair of tights or pantyhose.

Caring for Your Microphones

After investing hundreds, if not thousands, of dollars in microphones, you probably want to know how to take care of them properly. Caring for or storing your microphones isn't rocket science. Just follow the general guidelines and ideas that follow, and you'll keep your mics in tip-top shape.

A good microphone lasts a lifetime. Take care of your mics, and they'll give you years of service.

Daily care

The most important thing to keep in mind when using your mics is to resist the temptation to blow into them. I know you've probably seen someone on stage blow into a mic and yell "Test" to see whether it is working. And you figure that's how the pros must check their mics. Well, it isn't. Blowing into a mic is a sure way to literally blow out the diaphragm in some mics, especially those expensive ribbon mics. To determine whether a mic is working, just speak into it in a normal voice.

You don't need to blow or yell into any mic unless, of course, your singer's style is to yell into the mic and you're trying to set the input level. In this case, offer him or her your trusty dynamic mic and keep that expensive ribbon mic hidden.

Another thing to remember when handling your mics is that they can be fragile. Condenser and ribbon mics don't survive rough handling well. In fact, if you drop a condenser or ribbon mic, you may break it (this is another good reason to have a sturdy stand). Dynamic mics, on the other hand, are more durable, which is why they are often used for live applications and on drums. (It's not uncommon for an overzealous drummer to whack them by accident — as a drummer, I know about this firsthand).

Try to keep your mics away from dust and high humidity. Dust is probably the number-one enemy of a microphone because the dust can settle on the diaphragm and reduce the sensitivity of the mic — and even alter its frequency response. Always cover your mics or put them away when you're not using them.

Storage

Most professionals have mic lockers, where they can safely keep their mics when they're not in use. Mic lockers come in several varieties. You can make a special locked box fitted with foam padding that has a cutout for each mic, or you can keep your mics in their pouches or cases (if the mic came with a case) in a closet or cabinet.

Regardless of the type of storage cabinet that you have, try to handle your mics as little as possible. In fact, if you have a mic that you use a lot, I recommend leaving it on a secure stand rather than repeatedly dragging it out of its case or storage cabinet.

If you do leave your mic out on its stand, cover the mic with a plastic bag and close the open end around the mic when it's not in use (see Figure 6-9). This keeps out the dust.

Humidity can also be a problem for microphones. If you live in a humid environment, store your mics with a bag of silica gel next to them. (Silica gel, which absorbs moisture, is the stuff that comes in the packaging of a lot of electronic gear.) You can find silica gel listed as desiccant packets (Desi Paks) by the manufacturer. You can order silica gel in quantities of as little as ten from the following manufacturer:

Hydrosorbent Products, P.O. Box 437, 25 School Street, Ashley Falls, MA 01222 (www.dehumidify.com/desipak.html)

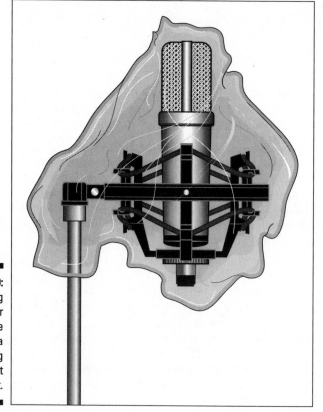

Figure 6-9:
Covering
your
microphone
with a
plastic bag
keeps out
the dust.

You can also do an Internet search by typing **"Desi Pak"** (include the quotation marks) into your favorite search engine.

Part III
Getting Ready to Record

The 5th Wave   By Rich Tennant

How much more bass do you want?

In this part . . .

Part III helps you get the best source sound, from instruments that are plugged directly into your system to acoustic instruments that you mic. Chapter 7 explores the process of setting the best levels for both plugged-in and miked instruments. Chapter 8 shows you the fundamentals of microphone placement and introduces you to common approaches. Chapter 9 digs into the specifics of microphone placement for a variety of common instruments to give you a leg up on getting nice-sounding tracks.

Chapter 7

Getting a Great Source Sound

The quality of your recording relies heavily on two things: how your instruments sound and how well you get that sound into your computer without messing it up. The problem is that anyone can easily mess up the sound or at least fall short of getting the best possible sound.

This chapter gives you the knowledge to keep bad sound — or sound that's not as good as it could be — from happening. In this chapter, I describe signal flow and the role that it plays in shaping the sound of your instrument. I also give you tips on how to get great guitar sounds and killer keyboard sounds without hassle. To top it off, I spend a few pages getting you up to speed on miking effectively.

Making Sense of the Signal Chain

The *signal chain* is the path that your sound travels from its creation (your guitar, keyboard, or voice) to your recorder. This path often includes several steps — and pieces of gear — that need to be optimized so that you don't end up with too much or too little sound going to your system. I cover the flow of various signal chains in detail in Chapter 4, but here's an overview of the process. Figure 7-1 shows the straightforward signal chain for a mic going into a studio-in-a-box recorder.

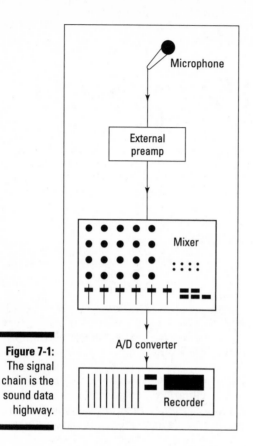

Figure 7-1:
The signal
chain is the
sound data
highway.

In this example, the sound originating from your voice enters the microphone, travels to a preamp-equipped input in your device where it's amplified, is converted into digital information within the device, and finally gets
sent into the recording software section of your recorder and the hard drive,
where it's stored.

The key to a good instrument or mic sound is getting each signal in the chain
set to its optimal level. This particular signal chain involves just two places
where you can make adjustments to your signal levels, as follows:

✔ **The source:** In the example shown in Figure 7-1, the microphone's placement has a huge effect on the signal level that goes into your computer.
Moving the mic just a couple inches can have a significant impact on your
signal level at the preamp. A good, solid level keeps you from having to
crank up your preamp too far, which causes noise. If the level is too hot,
though — *hot* in the sense of a solid signal between –12dB and –6dB —
you risk getting distortion at the mic. This same concept holds true for
keyboards or other electronic instruments, as well as guitars plugged
directly into your interface.

✔ **The preamp-equipped input:** You adjust this level to get the right level in your recorder. I discuss the optimal signal level for different systems in the next section.

Setting Optimal Signal Levels

Getting a sound signal to the recorder takes several steps. The path that the sound takes from the instrument or microphone to the recorder is called the *signal chain* (see the previous section). You need to be aware of the signal level at all of these steps to get the best sound possible. Too much gain at one stage forces you to reduce the gain at another. Likewise, too little gain at one point may require you to *overdrive* (bump up the gain) during the next stage.

Incorrect gain structuring results in a signal that's too low, which creates noise, or a signal that's too high, which causes distortion. In fact, with poor gain structuring, you can have a signal that is both too quiet and distorted.

How you set the levels that you record to disk has a lot to do with how good (or bad) your performance sounds. The key to getting good recording levels is to get as hot (high) a signal as you can without going over the maximum that the converter or recorder can handle. If you use analog tape, you have some leeway in how hot your signal can get, but if you record digitally, you don't have that luxury. Anything over the baseline of 0dB is going to *clip* — a nice recording term that means *distort*. 0dB, by the way, doesn't mean "no sound." Instead it refers to the highest level that a digital system can handle without clipping the signal.

How hot is hot enough, you ask? Well, it depends on who you talk to and at what bit depth you record. Because you're reading my book, here's my take on the best levels at which to record:

✔ **16-bit systems:** By this point in the book (assuming that you've read other sections on digital recording), you know that I'm not a fan of 16-bit recording. This is because to record with enough headroom, you need to turn the incoming level down so much that you start to lose sound quality; that is, you're using fewer than 16 bits and lowering the resolution of your system. In this case, I usually recommend setting your level higher in a 16-bit system than in a 24-bit system — usually with peaks no higher than –6dB. This allows some room for transients (check out the section "Making the Most of Microphones," later in this chapter) while preserving as much resolution as possible.

✔ **24-bit systems:** Because plenty of bits are available, you have more wiggle room before you start to lose sound quality. For 24-bit systems, I suggest that you record with your peak level at or below –12dB. This gives you enough room for transients to sneak through without clipping your system.

When you set your recording levels (do this by playing a section of your song), keep the following points in mind:

- **Keep an eye on the clip light on your preamp/input.** Not all inputs have a clip light, but if yours does, it's most likely located next to the trim knob. Sending too hot a signal through your preamp/input is the first way you can create distortion. Your clip light should illuminate only faintly once in a while, if at all. If your clip light is glowing red, your signal is way too hot, and you may end up with distortion. (Check the owner's manual for your preamp to see when the clip light is set to activate. Some clip lights are set to go off at –6dB, others illuminate at –3dB, and still others light at 0dB.)

- **Use the meters as a guide.** Both your mixer and recorder have meters that show you the level of the signal going in. Both of these levels are important, so keep an eye on them. Make sure that the meters never go above 0dB and that they peak out at a maximum of –12dB to –6dB. Also, be aware of whether you're monitoring pre or post levels, which I discuss in the next section.

- **Trust your ears.** Even with the clip light and meters, you still need to listen carefully to the signal. Many of the level meters on digital recorders are fairly slow to respond and can often miss sudden, extreme transients. If you hear any clipping or occasional harshness in the sound, turn the level down, regardless of what your meters tell you.

- **When in doubt, turn down the level.** If you can't tell whether the sound is clean, don't be afraid to turn the level down a little. Recording at –16dB instead of –12dB isn't going to ruin your track, but a clipped note can.

The straight-line rule

Most professional engineers are taught to record by using the *straight-line rule*. This rule comes from the old days of analog recording. It is thought of as being not only good engineering practice but also a courtesy to any other engineer who may handle your tracks.

The straight-line rule basically involves setting up your input levels so that they roughly match the levels that you want when you mix the song. You do this by setting your channel fader at 0dB (also marked as Unity on some mixers) and adjusting your input gain (the trim knob on your mixer or preamp) until you have a clean signal (no distortion) on the recorder's meters. The signal's level needs to be approximately the same as the level of the instrument in the final mix. For some instruments, such as a snare drum, the level peaks close to 0dB, but on other instruments, such as the string section, the level may be near –10dB. If you follow the straight-line rule, when you're ready to mix your tracks, set all your faders at 0dB — and you'll have a rough mix.

The courtesy is that if someone then takes your recorded tracks to another system with another engineer, that engineer only has to set the faders at 0dB and everything is ready for final adjustments.

Understanding Pre and Post Levels

Most digital systems provide several options for monitoring meter levels. You can have prefader input levels, postfader input levels, prefader track levels, postfader track levels, and master bus levels (see Figure 7-2). Even with the same signal, different kinds of levels (prefader, postfader, input, track master bus, and so on) may end up showing different readings on your meters.

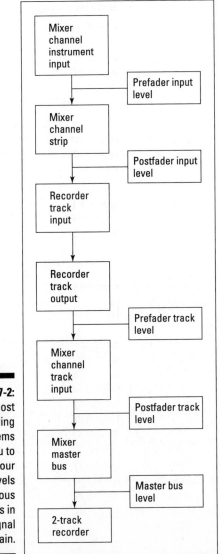

Figure 7-2:
Most recording systems allow you to monitor your signal levels at various places in the signal chain.

Interpreting the various levels

I try to clear up what all these different levels mean in the following list:

- **Prefader input levels:** The prefader input level shows you the level of the signal going into the mixer's channel strip before the signal hits the EQ or fader (hence the term *prefader*). Your sound source and trim adjustment (either on the mixer or a separate preamp) control the level shown on this meter.

  If your signal is too low or too hot and you don't have a separate preamp, adjust the trim knob on your mixer. If you're using a separate preamp, adjust the trim knob on your outboard preamp. You can also make adjustments to this level at the sound source. This could be either the output level of your instrument or the placement of your microphone.

- **Postfader input levels:** The postfader input level shows your signal level after the signal has traveled through the input channel's channel strip, that is, after the EQ and fader settings.

  This level is different from the prefader input level only if your fader is somewhere other than unity gain (or 0dB) or if you've made some adjustments to the EQ. To be specific, if you've removed any frequencies with the EQ or set your fader below 0dB, your postfader level is lower than the prefader level. Likewise, if you've added frequencies with the EQ or placed your fader above unity, your level is higher than it was going in.

- **Prefader track levels:** This is the most important level of your input signal chain (that is, if a most important level exists). This meter shows you what is actually recorded to the hard drive of the recorder.

  If you're using an analog mixer and a stand-alone recorder, you see this level on the recorder, not the mixer.

  This level matches the level of the postfader input channel routed to the recorder channel. If you have more than one input channel routed to a recorder track, this level is generally higher than each of the individual input postfader levels. This is because the signals combine to produce a higher overall level (called *summing*). If this is the case and the prefader track level is too high, you need to adjust the levels on all the tracks that are routed to this channel in order to drop the level coming in (the submix fader level, if you have these tracks run through the submix bus).

- **Postfader track levels:** The postfader track level shows you the level after you make adjustments to the track channel's fader or EQ settings. Like the postfader input level, the postfader track level is different from the prefader track level if you've made adjustments to either the EQ or the channel fader settings.

✔ **Master bus levels:** This level shows you the sum of all the levels being routed to the master bus. Unless you have only one channel going to the master bus, this level is different than any of the individual levels going to it because all levels from all the instruments are taken into account (summed). This is the level that is most important when you're mixing because this is the level that the 2-track master records.

Not all types of systems have all these level-monitoring options. For example, if you have an analog mixer, you may not have meters on anything except the recorder (prefader track level) and the master bus (master bus level).

Looking at some examples

You can use the various monitoring sources to find out where in your signal chain you may be introducing distortion or where you need to boost the signal. If you find the source of the signal problem, you don't have to over-compensate at a different part of the signal path. For example, perhaps you connect a microphone to an external preamp and set the trim on the preamp for a good, hot signal. The prefader track level going to the recorder, however, is too low. In this case, you can check the postfader input level to see whether something is squashing your signal. The fader may be set too low, or some EQ may be set to reduce some frequencies. To fix the problem, you can either raise the fader or adjust your EQ until your level at the prefader track meter is where you want it to be.

Another scenario is when you have a recorded track that has even levels (as seen on the prefader track level) but you're getting distortion at the master bus (master bus level). In this case, check the postfader track level to see whether it looks different than the prefader level. It most likely will, and you can fix the problem by adjusting either the fader or the EQ until the level is tamed. If both the prefader and postfader track levels look the same, the combined levels that come from more than one track to the master bus are probably causing the distortion. In this case, you need to reduce the levels from all the tracks going to the master bus to bring the master bus level down a bit.

Don't get too stressed about your levels. Use your ears and trust yourself. If you get noticeable digital clipping (distortion), just record the part again. One of the great things about digital recording is that you can erase and rere-cord a performance as many times as you want without compromising sound quality.

Getting a Great Guitar Sound

Do you wanna know how to get the absolute best, most rich, engaging guitar sound? Well, I wish I could tell you, but alas I can't. This is something you're going to need to figure out by listening as you tweak your gear. That said, you can get your sound into your computer in four ways, and each way has its plusses and minuses, as I describe in the following list:

- **Directly from your guitar into your instrument input:** The instrument input in your system could be located in your analog mixer (stand-alone systems), your recorder (SIAB systems), or your audio interface (computer-based systems). This assumes that your instrument input can handle a direct connection from a guitar. (Most can, but check to make sure that the one you have or want has this capability. If it doesn't, you need to get a direct box to put between your guitar and your instrument input. I talk about direct boxes in Chapter 1.) By using this method, the sound you get from your guitar is pretty much the same sound you're going to get recorded.

  You may not like the sound — in fact, I'll bet you won't. The solution to this unfortunate state of affairs is to use a plug-in (or more than one) in your recording program to get the sound you want. This is a common way to get a guitar sound, and tons of good plug-ins can help, including plug-ins for providing distortion, delay, chorus, and even special amp simulators that are designed to sound like popular guitar amplifiers. One advantage to this approach is that you can tweak the sound of your guitar as much as you want after it's recorded. The disadvantage is that you can easily become afflicted with indecision disorder and be unable to pick the sound you want. Also, many guitar-tone connoisseurs feel that getting the sound this way isn't as good as miking up an amp with the sound you want.

- **From your guitar to an amp simulator and from the amp simulator into your instrument input:** Amp simulators are like the plug-ins that you can get for your software, only they're stand-alone units that already have the various sounds in them. A bunch of stand-alone amp simulators are available on the market, and most offer decent simulations of the most popular guitar amps. This can be a good solution for many people, but the disadvantage of doing this — instead of adding your effects in the computer — is that after you record your sound through an amp simulator, you're stuck with that sound. Of course, if you often get hit with indecision disorder, this may be a good solution for you.

- **From your guitar into your amp and from your amp's line output to your instrument input:** Recording a guitar this way is great for people who have an amp that they like the sound of but who don't want to mic a speaker. When you follow this approach, you have three volume controls to adjust to get your level into your recorder — your guitar, your amp, and your interface. You may have to take some time tweaking these settings to get the best possible sound.

> ✔ **From your guitar into your amp with a mic picking up the speaker's sound:** This is the old standby approach because you get to record the actual sound you're used to hearing coming out of your amp. With this method, having the right mic and mic placement makes all the difference in the world. I offer some specific guitar-amping mic techniques in Chapter 9.

There is no single way to get a great guitar sound. Don't be afraid to experiment. You may just come up with a sound that really moves you.

Creating a Killer Keyboard Sound

The key to getting a killer keyboard sound is making sure that you get the sound into your system without messing it up (no pressure here). Depending on your gear, keyboard sounds can be brought into your system in one of the following ways:

> ✔ **Using the analog outputs in your keyboard:** For an external keyboard that contains the sounds you want to record, plug an instrument cord from the main outputs of your keyboard to the corresponding number of inputs in your system. Turn your keyboard volume up between ½ and ¾ or until you get a decent signal to register in your recorder. If your instrument input has a volume (gain) control, adjust it and the volume of your keyboard until you get a solid sound without distortion.
>
> Follow the guidelines that I list in the section "Setting Optimal Signal Levels," earlier in this chapter, to get your best signal levels.
>
> ✔ **Recording MIDI data and adding the sound later:** If you have a MIDI-capable keyboard and a MIDI sequencer, you can record your musical performance as MIDI data and assign the sound later. In this case, connect your keyboard to your MIDI sequencer. This can be done using a MIDI cable connected to MIDI ports in each device, or it can be done with a USB connection if you have a USB-equipped keyboard and MIDI sequencer (such as a software program in a computer). Chapter 5 explains how to make the connections for this.
>
> Because you're recording MIDI data instead of an audio signal, you don't need to worry about setting the record level. Chapter 12 explains the process of recording MIDI sequences in detail.

Making the Most of Microphones

Finding a great sound from a mic is key to getting a great-sounding recording. To do this, you need to use the best mic for the application and place it where it can sound its best. This requires not only knowledge of the different types of mics that are available (see Chapter 6) but also an understanding of how these mics are used for a variety of instruments (see Chapter 9). In the following sections, I give you a quick tutorial on setting optimal levels of your microphones to help you get the most out of the mics and techniques I present in the other miking chapters.

The most difficult part of getting a good sound by using a microphone is dealing with sudden, extreme increases in the sound signal. These blips are called *transients,* and they regularly happen when a drum is first struck, when a vocalist sings certain syllables (for example, those that begin with a *P*), and when a guitar player picks certain notes. In fact, because you can't always control the amount of force that you apply to an instrument, transients can happen at any time, with any instrument, and without warning. (Highly trained musicians produce fewer extreme transients because they have a greater mastery over their muscular movements.)

In digital recording, all it takes is one slight, unexpected note to cause clipping and distortion, ruining what may otherwise be a perfect musical performance. Believe me, nothing is so heart-wrenching as listening to the perfect take (recorded performance) and hearing the unmistakable sound of digital distortion. Although you can't eliminate transients (they are part of an instrument's character), you can tame extreme transients that often cause clipping (distortion). You can do this in the following three ways:

✔ **Set your levels with enough headroom to handle these transients.** I cover this step in the section "Setting Optimal Signal Levels," earlier in this chapter.

✔ **Minimize transients with proper mic placement.** I explain this process in the next section.

✔ **Run the signal through a compressor when recording.** The section "Compressing carefully," later in this chapter, gives you the lowdown on this process.

Placing mics properly

A microphone that's placed too close to a loud sound source or pointed too directly toward the point of attack can easily pick up extreme transients. In most cases, you just need to pull the mic away from the instrument a little or turn it ever so slightly to avoid a signal that's too high. I don't go into detail here because I cover mic placement thoroughly in Chapter 9.

The main thing to keep in mind when placing your microphones is to experiment. Don't be afraid to spend time making small adjustments. After all, the track you save could be your own.

Compressing carefully

Compressors are processors that allow you to control the dynamics of a signal — and boy, are they ever versatile. You can use compressors on the front end while tracking (recording) instruments to make sure that you don't have stray transients. You can use them to level off an erratic performance. And you can use compressors to raise the overall apparent level of a mixed song. In the following sections, I discuss the first use of compression: the control of transients. (You can find out about the other ways to use compression in Chapters 14 and 15.)

If you have an SIAB (studio-in-a-box) system or a computer-based system, you probably have a compressor included with the effects in the unit. Although you can use this compressor to track with, your signal has to go through the A/D converter first. (The A/D converter changes your signal from analog to digital form.) Because these systems are digital, the A/D converter is the first in line after the preamp. This often defeats the purpose of using a compressor to control transients because the A/D converter is where you often get your first dose of distortion. If you're serious about using compression on the front end to tame transients, you may want to insert an external preamp into the signal chain before the A/D converter.

Getting to know compressor parameters

Compressors have a series of dials that allow you to adjust several parameters. They are as follows:

- **Threshold:** The threshold setting dictates the level that the compressor starts to act on the signal. This is listed in decibels (dB). For the most part, you should set the threshold level so that the compressor acts only on the highest peaks of the signal.

- **Ratio:** The ratio is the amount that the compressor affects the signal. The ratio — such as 2:1, for instance — means that for every decibel that the signal goes over the threshold setting, it is reduced by two decibels. In other words, if a signal goes 1dB over the threshold setting, its output from the compressor will only be ½dB louder. The ratio is the one parameter that varies considerably from instrument to instrument because the level of the transient varies.

- **Attack:** The attack knob controls how soon the compressor starts, well, compressing. The attack is defined in milliseconds (ms), and the lower the number, the faster the attack. For the most part, you're trying to control transients, and they happen at the beginning of a note. Therefore, you should set the attack to act quickly.

- **Release:** The release parameter controls how long the compressor continues affecting the note after the note starts. Like the attack, the release is defined in milliseconds. Because transients don't last for very long, you usually use a short release time when using compression on the front end.

✔ **Gain:** The gain knob allows you to adjust the level of the signal coming out of the compressor. This is listed in decibels. Because adding compression generally reduces the overall level of the sound, you use this control to raise the level back to where it was going in.

✔ **Hard knee or soft knee:** Most compressors give you the option of choosing between a *hard knee* and a *soft knee* (or they do it for you based on the setting that you've chosen). Hard knee and soft knee each refer to how the compressor behaves as the input signal passes the threshold. More details descriptions are as follows:

- **Hard knee** applies the compression at an even rate, regardless of the level present over the threshold. So if you choose a compression setting of 4:1, the compressor applies this ratio for any signal over the threshold limit. Hard knee compression is used for instruments like drums, where you need to quickly clamp down on transients.

- **Soft knee** applies the compression at a varying rate depending on the amount the signal is over the threshold setting. The compressor gradually increases the ratio of the compression as the signal crosses the threshold until it hits the level that you set. Soft knee compression is used on vocals and other instruments where the signal doesn't have fast peaks.

Creating compressor settings

When you use a compressor to keep transients at bay, you only want to compress the highest transient levels — the ones that would overload your system or eat up your headroom — and you want to do this so that you don't hear the compressor kicking in. Even though every instrument contains different levels of transient signals and each person who plays an instrument creates different amounts of extreme transients when he or she plays, here are some things to keep in mind as you create your settings:

✔ **Keep the threshold high.** With a high threshold setting, your compressor only kicks in as the signal gets close to distorting. For most instruments, I would use a setting of about –6dB. Some instruments with very high transients, such as percussion and drums, can handle a setting like –10dB. Set your threshold so that when the extreme transient happens, it only triggers the compressor a couple of decibels, and the nontransient material (the main sound of the instrument) doesn't trigger the compressor.

✔ **Adjust the ratio to the material.** For high-transient material (such as drums and percussion), choose a higher ratio, and for lower-transient material (like strummed or bowed string instruments), choose a lower ratio setting. Try to use a ratio that relates to the level of the transient over the nontransient signal. Because percussion instruments have initial signal peaks (transients) that are much stronger than the body of the instrument's sound, you can compress this peak without affecting the main sound of the instrument. By matching the ratio to the degree of the transient this way, you can create a more even level without changing the sound characteristics of the instrument.

✔ **Use a short attack.** Transients happen at the initial attack of the instrument. This means that if you want to compress the transient, the compressor must kick in right away when this signal happens. A setting of 1 millisecond or less is optimal.

✔ **Use a short release.** Transients happen quickly and they last a very short amount of time. When you try to control these signals during tracking, you only want to catch the transient itself — and no other part of the instrument's sound. Setting a short release time — start with about 10 milliseconds — ensures that your compressor doesn't linger on to affect the body of the instrument.

✔ **Don't mess with the gain.** Because you're only catching the highest transient signals and you're only compressing them a tiny bit, you don't need to add or reduce any of the signal that's going through the compressor. Leave the gain control at 0dB.

When using a compressor during tracking, keep the following two points in mind:

✔ **You can always add compression to a recorded track, but you can never take it away.** If you're not sure how much compression to apply to a particular situation, you're much better off erring on the side of too little because you can always run the sound through another compressor later.

✔ **If you can hear a change in the sound of your signal, you probably have the compressor set too high.** The reason that you use a compressor on the front end is to eliminate extreme transients, which you can't hear when you play. If your compression setting changes the sound, you should slightly reduce the compression setting (unless you're going for that effect).

Chapter 8

Taking a Look at Microphone Techniques

*T*o record acoustic instruments — that is, any instrument that doesn't have an electronic output — you need to use a microphone. The sound that you ultimately get can vary considerably based on where you place the mic in relation to the instrument and the room that you record in. I spend quite a bit time — three chapters, in fact — talking about microphones because they're so important to the quality of your final recordings. See Chapters 6 and 9 for more miking details.

In this chapter, I take a look at some of the most common microphone techniques that are used in professional recording. You get a chance to see, up close, how spot miking works. You also get a broad view of distant miking and take a look at the big picture on ambient miking. As well, this chapter explores some common stereo miking techniques and explains what to look for when combining these various approaches.

Regardless of the style of microphone that you use or the type of instrument that you record, you can use one or more of the following mic-placement techniques to capture the sound that you want:

✔ **Spot (or close) miking:** Put your microphone within inches of the sound source.

✔ **Distant miking:** Pull your mic back a few feet from the sound.

✔ **Ambient miking:** Place your mic way back in a room.

✔ **Stereo miking:** Set up two mics at various distances from one another.

✔ **Combined miking:** Use a combination of the four traditional placement strategies listed here.

This chapter introduces you to the four traditional mic-placement strategies that are used in recording. You discover the characteristics and purposes of each of these four methods and gain an understanding of how each relates to a particular tonal or sound quality. I also discuss how you can combine these strategies.

Singling Out Spot Miking

Spot miking (also called *close miking*) involves placing your microphone within a couple of feet of the sound source. Home recordists use this technique most often because it adds little of the room (the reverb and delay) to the recorded sound. Figure 8-1 shows the close miking placement.

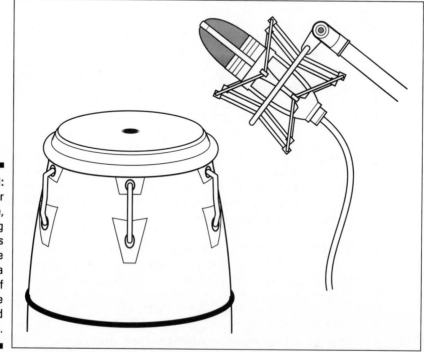

Figure 8-1: Spot, or close, miking involves placing the mic within a couple of feet of the sound source.

Spot miking tends to create a less natural sound and can compromise the quality of your recordings if you're not careful. It can also offer you some advantages if you record multiple instruments in one pass or if your room doesn't sound good. Here are some things to consider when using spot miking:

✔ **Transients are more extreme.** Distance from a sound source tames the initial attack of an instrument. Spot miking picks up more transient material, which can make the sound of the instrument seem harsh and can overload your mic, preamp, or converter without your seeing it on your level meters. You need to listen closely to your recorded sound to make sure that you don't have distortion. A solution to this problem is to move the mic back a bit or point it slightly away from the instrument.

✔ **The room isn't part of the recording.** This can be good or bad depending on the sound of your room:

- On the plus side, it can keep a bad-sounding room from ruining the sound of your track by putting it so far in the background of the recording that it isn't really heard on your tracks.

- On the downside, you lose the natural ambience of an instrument that gives it its character, so if you have a nice-sounding room, this technique may not be the best choice (depending on how many instruments are playing at once — see the next bullet).

✔ **You can isolate each instrument.** Spot miking can help you keep multiple instruments separated in your tracks, so if you record your band live, you can create some isolation among instruments. (This assumes that you use a microphone with a cardioid polar pattern. Chapter 6 has more details on this). This makes mixing a lot easier. Because of the downside that I list in the previous bullet, I'm a big fan of using room mics (using the ambient technique described in the section "Assessing Ambient Miking," later in this chapter) in conjunction with spot mics to create a more realistic sound.

✔ **Even minor adjustments in mic placement can have a huge impact on your recorded sound.** Because the mic is so close to the sound source, small adjustments to the mic's placement make a noticeable difference, and the mic may not capture the complete sound of the instrument. Finding the spot that sounds the best may take you a while.

✔ **The closer you put your mic, the more bass you record.** I mention this in Chapter 6, but it bears repeating here. As you move a mic with a cardioid polar pattern in close to the sound source, the mic picks up more bass energy. This is called the *proximity effect.* It can be an advantage for some applications — rounding out the sound of a vocal, for instance — but it can also cause problems with some instruments such as acoustic strings, where you don't want the extra bass muddying the sound. To counter this effect, use an omnidirectional or figure-8 mic or move the cardioid-pattern mic away from the sound source until the bass is more manageable. (See Chapter 6 for a rundown of the different types of mics.)

Detailing Distant Miking

When you use *distant miking,* you place mics about 3 or 4 feet away from the sound source, as shown in Figure 8-2. Distant miking enables you to capture some of the sound of the room along with the instrument. An example of a distant-miking technique is the overhead drum mic. With it, you can pick up the whole drum set to some extent. Coupling the distant mic with a few select spot mics, you can record a natural sound.

Figure 8-2:
The micro-phone is placed 3 to 4 feet from the instru-ment in the distant-miking technique.

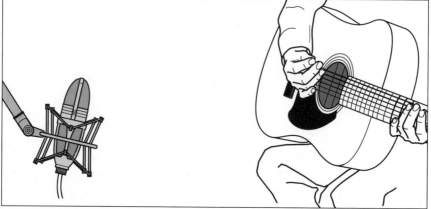

Distant miking has its plusses and minuses. Here are some things to remem-ber if you use this technique:

- ✔ **You can get a more natural sound.** By moving the mic back a few feet from its source, you give the instrument a chance to breathe a bit and allow the sound to blend a little with the room in which it's played. You also eliminate the impact of the proximity effect (see the previous sec-tion) and correct the balance between the body of the instrument's sound and the transient from the initial attack. This often creates a more pleasing, natural sound.

- ✔ **Other instruments may bleed into your track.** If you record more than one instrument at the same time, distant miking increases the bleed of other instruments into the track of the instrument that you want to record. The solution to this is to use the spot-miking technique instead, move the instruments farther apart, adjust the mics so that the blind spot of the mic is facing the instrument you don't want to record, or place gobos (acoustic baffles, as discussed Chapter 3) between the instruments.

- ✔ **The sound of the room is important.** With the mic farther away from the instrument, more of the room sound is picked up in relation to the instrument. As a result, you hear more of the room in your tracks. This can be nice if your room sounds good, but it can get in the way if your room doesn't.

✔ **Multiple mics can cause phase problems.** Whenever you use more than one mic on a source such as a band or drum set, the relationship of these mics to the source and to one another plays a significant role in the sound you get. If the mics are not placed properly, some frequencies may drop out. Called *phase cancellation,* this is the result of the recorded waveforms reaching each mic at slightly different times. The sidebar "Problems with stereo miking" and the section "Creating Miking Combinations," later in this chapter, explain this phenomenon in more detail.

Assessing Ambient Miking

Ambient miking is simply placing the mic far enough away from the sound source so that you capture more of the room sound (the reverb and delay) than the sound of the actual instrument (see Figure 8-3). You may place the mic a couple of feet away from the source but pointed in the opposite direction, or you may place it across the room. You can even put the mic in an adjacent room, although I admit this is an unorthodox technique. The distance that you choose varies from instrument to instrument.

Ambient miking definitely has its place, but using this technique requires some forethought. Consider the following items when you use this technique:

✔ **You lose the attack of the instrument.** Because the mic is so far from the sound source, it picks up more of the ambience of the room than the attack of the instrument (hence the name of the technique). To counter this effect, use distant or spot mics for the instruments that you want to have a more pronounced presence and blend these mics with the ambient mic when you mix.

✔ **You need a good room.** Ambient miking relies on the sound of the room to create a pleasing ambience. If your room doesn't sound great, you're better off using a closer miking technique instead. On the other hand, if you can find a great room in which to record — a church or auditorium, for instance — setting up a mic in the middle of the room (you must listen for the best placement by walking around the room as the music plays) can give your tracks that extra something that can set them apart from the run-of-the-mill home recordings.

✔ **Placement is key.** Just as each instrument has a sweet spot, each room has a place that sounds best. Take your time finding this location and put your ambient mic there.

✔ **Watch for phase problems.** Because an ambient mic is typically used in conjunction with another mic or two (or more), you must keep the relationship among the mics correct; otherwise, you'll have problems with the phase of the recorded waveforms.

Ambient mic placement works well in those places where the room adds to the sound of the instrument. The sound that you record is ambient (hence the name). If you mix an ambient mic with a spot mic, you can end up with a natural reverb. So if your room doesn't add to the sound of the instrument, you're better off not using an ambient mic. You can always add a room sound by using effects in the mixing process (see Chapter 15 for more details).

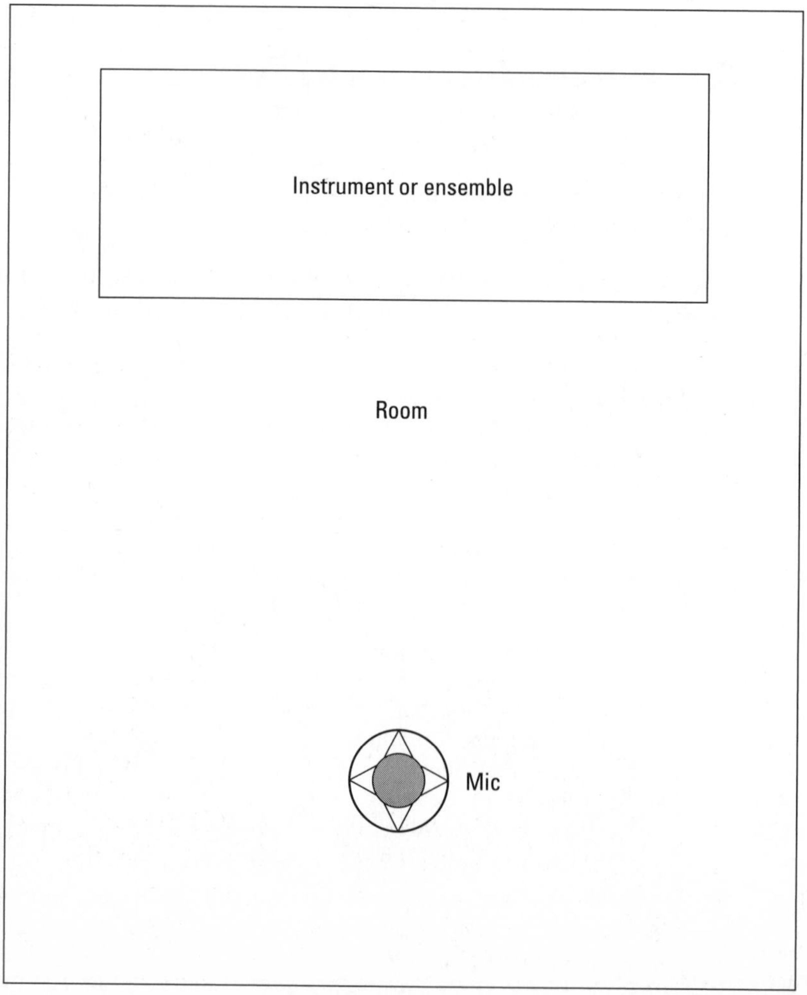

Figure 8-3:
Ambient
miking
involves
placing the
mic so that
it picks
up more of
the room's
sound
than the
instrument's
sound.

Instrument or ensemble

Room

Mic

Selecting Stereo Miking

Stereo miking involves using two mics to capture the stereo field of the instrument. You find a variety of stereo-miking techniques and some pretty complicated ways of using two mics to record. The three most common approaches are X-Y (coincident) pairs, the Blumlein technique, and spaced pairs. You can also find stereo mics that do a good job of capturing the stereo field of an instrument.

Stereo miking has the advantage of capturing a fairly natural stereo image, though not as good as what your ears capture. When you listen to performances that were recorded with well-placed stereo miking, you can hear exactly where each instrument performed on the stage. Of course, such wonderful stereo miking is an art. You can't just set up a couple of mics in a room and automatically get a good stereo sound. Capturing a stereo image with two mics requires some careful planning.

X-Y pairs

X-Y (coincident) stereo miking consists of using two mics that are placed right next to each other so that the diaphragms are as close together as possible without touching one another. X-Y stereo miking is the most common type of stereo mic setup and the one that you'll likely use if you do stereo miking. Figure 8-4 shows a basic X-Y setup. Notice how the mics in this figure are attached to a special mounting bracket. This bracket makes positioning the mics easy.

Figure 8-4:
The X-Y stereo mic approach uses two matched microphones placed close together.

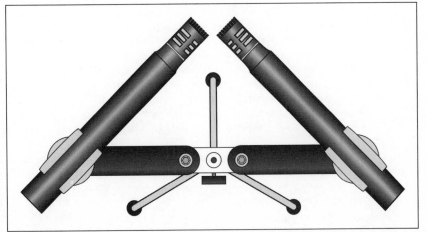

When you record using the X-Y technique, keep these points in mind:

✔ **The stereo image (the placement of the instruments in the sonic environment) isn't as wide or realistic as it is in real life.** The X-Y technique is easy to set up and get a decent sound, so like all things in life, you have to deal with the compromise this ease creates. No solution to this exists, so if a wide stereo image is important to you, consider using a different stereo technique, such as the spaced pair or perhaps a Jecklin disk. (For details on building a Jecklin disk for less than $20, visit my Web site — www.jeffstrong.com.)

✔ **Don't use two mics when one is enough.** After you get a pair of nice mics to do some X-Y miking, you'll want to use them on everything. A stereo-mic approach to a classical guitar composition is nice, but honestly, recording the acoustic guitar in a rock ballad with five other instruments playing isn't necessary and just makes life more complicated when you mix the song (see the section "Creating Miking Combinations," later in this chapter).

✔ **Keep some distance between the mics and the sound source.** The X-Y technique has no benefit over a single mic if you place your mics within a couple feet of the sound source. You simply don't have enough space for a stereo image to develop until you're at least 6 feet from the instrument or group of instruments. In fact, I would be at least 10 feet from the sound source before I use this approach.

Blumlein technique

The Blumlein technique is named after Alan Dower Blumlein, who patented this approach in 1931. Blumlein stereo miking involves placing two figure-8 mics in much the same way as the X-Y pattern (at right angles to one another with the diaphragms as close together as possible). The two mics are mounted on separate stands, one above the other. Figure 8-5 shows this technique.

The advantage of this technique is that the figure-8 mics pick up signals from both the front and back. This produces a natural sound. You also don't have to contend with proximity effects (enhanced bass response due to being close to the sound source) because figure-8 mics don't produce these effects. Here are some suggestions for when you should use this technique:

✔ **The room sound is important.** Because the Blumlein technique uses figure-8 mics that can pick up the sound on the other side of the mics than your instruments, you end up recording quite a bit of room sound with your instruments. This is one of the reasons that this technique sounds as good as it does, but your room must add to the quality of your sound, not hinder it.

✔ **Find the best place in the room.** Take some time to find the best place to put the mics. The placement may not be in the center of the room or the front of the band. Instead, it may be off to one side or closer to the back or front. This advice holds true for all miking, but with the Blumlein technique (or when using omnidirectional mics with the other techniques), correct mic placement can make the difference between a decent recording and a truly awesome one.

✔ **Get a sturdy stand that can handle both mics.** Using two stands to hold both mics makes moving them around (to find the sweet spot in the room) a real pain in the you-know-what. You can easily find mic-stand adapters that hold both mics. These can be an invaluable investment.

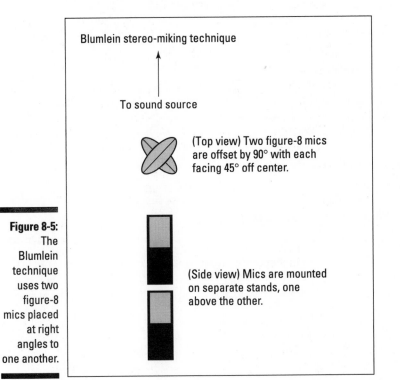

Blumlein stereo-miking technique

To sound source

(Top view) Two figure-8 mics are offset by 90° with each facing 45° off center.

(Side view) Mics are mounted on separate stands, one above the other.

Figure 8-5: The Blumlein technique uses two figure-8 mics placed at right angles to one another.

Spaced pairs

Spaced-pair stereo miking involves placing two mics at a distance in front of the instrument(s) that you want to record and at a distance from one another. This approach can work well if you record an ensemble that takes up a lot of room. Figure 8-6 shows a top view of a typical spaced-pair stereo mic setup.

Problems with stereo miking

When you do stereo miking, watch out for phase cancellation and poor stereo imaging. I describe these thorny issues in the following paragraphs.

Phase cancellation happens when the two microphones are placed so that they each receive the sound at slightly different times. When this occurs, you don't hear the bass as well because the low frequencies drop off. Improper mic placement or two mics that are out of phase with one another can cause phase cancellation.

Most digital recorders have a phase switch that allows you to reverse the phase of the signal (even after it's recorded). To test whether two mics are out of phase, just reverse the phase on one mic (don't do both) and listen to see whether the low frequencies become more apparent:

✔ If they do, you've corrected the problem and you're good to go.

✔ If this doesn't correct the problem, try changing cords on one of the mics because

some mic cords are wired differently than others. If this doesn't work either, you need to adjust the relationship between the two mics. Just move one mic around a little and listen for changes in the bass response. When the missing bass appears, you know you've solved the problem.

Poor stereo imaging occurs when you can't tell where things fall from left to right (or right to left, if that's the way you think) or when you can't hear a clear center point in the sound. Poor stereo imaging is a little more difficult to correct than phase cancellation, but you can fix it.

The solution depends on the stereo-miking technique that you use. If you use the X-Y technique, you've probably placed your mics too close to the sound source. If you use the spaced-pair technique, you've probably placed the mics too close to one another in relation to the distance from the instruments. In either case, adjusting the placement of your mics should clear up the problem.

Figure 8-6:
To use the spaced-pair approach, place two mics away from the sound source and apart from one another.

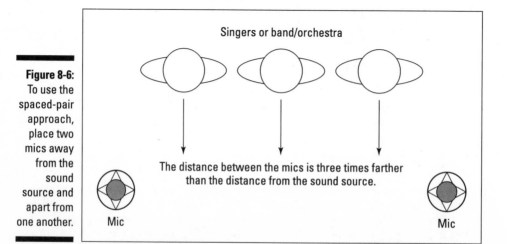

Singers or band/orchestra

The distance between the mics is three times farther than the distance from the sound source.

Mic

Mic

Keep the following things in mind when using the spaced-pair stereo-miking technique:

- ✔ **Follow the rule.** One of the most important things to consider when stereo miking with spaced pairs is that you will experience phase problems if you don't space the mics properly. Fortunately, experienced recordists have discovered a basic guideline that makes it easier to place the mics. Called the 3:1 rule, this guideline says that you should place the mics three times farther apart than they are from the sound source. Doing so minimizes potential phase problems.

- ✔ **Break the rule if necessary.** As handy as the 3:1 rule is, it isn't foolproof. At times, this rule doesn't produce the best sound. In the next chapter, I offer one of these instances for placing drum overheads in a three-mic technique. Use the rule as a guide, but trust your ears to determine the best place to put a spaced pair of mics (or a single mic, pair, or group of mics).

Stereo microphones

If you want to record an instrument in stereo and don't want the hassle of learning how to set up stereo pairs, you can use a stereo mic. Stereo mics have two diaphragms in them and use a special cord that allows you to record the output from each diaphragm on a separate track. An inexpensive stereo condenser mic is shown in Figure 8-7. This type of microphone acts like an X-Y pair, so follow the guidelines and suggestions that I offer in the section "X-Y pairs," earlier in this chapter, when using one of these.

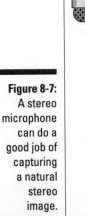

Figure 8-7:
A stereo
microphone
can do a
good job of
capturing
a natural
stereo
image.

Creating Miking Combinations

Many times, you'll want to use more than one mic. The possible combinations are almost limitless: You can use several spot mics on one instrument, you can use a spot mic and an ambient mic, you can have a distant mic and a spot mic, or . . . well, you get my point. As exciting as these possibilities can be, keep the following points in mind to get the best sound when you combine multiple mics:

- ✔ **Be aware of phase relationships.** Each mic interacts with all the other ones when you record, and you need to take the time to set up each mic so that it doesn't interfere with any others. This means honoring the 3:1 rule for stereo mics (see the section "Spaced pairs," earlier in this chapter). The only way to ensure that your phase is good is to record a snippet of a song (or a whole song if you want) and then listen to your tracks.

  Listen to each mic individually and then together to see whether any frequencies drop out. If frequencies drop out, finding the problem mics will take some detective work. You need to play pairs of mics that you recorded and until you find the problem; then you need to adjust each mic until the problem goes away. If you do this enough, you'll get pretty good at placing mics and making phase relationships work.

- ✔ **Be aware of bleed between mics.** This is mainly for bands that want to play together while still maintaining as much isolation as possible. A string quartet rarely needs isolation because all the instruments blend well together live; this blending is integral to the overall sound. However, a rock band with miked amps usually needs enough isolation so that you can do some tweaking to each instrument when you mix.

  As well, a band that plays well together and can nail the performances can have more bleed, whereas a band with a marginal player or two (you know whether you have one in your band) that needs to perform additional takes or punch-ins to fix a weak performance requires much more isolation. Doing a punch-in of your bass player (for instance, someone who flubbed a few notes into a live bleed-filled performance) can sound wrong in the mix.

- ✔ **Use only as many mics as you need.** Every additional mic that you add to your setup complicates your recording process considerably. To keep things simple, use as few mics as possible to get the sound that you want.

If you're using a digital recorder, it probably has a phase switch that enables you to fix the phase problems later if you missed them as you recorded. This isn't as optimal as recording without this problem, but it may allow you to save an otherwise good set of tracks.

Chapter 9

Miking Your Instruments

● ●

In This Chapter

▶ Exploring microphone techniques

▶ Miking drums

▶ Miking amplified instruments

▶ Miking acoustic instruments

● ●

*T*he location of a microphone in relation to your instrument or a singer has a huge impact on the sound of your recording. In fact, just a movement of an inch or two or even a slight turn of the mic can bring out different characteristics in the sound. The art of placing mics is one that you will undoubtedly spend a lifetime discovering.

In this chapter, you discover the fundamentals of using microphones to get a good source sound. You explore tried-and-true miking methods along with some practical miking tips and tricks that you can use right away. You also examine the use of compression and mic placement to control and eliminate *transients* — the usual peaks in the instrument's sound.

In Chapter 7, I present ways to get the best sound from your mics and to keep extreme transients from ruining an otherwise nice recording by overloading your inputs and clipping your audio, so check it out if you haven't done so yet.

Just remember, you don't need to use a compressor when tracking — simply keep your levels low enough to leave room for these unexpected signals. If you do decide to use a compressor during tracking, keep the attack and release times short (Chapter 7 has more on this). You only want to catch the initial signal and not mess with the rest of the instrument's sound. If you want to use a compressor to sculpt the sound of your instruments, you can do that easily during the mixing stage of producing your song. I cover this approach in detail in Chapter 15, where I offer a bunch of sample settings to get you started.

Getting a Great Lead Vocal Sound

Regardless of the type of home studio you have or the style of music that you record, you'll probably record vocals at some point. And unfortunately, vocals are one of the most challenging sounds to do well. You have to find the right mic for the person who's singing, and then you need to try different approaches to get the best sound out of him or her. Fortunately, you're in luck. In the following sections, I lead you through the (sometimes complicated) process of getting good lead vocal sounds.

Making the most of the room

To get the best possible recording of vocals, you need a dead room, which is another way of saying a room that has no reverberation. (Chapter 3 has some tips on how to deaden your room.) Recording vocals in a dead room gives a sense of "presence" and allows you to add compression to the vocals without making them sound distant (this is because the compressor raises the level of the background noise, particularly the reverberation from a live room).

 The easiest way to deaden your room for vocal recording is to hang curtains, carpet, or blankets around the room or to use the absorbent side of the reflector/absorber panels that I discuss in Chapter 3. Try to get the front and both sides of the vocal area covered with absorbent materials. If you use the reflector/absorber panels that I describe in Chapter 3, you need to use the stands, because the panels are only 4 feet tall.

Choosing the best mic

You have a lot of options for miking vocals. The type of mic that you use dictates where you place it.

Dynamic mic

Dynamic mics sound best when you place them close to the singer's mouth. The effect that you get is gritty. Huh? Okay, by gritty I mean dirty. That's no help either? Let me see . . .

Sound: Dynamic mics produce a midrange sound (the high frequencies aren't reproduced well). When someone sings with the mic right in front of her mouth, the sound lacks even more high frequencies due to the proximity effect (an enhanced low-frequency response at close range). What you get is a deep, bass-heavy sound that's often described as gritty or dirty. This type of sound can be great for some styles of rock and blues music.

Setup: To set up a dynamic mic for this purpose, just put it on a stand so that the singer can get his mouth right up against the windscreen.

Large-diaphragm condenser mic

Large-diaphragm condenser mics are the most common types of mics for vocals.

Sound: These mics can clearly reproduce the entire audible frequency spectrum and slightly accentuate the low mid frequencies (200–500Hz) at the same time. What you get is a nice, warm, full-bodied sound (that sounds like I'm describing a wine). The proximity effect (how close the singer is to the mic) determines how nice and warm-bodied the sound is. The closer the singer, the deeper and richer the tone.

Setup: When you set up a large-diaphragm condenser mic for vocals, you need to place the mic so that nasty sibilances (the sound from singing *s* and *t* sounds) and pesky plosives (pops from singing *p* syllables) don't mess up your recordings. To deal with plosives and sibilance, you can either use a pop filter (see Chapter 6) or have the singer sing past the mic. If you want the singer to sing past the mic, you can do one of the following things:

✔ Place the mic above the singer and set it at an angle pointing away from him (Figure 9-1, left).

✔ Set up the mic below the singer and angle it away from him (Figure 9-1, right).

✔ Put the mic off to the side and face it toward the singer (Figure 9-1, center).

Figure 9-1:
You can place the mic at different angles to control sibilance and plosives.

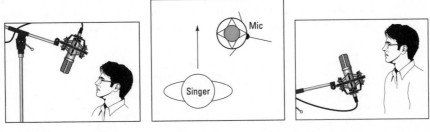

Small-diaphragm condenser mic

The small-diaphragm mic won't be your first choice in a vocal mic, unless you are recording a female vocalist with a soprano voice and you want to catch the more ethereal quality of her higher frequencies.

Sound: The small-diaphragm condenser mic creates a much more bright or airy sound than the large-diaphragm mic. This means that it doesn't contain the low-mid (200–500 Hz) warmth of its larger-diaphragm counterpart.

Setup: You set up the small-diaphragm mic in the same way that you set up the large-diaphragm mic.

Ribbon mic

The ribbon mic is a good choice if you're looking for a crooner-type sound (think Frank Sinatra).

Sound: The ribbon mic is thought to add a silky sound to the singer's voice. By silky, I'm referring to a slight drop-off in the high frequencies (not as severe as a dynamic mic, though). To my drum-abused ears, ribbon mics have a kind of softness that the large-diaphragm condenser mics don't have. The sound is more even, without the pronounced low-mid effect.

Setup: If you use a ribbon mic, you can set it up in the same way that you set up a condenser mic. Just be more careful about singing directly into a ribbon mic because the ribbon can break if you sing, speak, or breathe too hard into it.

 Many digital studios (the SIAB and computer-based systems, especially) contain mic simulator programs as part of their effects packages. Mic simulators allow you to use a relatively inexpensive mic (a Shure SM57, for instance) and make it sound like a much more expensive vocal mic. The mic simulator doesn't match the sound of a great mic perfectly, but it does give you more options, especially if you don't have the bucks to buy a handful of top-notch vocal mics.

One of the great things about using a mic simulator is that you can choose the exact sound you want *after* you've recorded the vocal part. This way, you can spend less time trying to choose the perfect mic and get down to the business of recording before your singer gets worn out.

Getting Good Backup Vocals

To record backup vocals, you can either track each part separately by using the same mic-placement techniques that I describe earlier or you can have all the backup singers sing at once into one or two mics. If you do the latter, you can either use a stereo pair of mics, a figure-8 mic, or an omnidirectional mic.

If you use a stereo pair of mics, I recommend setting them up in a coincident X-Y pattern. Have the vocalists stand next to each other facing the mics at 3 or 4 feet away. Either large- or small-diaphragm mics work best for this setup. Check out Figure 9-2 for a neat top view of this arrangement.

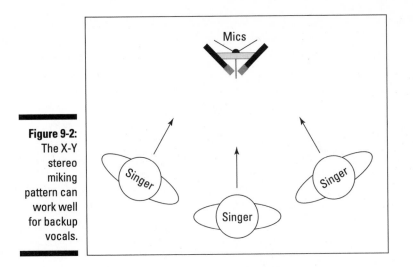

Figure 9-2:
The X-Y
stereo
miking
pattern can
work well
for backup
vocals.

If you choose to use a figure-8 mic, the singers can stand on opposite sides of the mic (Figure 9-3). The advantage of this setup is that the singers can look at each other while they sing.

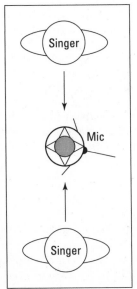

Figure 9-3:
Backup
singers can
stand on
either side
of a figure-8
mic and see
each other.

An omnidirectional mic can also work well for backup vocals. In this case, the singers stand in a circle around the mic, as shown in Figure 9-4.

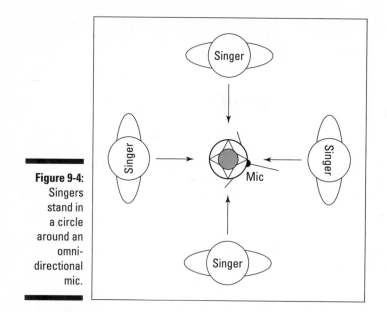

Figure 9-4:
Singers
stand in
a circle
around an
omni-
directional
mic.

Examining Electric Guitar Miking

Miking your electric guitar is a personal thing. It seems to me that every guitar player spends a lot of time getting his or her "sound" (although I don't play guitar, so what do I know?). If you're a *real* guitar player, you undoubt-edly take great pride in getting your sound exactly right on tape, er, disk. You likely spend countless hours tweaking your amp and adjusting the mic to get the sound just right. On the other hand, if you're not a real guitar player, you may just want to record the part and get it over with. Either way, you can start looking for that perfect guitar sound by placing your mics in one (or more) of the ways that I outline later in this chapter.

Using the room

Whether you play through a small jazz chorus amp or power-chord your way through a six-foot-tall Marshall stack, the room that you play in has less impact on your sound than if you play drums or sing. For the most part, look for a room that is fairly dead — a room without natural reverberation. You can always add effects later.

Guitar miking involves mostly spot mics, so your only consideration when recording a guitar using an amp is how your neighbors feel about noise, er, your most-excellent guitar playing.

TIP

If you have finicky neighbors, you can put your guitar amp inside an amp-isolator box (see Chapter 3) to reduce the noise. You can find the plans to build one of these boxes on my Web site: www.jeffstrong.com.

Getting the most out of the mics

The type of mic that you choose largely depends on the type of sound you're looking for. For example, if you're looking for a distorted rock guitar sound with effects, you can get by just fine with a dynamic mic. If you favor a clean sound, a small-diaphragm condenser mic may work better for you. If you're going for a warm, full-bodied sound, try using a large-diaphragm condenser mic.

No matter which type of mic you use, you get the best sound from your amp speakers by putting a mic about 2 to 12 inches from the cabinet, with the mic pointing directly at the cone of one of the amp speakers (the cone is located in the center of the speaker). You can see this positioning in Figure 9-5.

You may want to experiment with how far the mic is from the amp and the angle at which you point it. Sometimes just a slight movement in or out, left or right, can make all the difference in the world. You can even try pointing the mic at different speakers if your amp has more than one, because each speaker has a slightly different sound.

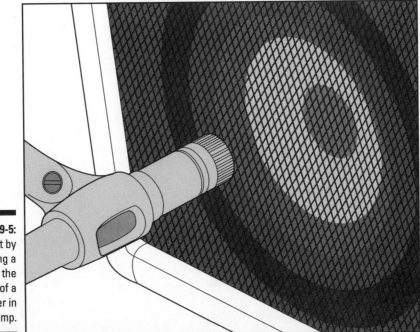

Figure 9-5:
Start by placing a mic near the cone of a speaker in your amp.

I know some engineers who disconnect all but one speaker in the cabinet (assuming that you have more than one speaker) to lower the volume and still have an intense, distorted sound. This can be especially beneficial if you have one of those amp stacks with a volume knob that goes to 11, and you need to crank the amp to get your "tone" (come on, rockers, you know who you are). This way you don't overdrive the mic — creating distortion — and you can still get that nasty sound that you're looking for.

If you can't quite get the sound that you want from your amp with the one mic pointed at the speaker cone, you may want to add a second mic 3 or 4 feet away. You also point this mic directly at the speaker cabinet for a more ambient sound. This may also give your sound more life, especially if you have a room with natural reverberation. If you add a second mic, remember to watch for phase differences between the mics and make adjustments accordingly. (I discuss phase cancellation in Chapter 8.)

Are you sick of the same old sound coming out of your amp? Do you wanna really shake things up (and I mean this literally)? Well, put your guitar amp in a tiled bathroom and crank it up. You can put a mic in the bathroom with your amp (a couple of feet away) and maybe another one just outside the door (experiment by how much you close or open the door). The effect is, well . . . try it and find out for yourself.

On most digital recording systems, you can use an effect called an *amp simulator* to give your guitar a variety of sounds. The amp simulator can make your guitar sound like it was played through any number of popular amplifier setups. This can save you the hassle of trying to mic your guitar amp and keep your neighbors happy. Just plug your guitar into the Hi-Z jack in your mixer. If you don't have a Hi-Z jack, you can use a direct box or the line-out jack of your amp (more on this in Chapter 4).

Exploring Electric Bass Miking

When you mic an electric bass, getting a good sound can be a real bear. Your two adversaries are muddiness (lack of definition) and thinness (a pronounced midrange tone). These seem like almost polar opposite characteristics, but they can both exist at the same time. I outline the best way to avoid these problems in the following sections.

Running your bass guitar directly into the board — via a direct box, your amp's line-out jack, or a Hi-Z jack on the mixer — gives the guitar a punchier sound. Some recorders have amp-simulator programs for bass guitar as well as guitar. So don't be afraid to skip the amp and go directly into the mixer.

Managing the room

The sound of an electric bass guitar can quickly get muddy. Your best bet is to choose a room that doesn't have a lot of reflective surfaces (for example, paneled walls and wooden floors that the sound can bounce off of). A dead room is easier to work with. Don't make your room too dead, however, or it just sucks the life out of your amp's tone. If you can get your amp to sound good in your room, placing the mic properly is easy.

Don't be afraid to be creative and to try recording your bass in different rooms. Look for a room with a warm sound to it. One thing though — the bathroom amp trick doesn't work well on bass guitar (but it can be fun to try anyway).

Getting the most from the mic

Because the bass guitar produces low frequencies, a dynamic mic or a large-diaphragm condenser mic works well. I avoid small-diaphragm condensers and ribbon mics for the electric bass, but try them if you want. Who knows — you may end up with an awesome bass track.

Mic placement for the electric bass is similar to the guitar: You place a single mic 2 to 12 inches away from one of the speakers. Sometimes with bass, if you angle the mic and let the speaker's sound kind of drift past the diaphragm, you can get a great sound. For a bass, skip the distant mic, which generally just adds muddiness to the sound.

Miking Acoustic Guitars and Similar Instruments

At the risk of offending banjo, dobro, harp, or ukulele players, I'm lumping all strummed or picked string instruments together. I know, they all sound and play differently, but the microphone-placement techniques for all these instruments are similar. Allow me to explain.

Because all these instruments have a resonating chamber, you can pretty much use the same mic placement for any of them. You use different types of mics for different instruments, and I get to that in a minute.

Making the most of the room

Because these are acoustic instruments, the room plays a role in the sound that you end up recording. Unless you have a great-sounding room, you want to minimize its impact on your instrument's sound. You can do this by recording with spot mics or by placing absorber/reflectors in strategic places around your room. Put the absorber side out if the room is too live or the reflector side out if the room is too dead.

For example, if your home studio resides in a spare bedroom with carpeting and that awful popcorn stuff on the ceiling, you can put a couple of the reflector panels around your guitar player and the mic. This adds some reverberation to your guitar. Any unwanted reflections from the ceiling or walls are shielded from the mics, because the absorber sides of the panels are facing the rest of the room.

Using your mics

I often prefer to use condenser mics when recording acoustic instruments. The type of condenser mic you use depends on the overall tonal quality that you want to capture or accentuate. For example, if a guitar has a nice woody sound that you want to bring out in the recording, a large-diaphragm condenser mic is a good choice. On the other hand, if you're trying to capture the brightness of a banjo, a small-diaphragm mic is a better choice.

You can position your microphone in a variety of ways, and each accents certain aspects of the instrument's sound. Even a slight adjustment to the mic can have a significant impact on the sound. You may have to experiment quite a bit to figure out exactly where to put a mic.

To help with your experimentation, listen to the instrument carefully and move the mic around (in and out, left and right) until you find a spot that sounds particularly good. You need to get your ears close to the instrument to do this.

Here are some suggestions to get you started:

- **Put the mic 6 to 18 inches away from and 3 to 4 inches below the point where the neck meets the body of the instrument.** Then make minor adjustments to the direction in which the mic points. Pointing it toward the sound hole(s) often gives you a richer, deeper tone. (This can translate to muddiness on some instruments.) Turning the mic more toward the neck brings out the instrument's brighter qualities. See the image on the left in Figure 9-6.

- **Place the mic about 3 feet away from the instrument and point it directly at the sound hole.** At this distance, you capture the rich sound from the sound hole and the attack of the strings. See the center image in Figure 9-6.

✔ **Put the mic about 6 inches out from the bridge of the instrument.** Try pointing the mic in different directions (slight movements of an inch or less can make a huge difference) until you find the spot that sounds best to you. See the image on the right in Figure 9-6.

✔ **Set up the mic at about the same distance and angle from the instrument as the player's ears.** Point the mic down toward the instrument so that the mic is a couple of inches away from either side of the musician's head. This is an unorthodox approach that I like because the player adjusts his playing style and intonation to correspond to what she is hearing when she plays. With this technique, you're trying to capture exactly what the musician hears.

Figure 9-6:
Positioning the mic in these ways can produce a good acoustic-instrument sound.

Getting a Handle on Miking Horns

There's nothing like the sound of a horn played by a skilled player. Sure, you can use a synthesizer or sampler to play horns, but it's not quite the same. Luckily, horns, such as trumpets, trombones, and saxophones, use similar miking techniques, so if you want to mic some horns, you don't have to understand a ton of different techniques.

Understanding the role of the room

Because of the high volume levels of most horns and the fact that you mic them fairly closely, you don't get a ton of impact from the acoustics of the room. Unless your room sounds *really* bad (for example, a small spare bedroom with carpeting and a low ceiling), you can deal with any room sound that bleeds into the mic.

If you have a small room that adds an unwanted sound to the instrument, sur-round the horn player with acoustic panels, similar to what I describe in the section "Getting a Great Lead Vocal Sound," earlier in this chapter. You can experiment with using either the reflective or absorptive side of the panels to get the sound that you want. Generally speaking, err to the side of a more dead room — you can always add some reverb later.

Making the most of the mics

For most horns, a decent condenser mic — large- or small-diaphragm — works well. If you want a richer tone, a ribbon mic is the way to go. In fact, whenever I mic horns, I pull out a ribbon mic first, and it usually stays out until the session is over.

You can place the mic from 3 inches to a foot or more from the instrument, depending on the instrument and the sound you're looking for. For example, a trumpet, because of its high sound pressure levels (SPLs, or volume), would sound best with the mic a little farther away than the placement for a tenor sax. This is especially true with ribbon mics, where too much pressure can blow the ribbon.

Most horns generally sound better if the mic is placed just to the side of the bell (the part where the sound comes out). This keeps the SPL that the mic picks up low enough to avoid distortion and not blow your precious ribbon. For some of the louder instruments, choose a condenser mic with a high SPL rating and/or a pad switch, or move the mic away from the instrument a bit. (A *pad switch* reduces the amount of sound — usually by 10–20db — that the mic's internal circuits process, allowing you to have a louder signal without distortion.)

If you want to record more than one horn instrument at a time (a couple of trombones, for instance), you can use a figure-8 condenser mic and have each horn player positioned on either side of the mic. As an alternative, use one or more mics a couple of feet away from the players.

Placing Mics for a Piano

If you're lucky enough to have a real piano to record, you'll probably want to record it live rather than use some piano patch on a synthesizer. The follow-ing sections give you some suggestions on how to effectively mic a piano.

Harnessing the sound of the room

Pianos can be tough to record if your room doesn't sound great. Because of the size of the instrument — especially if it's a grand or a baby grand piano — you need a large room with a high ceiling to get the best sound. If you have an upright piano in a living room, for example, you may find it easier to just record a piano patch (sound) on a decent synthesizer.

If your room doesn't add to the sound of the piano, use a closer mic placement that you would if your room sounds great.

Managing the mics

Condenser mics are a must for recording piano. Either small- or large-diaphragm mics work well. Your mic placement depends largely on the sound you're going after. Here are a few examples:

- ✔ **Funky rock or ragtime sound:** Place your mic close in toward the hammers. In this case, I would use two mics — one over the higher register and one over the lower, 6 to 12 inches away from the hammers.

- ✔ **Natural classical-type sound:** Move the mics out from the instrument — 2 to 6 feet is usually good, depending on how much room sound you want in the mix. The farther you move the mics outside of the lid, the higher you should place the mics because the sound moves up as it goes out. A good reference is to use the lid as guide.

The farther outside the instrument you put the mics, the more room sound you pick up.

If you don't want to use a traditional condenser mic or if you want to try another approach to piano miking, you can use a boundary mic. A boundary mic is an omnidirectional mic that attaches to the instrument. You can find a decent-sounding boundary mic for about $50 from Radio Shack (Cat. #33-3022) or for a few more dollars from most other microphone manufacturers. Just mount the boundary mic to the underside of the piano's lid (consult your mic's manual for details on mounting it) to get the best sound. You can also use two boundary mics — one over the lower register and one over the higher one.

Setting Up Mics for Strings

Stringed instruments — violin and fiddle, viola, cello, and acoustic bass — can be a lot of fun to mic. They have a rich tone and produce an almost unlimited variety of textures. Each instrument has a different tonal spectrum, but because they all have the same basic shape and design (f-holes, strings, bows, and so on), they can all be thought of similarly. You can try any of the techniques that I describe for one of these instruments on the rest of them. For example, try the mic technique from the cello on the fiddle and see what you think. Your options are many, so experiment and use what you like.

Making the most of the room

As with any other acoustic instrument, the room can have profound impacts on the sound that you capture. Unless you have a really nice-sounding room, try to isolate the instrument from the room's sound. In this case, spot miking is the best choice. On the other hand, if you have access to a great-sounding room or concert hall in which to record, by all means add some room mics or use a stereo-miking technique.

Making sense of the mics

My favorite type of mic for classical string instruments is a small-diaphragm condenser unit, although on occasion I reach for a large-diaphragm condenser mic. A dynamic mic may produce an interesting effect, but it doesn't capture the most natural sound.

You can place the mic for each of the string instruments as follows:

- **Violin, fiddle, and viola:** These all sound great with a mic placed 1 to 2 feet above and behind the instrument and facing down at the instrument's body.

- **Cello and double bass:** For these instruments, place the mic several feet away from the instrument (between 4 and 8 feet) and point it toward the f-hole in the instrument. This allows you to capture the sound of the entire instrument. The only drawback is that you also get a fair amount of the sound of the room. If you don't want the effects of your room recorded, you can place acoustic panels on either side of the mic.

- **Ensembles:** Ensembles sound best when miked with a stereo pair placed between 8 and 20 feet away. You can use any of the stereo-miking techniques that I described earlier in this chapter. If you are miking soloists, you may also need to add a spot mic or two for their instruments. If so, follow the recommendations that I provide earlier in this list and watch for phase problems.

Digging into Drum Set Miking

If you're like most musicians, getting great-sounding drums seems like one of the world's great mysteries (you know, along the lines of how the pyramids were built or how to cure cancer). You can hear big, fat drums on great albums but when you try to record your drums, they always end up sounding more like cardboard boxes than drums. Fret not, for I have solutions for you.

First things first: Tuning your drums

The most important part of getting killer drum sounds is to make sure that your drums are tuned properly and that they have good heads on them (okay, those are two important things). Seriously, if you spend some time getting the drums to sound good in your room, you're halfway to the drum

---

What type of drum set?

If you want to buy a drum set for your home studio, here are some guidelines that have worked for me:

✔ **Smaller drums can sound bigger.** At one point, I had two top-notch Gretsch drum sets in my studio. One was a rock kit that had a 24-inch kick; 13-, 14-, and 18-inch tom-toms; and a 6½-inch deep metal snare drum. The other was a small jazz kit consisting of an 18-inch kick, 10- and 14-inch tom-toms, and a 5-inch deep-wood snare. Guess what? Even for the hardest rock music, the small kit sounded much bigger. You can tune the small drums down a bit and they just sing!

✔ **Choose your heads wisely.** Not all heads are equal. Some sound great on stage while others are better suited for the studio. Because the heads that come with a kit are most likely not the ones that sound the best on a recording, invest some money in testing different drumheads on your kit. I prefer either Remo pinstripes (great for rock and R&B) or coated Ambassadors (great for

jazz) on the top and either clear or coated Ambassadors (I choose based on aesthetics) on the bottom of the drum.

✔ **Use cymbals with a fast decay.** Cymbals that sound great on stage are different from those that sound great in the studio. Stage cymbals often have long decays and slow attacks. This causes bleeding, especially through the tom-tom mics, and correcting the problem can be a headache. If you buy cymbals for your studio, choose those that have a very fast attack and a short decay.

✔ **More expensive isn't always better.** For recording, my favorite drum sets are used kits from the late '60s and early '70s. My all-time favorite recording set is a late-'60s Gretsch jazz drum set with an 18-inch kick drum, a 10-inch mounted tom-tom, and a 14-inch floor tom. For a snare, I love old 5-inch wooden snare drums (for example, Gretsch, Ludwig, or Slingerland). The last one of these sets that I bought cost $350, including all the mounting hardware and the snare drum. It wasn't pretty, but it sure sounded great.

sound of your dreams. I don't go into detail here, but if you want specific drum-tuning guidance, you can do an Internet search or check out my book *Drums For Dummies* (published by Wiley).

You're looking for a clear, open tone on your drums. Resist the temptation to apply duct tape or other dampeners to the drumheads. Drums that are deadened and don't ring clearly definitely sound like cardboard boxes when you record them.

After you get your drums tuned as well as you can, the next step is to take care of rattles that may be coming from the stands or mounting hardware. Tighten any loose hardware and move any stands that may be touching one another. You may need to make some small adjustments to the pitches of your drums if they are causing hardware to rattle.

If you still have some ringing or unwanted overtones, you can damp them slightly. Cotton gauze taped lightly on the edge of the head (away from the drummer) is often enough. If you want a real dry sound on your snare drum, you can use the wallet trick: Have the drummer place his wallet on the head. (Use the drummer's wallet because it probably doesn't have any money in it.)

When your drums have been tuned perfectly, you're ready to start placing some microphones. You can choose from an unlimited number of miking configurations, only a few of which I can cover here (it would take a whole book to cover them all).

Using the room to your benefit

The room influences the drums' sound more than it influences that of other instruments. If you're looking for a big drum sound, you need a fairly live room (one with lots of reflection).

I know, you're thinking, "But I just have a bedroom for a studio, and it's carpeted." No worries, you can work with that. Remember, you have a home studio, so you potentially have your whole *home* to work with. Here are a couple of ideas to spark your imagination:

- Buy three or four 4-x-8-foot sheets of plywood and lean them against the walls of your room. Also, place one sheet on the floor just in front of the kick drum. This adds some reflective surfaces to the room.

- Put the drums in your garage (or living room, or any other room with a reverberating sound) and run long mic cords to your mixer. If you have a studio-in-a-box system, you can just throw it under your arm and move everything into your garage or, better yet, take all this stuff to a really great-sounding room and record.

> ✔ Set up your drums in a nice-sounding room and place an additional mic just outside the door to catch an additional ambient sound. You can then mix this with the other drum tracks to add a different quality of reverberation to the drums.

Picking up the kick (bass) drum

When recording a kick drum, most recording engineers choose a dynamic mic. In fact, you can find some large-diaphragm dynamic mics specifically designed to record kick drums.

No matter where you place the mic, you can reduce the amount of boominess that you get from the drum by placing a pillow or blanket inside the drum. Some people choose to let the pillow or blanket touch the inside head. I prefer to keep it a couple of inches away from the inside head, but I find it can be beneficial to let it touch the outside head.

That said, you can place your mic in several ways:

> ✔ **Near the inside head (see Figure 9-7, left):** If you take off the outside head or cut a hole in it, you can put the mic inside the drum. Place the mic 2 to 3 inches away from the inside head and a couple of inches off center. This is the standard way to mic a kick drum if you have the outside head off or if a hole is cut in it. This placement gives you a sharp attack from the beater hitting the head.

> ✔ **Halfway inside the drum:** You can modify the preceding miking technique by moving the mic back so that it's about halfway inside the drum. In this case, place the mic right in the middle, pointing where the beater strikes the drum. This placement gives you less of the attack of the beater striking the head and more of the body of the drum's sound.

> ✔ **Near the outside head (see Figure 9-7, right):** If you have both heads on the drum, you can place the mic a few inches from the outside head. If you want a more open, boomy sound (and you have the drum's pitch set fairly high), point the mic directly at the center of the head. If you want less boom, offset the mic a little and point it about two-thirds of the way toward the center.

If your drum sounds thin after trying these mic-placement approaches, you can try these two things:

> ✔ **Tune the drum slightly up.** In your quest for a deep bass tone, you may have tuned the drum too low. (This is especially common if you have a large bass drum.) In this case, the drum's fundamental tone may be too low to be heard clearly. Raising the pitch a bit usually solves the problem.

✔ **Create a tunnel with acoustic panels.** Putting the mic in the tunnel often helps if you have a room that's too dead. Place two of the panels on their sides (reflective surfaces facing in) with one end of each panel near the outside of the drum. Angle the panels out so that, where they are farthest from the drum set, the distance between them is just under 4 feet. Then lay the other two panels (reflective surface facing down) across the side panels to create a tunnel. You can also place a piece of plywood on the floor under these panels to further increase the resonance. Place the mic halfway into the tunnel, facing the center of the drum.

Figure 9-7:
You can place a mic in several places to get a good kick drum sound.

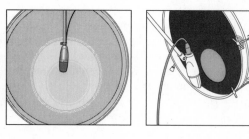

Setting up the snare drum

The snare drum is probably the most important drum in popular music. The bass guitar can cover the kick drum's rhythm, and the rest of the drums aren't part of the main groove. A good, punchy snare drum can make a track, whereas a weak, thin one can eliminate the drive that most popular music needs.

Because the snare drum is located so close to the other drums, especially the hi-hats, a cardioid-pattern mic is a must. The most common mic for a snare drum is the trusty Shure SM57. The mic is generally placed between the hi-hats and the small tom-tom about 1 or 2 inches from the snare drum head (see Figure 9-8). Point the diaphragm directly at the head. You may need to make some minor adjustments to eliminate bleed from the hi-hats. This position gives you a nice punchy sound.

If you want a crisper tone, you can add a second mic under the drum. Place this mic about an inch or two from the head with the diaphragm pointing at the snares. Make minor adjustments to minimize leakage from the hi-hats.

If you have the available tracks, record each snare mic to a separate track and blend the two later during mixdown. If you don't have the available tracks, blend them until you have the sound that you want.

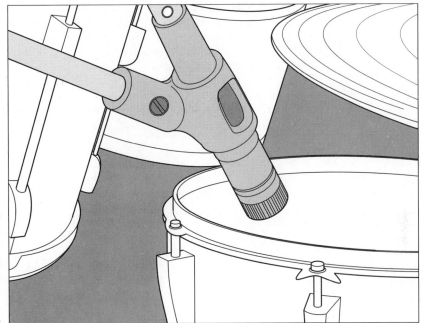

Figure 9-8:
The proper
placement
for the
snare
drum mic.

Tackling the tom-toms

The tom-toms sound best when using a dynamic mic. For the mounted toms (the ones above the kick drum), you can use one or two mics. If you use one mic, place it between the two drums about 4 to 6 inches away from the heads (Figure 9-9 shows this placement option). If you use two mics, place one above each drum 1 to 3 inches above the head.

If you want a boomy sound with less attack, you can place a mic inside the shell with the bottom head off the drum.

Floor toms are miked the same way as the mounted tom-toms. Use the following setup:

- Place a single mic a couple of inches away from the head near the rim.
- If you have more than one floor tom, you can place one mic between them or mic them individually.

If you want to apply compression to the tom-toms, you can start with the settings that I listed for the snare drum in the preceding section.

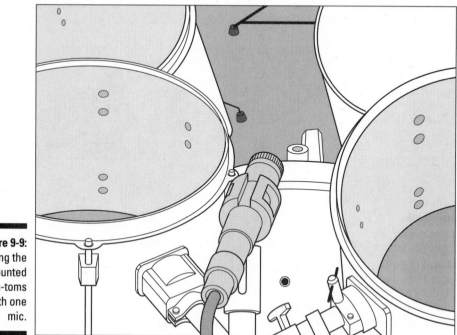

Figure 9-9:
Miking the
mounted
tom-toms
with one
mic.

Handling the hi-hats

The hi-hats are generally part of the main groove, and as such, you want to
spend time getting a good sound. You may have problems with a few other
mics on the drum set picking up the hi-hats, particularly the snare drum mic
and overhead mics. Some people don't bother miking the hi-hats for this
reason.

I like to mic hi-hats because, to me, these cymbals often sound too trashy
through the snare drum mic. If you mic hi-hats, make sure that the snare
drum mic is picking up as little of the hi-hats as possible by placing the mic
properly and/or using a noise gate (a dynamic processor used to filter
unwanted noise).

You can use either a dynamic mic or, better yet, a small-diaphragm condenser
mic for the hi-hats. The dynamic mic gives you a trashier sound, and the small-
diaphragm condenser mic produces a bright sound. You can work with either
by adjusting the EQ. I usually add just a little bit (4dB or so) of a shelf EQ set at
10 kHz to add a little sheen to the hi-hats.

Place the mic 3 to 4 inches above the hi-hats and point it downward. The
exact placement of the mic is less important than the placement of the other
instrument mics because of the hi-hats' tone. Just make sure that your mic
isn't so close that you hit it.

Creating the best cymbal sound

You want to know one secret to the huge drum sound of Led Zeppelin's drummer, John Bonham? Finesse. He understood that the drums sound louder and bigger in a mix if the cymbals are quieter in comparison (I'm guessing this is true, because I never really talked to him about this). So he played his cymbals softly and hit the drums pretty hard. This allowed the engineer to raise the levels of the drums without having the cymbals drown everything else out. Absolutely brilliant.

Because having the drums bleed into the overhead mics is inevitable and the overhead mics are responsible for providing much of the drums' presence in a mix, playing the cymbals softly allows you to get more of the drums in these mics. This helps the drums sound bigger.

Ask (no, demand) that your drummer play the cymbals quieter. Also, use smaller cymbals with a fast attack and a short decay. Doing these things creates a better balance between the drums and cymbals and makes the drums stand out more in comparison.

Small-diaphragm condenser mics capture the cymbals' high frequencies well, though many digital recordists like the way a ribbon mic mellows the cymbals. You can mic the cymbals by placing mics 12 to18 inches above each cymbal or by using overhead mics set 1 to 3 feet above the cymbals (see the next section).

Miking the whole kit

Most of the time, you want to have at least one (but preferably two) ambient mics on the drums, if for no other reason than to pick up the cymbals. Assuming that you use two mics, they are called *overhead mics,* and as the name implies, they are placed above the drum set. The most common types of mics to use for overheads are large- and small-diaphragm condenser mics because they pick up the high frequencies in the cymbals and give the drum set's sound a nice sheen (brightness). You may also want to try a pair of ribbon mics to pick up a nice, sweet sound on the overheads.

To mic the drum set with overhead mics, you can use either the X-Y coincident technique or spaced stereo pairs. Place them 1 to 2 feet above the cymbals, just forward of the drummer's head. Place X-Y mics in the center and set up spaced stereo pairs so that they follow the 3:1 rule (for example, the mics should be set 3 to 6 feet apart if they are 1 to 2 feet above the cymbals). This counters any phase problems. Point the mic down toward the drums, and you're ready to record. Figure 9-10 shows both of these setups.

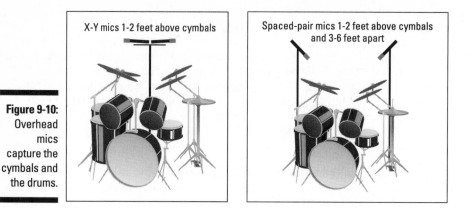

Figure 9-10:
Overhead
mics
capture the
cymbals and
the drums.

Getting Your Hands on Hand Drums

Hand drums can be anything from the familiar conga to unusual drums, such as the North African tar. Because you may encounter many types of hand drums, this section gives you some general guidelines when recording any hand drum.

Your selection in mics depends on the type of drum and its tonal characteristics. For example, conga drums occupy the middle of the frequency spectrum and produce a loud sound that a large-diaphragm condenser mic can capture well. Or, if you want a tighter, drier sound, you can use a dynamic mic. If you choose the dynamic mic, the mic colors the sound of your recording.

If you want to record any of the smaller, higher-pitched hand drums, use either a large- or small-diaphragm condenser mic and skip the dynamic mic altogether.

Mic placement also varies considerably among the various hand drums. Listen to the sound of the drum, and find a place where you like what you hear. For the most part, placing the mic from 1 to 3 feet from the drum creates the fullest sound. If you want a lot of attack, you can place the mic closer. You lose some of the drum's depth, however, when you place the mic closer than a foot.

Perfecting Percussion Miking

Miscellaneous percussion instruments, such as shakers and triangles, are nice additions to many styles of music. These instruments sound best with a good condenser mic. I choose a large- or small-diaphragm mic, depending on the characteristics that I want to pick up. For instance, a shaker can sound great with a large-diaphragm mic because this mic slightly brings out the lower frequencies of the instrument and softens the overall sound a bit.

Exploring the impact of the room

Most of the time, the room doesn't have a huge impact on percussion instruments because you mic them closely. If your room does get in the way, use the acoustic panels in much the same way that I suggest for vocals earlier in this chapter in the "Getting a Great Lead Vocal Sound" section (partially surround the mic and musician with baffles).

Choosing and using the mics

Both large- and small-diaphragm mics work well for percussion. When recording percussion instruments, the main thing to remember is that they can have a high SPL (sound pressure level, or just plain volume), so you may need to pad the mic, move it back, or turn it sideways from the sound source.

I like to put a single mic from 6 to 36 inches away from percussion instruments, depending on the size of the instrument and how much room I want in the sound. For example, because maracas are loud, I put the mic back a bit (18 inches), whereas with an egg shaker, I find that 6 to 8 inches often sounds best. But when I record an agogo bell or an Afuche I like to have a little room in the mix to give the instrument more depth. In this case, I mic from a couple feet away.

Part IV
Laying Track: Starting to Record

The 5th Wave · By Rich Tennant

Don't worry. We can fix it in the mix.

QUACK. QUACK.

MOO. MOO.

OINK. OINK.

In this part . . .

Part IV gets you started recording your music. Chapter 10 explores the role of multitrack recording in modern music making and helps you get a song set up in your system. Chapter 11 walks you through the process of recording audio tracks, from the first track to overdubs, to punching in and out (you even discover what these terms mean). Chapter 12 gives you the lowdown on recording MIDI sequences and takes the mystery out of this often-misunderstood technology.

Chapter 10

Multitrack Recording

In This Chapter

▶ Understanding multitrack recording

▶ Setting up a song to record

▶ Monitoring your mix

▶ Saving and sharing files

As recently as the 1960s, when someone wanted to record a song, he or she had to assemble a band, rehearse, and then perform the song live. If one of the musicians made a mistake, the whole band had to start over and record the song again. Not so anymore. You're lucky enough to have gotten into recording in an age where you can not only write the song but also record it yourself and play all the instruments. If you like, you can make lush, layered music without involving anyone else. In other words, you can *multitrack*.

In this chapter, I introduce you to the basics of multitrack recording, a process that enables you to assemble a song by recording one part at a time. You discover how to set up a new song in a variety of systems, and you find out how to set up the monitoring source and sound to help you inspire a great performance. This chapter also walks you through the process of saving files and transferring data between systems.

Understanding Multitracking

Multitrack recording is the process of recording each instrument (or group of instruments) individually and keeping those performances separate until a later date. Consider the CD or cassette player that you have at home or in your car. All the instruments are contained on a pair of stereo tracks. You can adjust the volume or equalization of these tracks, but you can't adjust the sound qualities of the individual instruments contained on these two tracks. The multitrack recorder, on the other hand, allows you to keep all these instruments separate (see Figure 10-1). Multitrack recording lets you do the following things:

- ✔ Make adjustments to the sound of the instrument on each track
- ✔ Adjust the levels (volume) of the instruments in relation to one another
- ✔ Assemble a "performance" that never happened

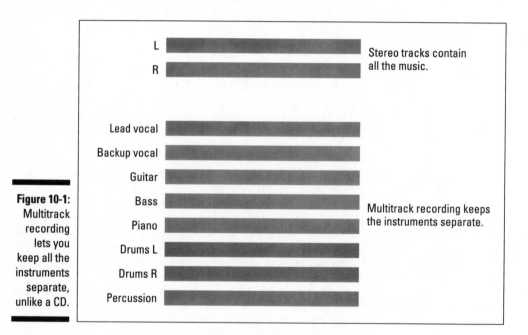

Figure 10-1: Multitrack recording lets you keep all the instruments separate, unlike a CD.

Getting Ready to Record

Before you can press the Record button on your system, you need to set up a few things. First, you need to find and choose the instrument or sound that you want to record, then you need to set the optimum volume level going to the recorder, and last, you need to decide what you want to hear while recording your performance. These steps are covered in detail in the following sections.

Setting up a song

If you're using a digital recording system, you need to open a new song file. When you do this, you may be asked (or prompted) to choose the sampling rate and resolution of this new song. (Some systems have you provide this information when you choose a track to record to rather than when opening a song file.)

You generally have the option to choose a *sampling rate,* which is the number of times every second that the digital recorder or converter takes a snapshot of the sound (check out Chapter 2 for details on sampling rates). Your options include 32, 44.1, 48, 88.2, or 96 kHz. Some digital recorders don't allow you to make a CD if you record with anything but a 44.1-kHz sampling rate. Check your owner's manual if you intend to eventually put your music on a CD.

Some systems may also let you choose the *bit depth* — the size, in binary digits, of the sample that the converter or recorder takes — that you want to record in. For this parameter, I usually choose the highest bit depth available to capture the best sound possible. If you choose 20 or 24 bits, you need to convert the final mix to 16-bit if you want to put your music on a CD, but the advantages you gain from recording at a higher bit depth far outweigh the conversion factor. (Go to Chapter 2 for more on bit depth.)

Finally, name your file, and you're ready to select a source signal to record.

Selecting a sound source

When you select a sound source, you simply set up your instrument or microphone so that it records to the track of your choice. Here's how to select a sound source:

1. **Turn the input trim knob and fader on the channel strip of your mixer all the way down to avoid hearing an unpleasant noise.**

2. **Plug your instrument or microphone into the appropriate input jack of your system.**

   For a microphone, this may be a separate preamp or the internal preamp in your mixer, SIAB system, or audio interface. For an electric guitar or bass, use the Hi-Z input or a direct box, and for a keyboard or other electronic instruments (such as a drum machine or sound module), use any of the instrument inputs.

3. **Choose the track that you want to record the signal to.**

   This procedure varies from system to system. Here's how to route the signal in the following systems:

   Studio-in-a-box (SIAB) systems: You can route the signal from any mixer input to any recorder track by pressing a button. For example, on the Roland VS-1680, just press and hold the Status button for the track that you want to record to. When the routing screen appears, continue holding the track's Status button and press the Select button for the input channel that you want to route to that track. Release the Status button, and you're all set.

Computer-based systems: You need to open the Input window to choose your input source. This process is pretty simple and is similar for most programs. Here's how you do it in Pro Tools:

    a. Choose Display⇨Edit Window Shows⇨I/O View.

        The I/O section of the Edit window appears, showing the inputs and outputs for each of your tracks.

    b. Click and hold your mouse button on the Input selector until the Input menu pops up.

    c. While still holding down your mouse button, move the mouse over the Input menu until it rests on the input listing you want.

    d. Release the mouse button to select the input listing.

        This menu closes, and the input you've selected appears in the Input selector.

Stand-alone systems: If you have a stand-alone recorder with a separate analog mixer, you need to connect a cord from the input channel that your instrument is plugged into to the track that you want to record to (use the direct line outputs from the input channel).

4. Arm the track that you want to record to (that is, set it to the Record mode).

This procedure also varies from system to system. Here's how to arm the track on the following systems:

Studio-in-a-box systems: A Selector button glows various colors, depending on the mode that the channel is in. Press the button on the track number that you're recording to until you see a red glow. This means that the track is ready to record.

If you are using an SIAB system and want to record to a different track number than the input channel you're plugged into, make sure that you arm the track that you want to record to and not the track associated with the input channel. If you don't do this, you either record your music to the wrong track (and possibly erase something else) or you don't record anything, depending on the routing of your system.

Computer-based system: Arm the track within the software by clicking the Record Enable button in the main window of your program. In Pro Tools, for example, this button is located in both the Edit window and the mix window for each track.

Stand-alone systems: Press the Track Selector button located near the Track Level meter on the front of the machine until the button blinks red.

Setting levels

Getting a sound signal to the recorder takes several steps. The path that the sound takes from the instrument or microphone to the recorder is called the *signal chain* (or the *gain structure*). For example, if you want to record your voice, you first capture your voice with a microphone and then you feed that signal to a preamp. From the preamp, you send the signal to the channel strip of your mixer, which sends the signal to the analog/digital (A/D) converter and then to the recorder. (Chapter 7 has more on this.) The signal chain may have all or just a couple of these steps, however. For example, a synthesizer is connected to the mixer, which is in turn connected to the recorder.

You need to be aware of the signal level at all of these steps to get the best sound possible. Too much gain at one stage forces you to reduce the gain at another. Likewise, too little gain at one point may require you to *overdrive* (bump up the gain) during the next stage. See Chapter 7 for more on setting optimal signal levels.

Getting the sound you want

After your levels are set, you can concentrate on fine-tuning the sound of the instrument before you record it. Here you can either adjust the EQ or apply effects to your sound.

EQ

I reserve EQ at this point for getting rid of any seriously unwanted frequencies that I'm picking up in a mic. For example, I generally cut some low midrange frequencies on the bass guitar and kick drum because I know that these frequencies will be a problem later. Otherwise, I pretty much leave the EQ alone when tracking.

Don't get too anal about getting the EQ of a recorded instrument just right at this point. All you want is a good, clean sound that approximates what you want in the final mix. You have another chance to make adjustments to the sound of your recorded instrument in the mixing phase.

Check the levels going to the recorder after you've made adjustments to the EQ because the levels may change.

Effects

The question of whether to record effects — reverb, delay, chorus, and so on — along with an instrument is a long-debated topic. Professional recording engineers caution you against recording your instruments *wet* (with effects) because this limits your options when you mix the song. On the other hand, by recording an instrument with an effect, you can use that effect processor on another instrument during the mixing process. Ultimately, you have to decide whether adding an effect to an instrument on the front end (before recording) is the way to go. (I describe effects in greater detail in Chapter 15.)

If you record using a computer-based system, adding an effect during tracking may stress your computer's processor to the point where it affects your recording. This can cause audio dropouts, pops, clicks, or other unwanted interruptions or corruptions to your audio data. If you have a slower computer or if you record a lot of tracks at once, you may find that you can't record with effects. In this case, your headphone mix while you track has no effect added to the sound, but you can still add effects during the mixing process (as described in Chapter 14).

If you're sure about the sound you want, you can add the effect on the front end. If you're not sure, you're probably better off waiting until later. You can always print (record) the effect during a *bounce procedure,* a neat trick where you re-record one or more tracks to another track. Bouncing is a common procedure if you don't have enough tracks in your system to record each of your instruments to its own track. I cover the bounce process in Chapter 11.

If you decide that you want to record your instrument with effects, you need to route the instrument through the effect processor and route the effect to the recorder. If you have an SIAB system, this is pretty easy. For example, to do this in a Roland VS-1880, follow these steps (most SIAB systems are similar):

1. **Select the input channel that your instrument is plugged into and route the channel to the track that you want to record to.**

   If you have a computer-based system, you need to use the Input menu on your screen to do this. On an SIAB system, your manual spells out the specific routing procedure.

2. **Arm the recorder's track (press the recorder's Status button until the button blinks red).**

3. **Select the effect that you want to use and assign it to one of your effects buses.**

   Go to the Effect A menu by pressing Shift+F3. Choose Effect 1 from the menu. Next, scroll through the Effects list and highlight the effect that you want to use. Press the Select button. Your chosen effect is now assigned to Aux Bus 1.

4. **Choose prefader or postfader on your Aux Send and turn the knob until you have the right amount of the instrument's signal sent to the effect.**

   You do this by going to the channel mixer settings menu on your screen.

5. **Route the effect return to the track channel that you want to record to.**

Press and hold the Status button for your track until the Routing menu pops up (this takes about 3 seconds). Next, while still pressing the Status button, press the Effect button for the effect number (1, 2, 3, or 4) that you want to use. ***Note:*** This step may not be necessary on some systems.

6. **Start recording.**

See Chapter 11 for the lowdown on recording.

On some systems, if you want to hear your recorded track, you may have to "unroute" the effect from that track. Your owner's manual spells this out for you.

Adding an effect in a computer-based system, such as Logic Pro, involves these steps:

1. **Select one of the buses from the Send selector in each track's channel strip that you want to route to the effect.**

   You can view a track's channel strip in the Environment window (choose Windows⇨Environment if the window isn't open) or in the Arrange window. To open a track's channel strip in the Arrange window, click the track name in the Arrange window to highlight it. The channel strip appears on the left.

   When you release your mouse button after selecting the bus, the bus is listed, and a trim pot (knob) appears next to the bus number.

2. **Adjust the trim pot to a moderate level.**

   I usually start with about –15dB.

3. **Double-click the bus number.**

   You're taken to the Bus Channel strip in the Environment window, where you can choose the effect to insert into the bus.

4. **By using the Insert selector pop-up menu in the Bus Channel strip, select the effects plug-in that you want to use from the Inserts pop-up menu.**

   The Effect Plug-In window opens. Here you set your parameters, such as predelay, reverb time, and room type (for a reverb plug-in, for example).

5. **Play your track by clicking the Play button in the Transport window.**
   Your session plays, and you hear the effect of your plug-in on your track. You can then tweak the plug-in parameters or the send level for your track as your song plays to get the sound that you want.

To record an effect with an analog mixer and a stand-alone recorder, you have to route things differently. You can do this one of two ways: by running cables from the master output of your mixer to the track input of your recorder or by creating a submix and connecting the recorder's track input to the submix output on your mixer. Your owner's manual should clearly explain these procedures.

Choosing a monitoring source

To record effectively, you need to hear what you're doing. This requires you to set up your monitoring source so that you can hear what you want to hear. You want to monitor the sound that's going through the recorder. This way, you can hear any distortion that may be present. Here's how monitoring works on the following systems:

- ✔ **Computer-based systems:** Set the output for your track(s) to the output that you have your monitor speakers plugged into. If you use the main outputs in your interface, these are usually assigned to outputs 1 and 2 in your system. (You can assign them however you want — check your manual for the specifics on doing this.) Set your outputs to channels 1 and 2 and turn on your monitors.

- ✔ **Studio-in-a-box (SIAB) systems:** Because SIAB systems have fader banks, make sure that you designate the track channel to monitor rather than the input channel. After you've chosen the track channel that you want to listen to, bring up the fader to a level that allows you to hear what's going to disk.

- ✔ **Stand-alone systems with an analog mixer:** You need to have the track output from the recorder connected to an input channel of your mixer. Check out your owner's manual or go to Chapter 4 to find out how to do this.

Saving Your Work

After you record a track that you want to keep, you can save the song. Stand-alone recorders automatically save a track after you record it (much like a tape recorder). If you use an SIAB system or a computer-based system, however, you need to save the file just as you save a file when you're working in a computer program. And like other files in other computer programs, it's a good idea to save your work often so that you don't lose any of the music that you worked so hard to record. Check your owner's manual for your system's procedures.

In addition to basic file-saving commands, most digital systems (computer-based and SIAB) allow you to save individual "scenes" or "snapshots" within each song that contain things such as mixer and effects settings.

Sharing Files with Others

Because your music is stored on a hard drive, you can transfer the data to other systems. The advantages of file sharing are far-reaching. You can collaborate with other people without ever being in the same room together. In fact, I'm working on several projects where I've never sat down with the other musicians. One such musician is even across the country from me. We just create CDs with our parts on them and send the CDs back and forth.

This disadvantage of file sharing is that digital recording technology is relatively new and, as such, a single standard for saving data hasn't emerged. Some recorders use proprietary file formats that only a system from the same manufacturer can open. This is the case for all the Roland SIAB systems except the newest machine, the VS-2480. Computer-based systems, on the other hand, often allow you to save your data in a number of file formats.

All is not lost if you have a system that has a proprietary file format. All digital recorders have jacks in them that enable you to transfer the data from one system to another. This means that you can send your file from your system to a computer and then use software to convert the file into a format that another person's recorder can read. (The software that you choose varies depending on the systems that you want to transfer the files to and from.) If you're doing a lot of transferring, this can be time consuming, but for the occasional transfer, it's no big deal.

If you work with a system that can save files in the WAV or AIFF format, you don't have this problem, and you can easily transfer your stuff from one machine to another. Also, if you're transferring songs from one system to another system of the same type (a Roland VS-890 to a Roland VS-1880, for instance), you don't have to worry about file conversion either.

Chapter 11

Recording Audio

· ·

· ·

*O*kay, you've plugged in your instrument, set up your routing the way you want it, gotten the levels just so, and chosen what you want to hear while you play. Congratulations, you're ready to record. Now the fun begins. . . .

In this chapter, I walk you through the process of recording some tracks for your song. You start with your first take, move on to some overdubbing by adding more tracks, and do some punching in and out to redo some parts. You also explore the process of submixing to record multiple instruments into just a couple of tracks.

Performing Your First Take

Your palms are sweaty, your pulse rate is up, and you're hands are shaking as you get ready to press the Record button. I know the feeling; I've been recording for almost 20 years and still get a little tense when the tape, er, disk starts to roll. There's something about knowing that what you're about to play is for keeps (or at least could be).

Relax. Take a deep breath and remember that you're both the artist and the producer. You can take as many "takes" as it takes you to get a good "take." (Sorry, I couldn't help myself. A *take,* by the way, is an attempt at a performance.) Anyway, it's normal to get a little nervous when you know the recorder is capturing every sound that you make.

To do your first take, follow these steps:

1. **Cue the beginning of the song.**

   Press 0 (zero) on a Roland VS-1680 or press the Stop button twice in Logic or Cubase, for example.

2. **Arm your track by pressing the Record Enable button or, in the case of a Roland SIAB system, the Status button until it blinks red. Next, arm the recorder by pressing the Record button until it flashes red, and then press the Play button.**

   Presto, you're recording.

3. **When you're done, press the Stop button and then press 0 or the Stop button again to rewind.**

4. **To listen to your recorded track, you need to disarm the track that you recorded to and set it to play. You accomplish this by pressing the Track Status button until it turns green (or by deselecting the track — just click the track bar).**

   Now you're in playback mode.

5. **Now, just adjust your channel fader on the track channel that you recorded to and press the Play button.**

Well, how does it sound? Good? Then you're ready to record a different track. If you don't like the sound, you can record the part over again by rewinding, rearming the track (press the Status button until you get the red blinking light again), and pressing the Record button followed by the Play button. If you're like I am and make lots of mistakes, you'll figure out how to do this procedure at lightning speed.

Punching In and Out

Punching in and out refers to being able to overdub a section of a performance (that guitar lick you keep missing, for example) while keeping the part of the performance that you like. Punching in and out can be pretty simple: Play the track and press the Record button when you want to start. Then press the Stop button when you're done. At least that's how it used to be done.

With a digital recorder, you can set up the system to punch in and out a number of ways. You can punch in and out manually either by using a nimble finger to punch buttons or by using a foot switch. You can also program the recorder to punch in and out automatically. If you go the automatic route, you usually set up your system to punch in and out once, but in some cases, you may want to re-record over the same part of the song a certain number of times — a process known as *loop recording*.

Manual punching

Manual punching in and out is exactly what it sounds like: You manually press the Record button when it's time to start the punch, and you manually press the Stop button when you're done. This is the type of punch you do if you have enough time between when you press the Record button and when you need to start playing as well as when you stop playing the part and when you can get to the Stop button. You may also do manual punching if you're acting as the engineer and someone else plays the instrument.

Punching with a foot switch

On most recorders, you can use a foot switch to punch in and out. This frees your hands so that you can play your instrument while you do the actual punching in and out.

Automatic punching

Automatic punching in and out is one of the many gifts from the digital recording gods. This process allows you to fully concentrate on getting your part right without having to worry about getting the punch right. With automatic punching, you can replace very small passages or get into really tight places with your punch.

For example, suppose you have one bad snare drum hit (I've been there many times) that you want to replace. With automatic punch in/out, you can set it to start recording right before that bad note and stop immediately after it, leaving the rest of the notes untouched.

Even though each recorder is a little different in its autopunch procedure, all recorders follow these basic steps:

1. **Select the track you want to punch in and out of.**

2. **Arm the track by pressing the Select button until you get the red blinking light.**

3. **Locate the punch-in point on your recorder.**

    You do this either by playing the song until you get to the point that you want to punch in or by keying in the numbers for that section of the song.

4. **Press the In Point (punch in) button on your recorder.**

5. **Locate the punch-out point on your recorder.**

    You do this either by playing the song until you get to the point that you want to punch out or by keying in the numbers for that section of the song.

6. **Press the Out Point (punch out) button on your recorder.**

7. **Press the Auto-Punch button on your recorder.**

8. **Rewind the recorder to just before the punch-in point.**

9. **Press the Record button followed by the Play button (some recorders don't require you to press the Record button first).**

10. **Play your part.**

When you're done, your newly recorded part is neatly placed in the song.

Repeated punching (looping)

If you have a tricky part to record and you know it will take you a few tries to get it right, you can use the repeated punching (also called loop recording) function. During the repeated punching procedure, the recorder keeps repeating the section within the loop until you press the Stop key, so you can try recording your part as many times as you want without having to set up the punch in and out procedure again.

This procedure uses the same basic steps as the automatic punch in and out procedure, except that you also need to choose the section of the song that the recorder plays before and after the actual punch times (called the *loop start* and *loop end* points). For some systems, you can do this the following way:

1. **Locate the place where you want to start the loop on your recorder.**

2. **Press the Locator button.**

    This stores the locate point you chose in Step 1.

3. **Locate the place where you want the loop to end.**

4. **Press another Locator button to store this value.**

5. **Press and hold the Loop button.**

6. **While still holding the Loop button, press the Locator button that you used to store the loop start point (Step 2).**

7. **While still holding the Loop button, press the Locator button that you used to store the loop end point (Step 4).**

8. **Follow the steps for the automatic punch in and out that I list in the previous section of this chapter.**

Multitrack abuse

You have a recording system with 16 or more audio tracks, a couple dozen MIDI tracks, and countless virtual tracks (additional tracks in a digital system that are hidden behind the main tracks for recording variations of a part). What do you do? Well, you do what anyone else in your shoes would do — you try to fill all your available tracks with instruments. After all, that's how you get really lush recordings, right?

Yeah, sometimes, but this could also be a recipe for a bunch of mud. In fact, you can end up with a super-lush recording by using just a handful of tracks. Lushness is a product of the song's arrangement (how all the parts fit together) rather than just the number of tracks.

One of the most difficult things about multitrack recording is knowing how to use your tracks most effectively and having the discipline to quit when the song is done, regardless of whether you've used all your tracks. So, remember that just because you have the tracks available to you, you don't need to use them all.

Exploring Overdubbing

After you record one useable track, you can move to the next step: overdubbing. *Overdubbing* is simply adding another track to an already-recorded one. Overdubbing is the heart of the multitrack recording process for most home recordists and a technique that you will undoubtedly use and occasionally abuse.

The overdubbing process is pretty straightforward. You simply follow the procedures for recording a take while making sure that you're monitoring the recorded tracks that you've already made.

When you record an overdub, hearing certain parts that you recorded earlier may throw you off. If this becomes a problem, you can turn down certain parts in a mix and only listen to those parts that help you to perform the overdub. For example, if you're overdubbing the lead vocal and a dobro part breaks your concentration on your lines or on hitting a note correctly, just slide the fader for the dobro's channel down a little (or a lot).

Submixing

At times, you may want to record a bunch of instruments, such as the drums of a drum set, to one or two tracks. In this case, you need to create a submix of the inputs before you commit them to disk.

Submixing is essential if you have a recorder with fewer tracks than you have instruments. The advantage with creating submixes is that you can get by with fewer tracks. The disadvantage is that you can't make many changes to the sound or volume of the individual instruments after you record them.

Recording by using submixes presents challenges that overdubbing doesn't. Here are some points to keep in mind:

✔ Make sure that each instrument sounds the way that you want it to sound on the final mix. You can make minor adjustments to EQ and effects, but only to the entire submix group.

✔ Before you record, make sure that each instrument's volume is where you want it relative to the volume of the other instruments.

✔ Decide where in the stereo field you want each instrument. This is called *panning* and it determines how far left or right each instrument can be heard. Panning is discussed in more detail in Chapter 14.

This can take time to set up, but if you're limited on available tracks, you can record a lot of instruments on few tracks.

If you're not sure exactly how you want the final submix to sound, you can record more than one version onto separate tracks and use a bounce procedure (see the following section) after you've recorded. This gives you more time to experiment with alternate versions of your submix.

Bouncing

Bouncing is like submixing, but you do bouncing after you record the tracks. For instance, you can record all your drum mics onto separate tracks initially and then bounce (or combine) all those tracks onto one or two tracks later. In most cases, you want to bounce to two tracks rather than one so that you can maintain panning information in your final mix.

Bouncing has some advantages over submixing. You can take your time getting each instrument to sound right before you group them together. On the downside, you may not have this option if you are recording live and can only put the drums on two tracks initially. In this case, you need to create a submix.

If you have the space to record the instruments to separate tracks initially, here's how you bounce the tracks down to two:

1. **Decide which tracks you want to bounce, and route these tracks to the tracks that you want to bounce to.**

2. **Adjust the EQ of each instrument to get the sound you want.**

3. **Adjust the panning of each instrument — use the panning knob located above your mixer's channel fader — so that the instrument is where you want it in the stereo field.**

   Remember that you need to be bouncing to two tracks for panning to work.

4. **Set the levels of each instrument relative to one another.**

5. **Add any effects that you want to record with the instruments.**

6. **Press the Record button.**

You can use virtual tracks (see the next section) to record several different versions of your bounce. This gives you some options later when you're mixing. For example, set the track levels differently for each bounce — raise the snare drum in one, change the EQ of the hi-hats in another, and so on.

Keeping Track of Your Tracks

One of the great things about digital recording systems is the number of tracks that are often available. Computer-based systems, for example, often have unlimited numbers of tracks (or obscenely high numbers), and many SIAB systems offer virtual tracks. *Virtual tracks* are additional tracks that are hidden behind the basic tracks of the system. They allow you to record various takes of a performance on separate tracks, but only one virtual track can be played at a time. Virtual tracks are great when you're not sure whether you like a particular take and it's not bad enough to record over.

Having all these tracks is great except it can be daunting to keep (ahem) track of all of them. My recommendation: Use track sheets to document all your tracks. *Track sheets* are forms where you enter basic information for each of your recorded tracks, such as what instrument, take, and performance section are included. This gives you a visual representation of your song's components and makes it easier to choose which performances to include in your final mix. Here are some Internet resources to get you started:

✔ **SilentWay.com** (`www.silentway.com/tips/equip/tracksheet.html`): This page offers free track sheets for 8- to 48-track sessions.

✔ **VS-Planet "User Track Sheet" Collection** (`www.vsplanet.com/Pages/ UsersArea/Downloads/index.html`): This page is part of The VS-Planet, which is a site dedicated to Roland VS-series recorders. Scroll down the page until you get to The VS-Planet User Track Sheet Collection. You can also find studio-organizing forms on this page (located just below the track sheet downloads).

Chapter 12

Recording and Editing MIDI Data

Recording and editing MIDI tracks are similar to the process you under-take with audio. The main difference is that MIDI tracks contain perfor-mance data instead of sound. This offers the advantage of being able to choose the sound or instrument you want to "play" your data on later, after you've finished recording. Of course, this also provides the temptation not to make a decision on your sound.

In this chapter, I get you started recording MIDI by walking you through the process of synchronizing a variety of MIDI devices. Then I give you the low-down on recording your tracks, adding to them with overdubs, and editing it all in some of the many ways that most sequencers allow you to. To top it off, I offer a little advice about saving and transferring MIDI data.

Synchronizing Your Devices

To do any kind of music with MIDI, you need to synchronize your devices to one another. The first thing you have to do is decide which device is going to send the MIDI commands (called the *master*) and which devices are to receive them (called the *slave*). The process for synchronizing MIDI devices varies slightly from configuration to configuration. You can get a glimpse into a few possibilities in the following sections.

Synchronizing two (or more) synthesizers

In this first scenario, you synchronize a synthesizer and a sound module (or another synthesizer). In this case, your keyboard is the master because this is the instrument that you actually play. Start by attaching the MIDI cable to the out port of the keyboard and to the in port of the sound module. Figure 12-1 shows the setup for two synthesizers. If you have more than two devices, you can run a cable from the thru port of the second device to the in port of the next one, and so on. You can connect up to 16 devices this way.

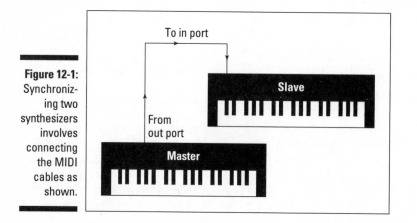

Figure 12-1:
Synchronizing two synthesizers involves connecting the MIDI cables as shown.

The next steps involve configuring each device in the chain so that each device recognizes its place and responds only to those messages that you assign to it. Keep in mind that all devices operate differently, so I can't walk you through the exact steps for your instruments. Be sure to read your owner's manual for your device's specific procedures. The following steps give you a general idea of the process involved in synchronizing two synthesizers:

1. **Go into your master keyboard's system parameters and choose Master.**

   This is generally a dialog box located within the software of your device.

2. **Choose Slave for each of your other devices.**

   You usually do this by going into the MIDI synchronization menu in your software.

3. **Make sure that each device in your chain is set to mode 3 or 4, depending on whether you want polyphony.**

4. **Assign a MIDI channel for each device that's down line (connected to the out port) from the master.**

You can find channel assignments within your device's system parameters. For example, in a ddrum4 sound module, you press the System button until the light next to the word "MIDI" illuminates. You then use the dial to choose the MIDI channel that you want to use.

You can choose from 16 channels (1–16), but if you have a drum machine, set it to channel 10 because this is the default drum channel for GM (General MIDI) devices.

5. **Play the master keyboard.**

   This makes your other MIDI devices play the appropriate sounds (hopefully). If you don't hear anything, make sure that you have the appropriate MIDI channel selected.

Synchronizing a computer sequencer and a synthesizer

If you're using a computer or sequencer and want to synchronize it to a sound module or synthesizer, you need to go through some additional steps. These are:

1. **Connect your synthesizer to the MIDI interface, and connect the MIDI interface to your computer.**

   Run the appropriate cable from the MIDI interface to the appropriate jack of your computer. For example, this can be a USB cable if you have a USB computer and USB MIDI interface.

2. **Connect the MIDI interface to your synthesizer.**

   You do this by connecting a cable from the MIDI out port of your synthesizer to the MIDI in port of the interface. Then connect another cable from the MIDI out port of the interface to the MIDI in port of the synthesizer. This allows the MIDI communication to go both ways, as shown in Figure 12-2.

3. **If you're using a synthesizer to play your MIDI sequences from your computer, you need to set your synthesizer to *local off* mode. Then enable the thru function in your sequencer program so that the MIDI information that you send from the keyboard to the sequencer is sent back to the keyboard.**

   Local off mode disables the keys from the sounds and makes the sequencing process go much smoother. Enabling the thru function in your sequencer program enables you to hear what you're playing while you record your part.

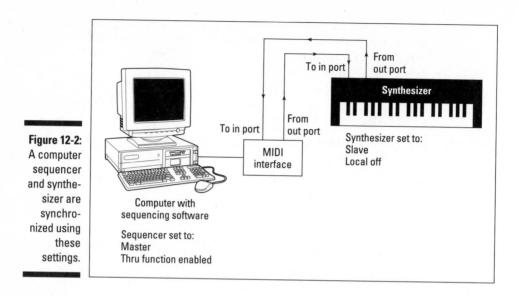

Figure 12-2:
A computer sequencer and synthe-sizer are synchro-nized using these settings.

If you don't set your synthesizer on local off, you create a *feedback loop*. In a feedback loop, both your synthesizer's keys and the sequencer are sending the same messages to the sound generator in your synthesizer and causing it to play each note twice. The best that can happen is that you trigger each note twice and use up your polyphony faster. The worst that can happen is echoed or stuck notes and possibly jammed messages, which may cause your system to lock.

4. **After you connect all the cables, be sure to choose the MIDI channel that you want the track recorded to and set both the sequencer and instrument to that channel.**

   You can find the MIDI channel selector within your device's software. Sometimes it is a combination of key commands (such as repeatedly pressing the System button in a ddrum4 sound module). Other times, it is a pull-down menu that you access from the top of your computer screen. In Cubase, the channel selector for the sequencer is located just to the right of the track name.

After you have your channel setup and your local off business out of the way, you can play your synthesizer, see it register in the sequencer, and hear it play. If you don't, check all your settings.

Synchronizing a sequencer and an audio recorder

If your system does the sequencing inside the computer and your audio tracks are recorded on either a stand-alone recorder or an SIAB (studio-in-a-box) system, like the Roland VS-1880, you need to synchronize them. In this case, your devices use timing data rather than communicating/responding with the help of performance data.

You need to get both your sequencer and your recorder to recognize the same timing data. You start this process by determining which device is the master and which one is the slave.

The process that I describe in this section also works if you're connecting a synthesizer to a drum machine. Select the sequencer as the master device and the drum machine as the slave.

You can choose either device to be the master. In this example, I outline setting up your system with the SIAB system as the master and the sequencer as the slave, as shown in Figure 12-3. You may be able to set up your system the other way around (particularly if you have a stand-alone recorder connected to a sequencer), but I chose this way because doing so allows you to use the faders and transport functions (play, record, stop, and so on) in your SIAB system. With some systems, you may be able to use your sequencer's transport and automation functions with this setup as well, which I discuss in the section "Sequencing," later in this chapter.

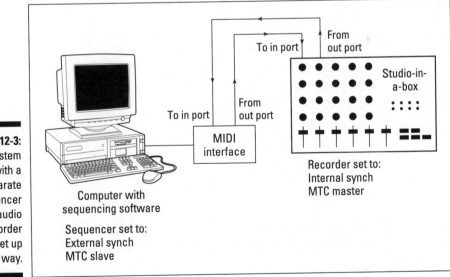

Figure 12-3: A system with a separate sequencer and audio recorder are set up this way.

After you've chosen which device is the master and which is the slave, you can start synchronizing your systems. These steps help you get going:

1. Choose Internal Synch in your master device's Synchronization dialog box.

Each device has a different procedure for this, so read your device's manual to find out how to choose the synchronization mode. In a Roland VS-1680, press Shift+F5. Then press Synch (F6). A dialog box appears. Use the dial to choose Internal Synch. Click the Exit button to return to the main menu.

2. **Choose External Synch in your slave device.**

   This can be a dialog box within the MIDI synchronization menu. For example, in Cubase, choose Options⇨Synchronization from the main menu on the top of your screen. The external or internal synch choice is on the upper left of the dialog box.

3. **Choose either MIDI Time Code (MTC) or MIDI Clock for the timing method.**

   In Cubase, for example, this option appears directly below the external or internal synch option.

   You ultimately want to choose the timing method that you prefer and the one that works best for your gear. You can find out about these timing methods in the nearby sidebar "MIDI Time Code, MIDI Clock, huh?"

4. **If you chose the MTC mode, you need to choose a frame rate to go with it.**

   For this example, set your frame rate at 24 fps (frames per second). You should be synchronized at this point.

5. **If you chose MIDI Clock in Step 3, you need to choose between tempo map and synch track.**

   For more on these options, see the nearby sidebar "MIDI Time Code, MIDI Clock, huh?"

6. **Press the Play key in your master device to see whether your slave device responds.**

   If it does, you're set to go; if it doesn't play, double-check your settings. Your timing settings probably aren't exactly the same.

Using the transport function from one device to control another

Another aspect of synchronization can enable you to use the transport function (play, stop, record, and so on) from each device to control the other. This is the MIDI Machine Control (MMC) function. The MMC function is located within the Synchronization menu of your device's software. (You can find this in the same place as the MTC synch in most systems.) MMC allows

TECHNICAL STUFF

MIDI Time Code, MIDI Clock, huh?

When you try to synchronize two devices using MIDI timing messages, you're met with several choices. One is between MIDI Time Code (MTC) and MIDI Clock. The other is frame rates and tempo map or synch track. This can be confusing, so this sidebar contains a brief overview of these options.

MIDI Time Code uses absolute time in its messages (the actual time on the clock from the beginning of the song or reference point in hours, minutes, seconds, frames, and subframes). This data can then be translated into SMPTE messages (the kind of synchronization data used in film and television). If you choose MTC, you also have to decide the frame rate for the time code. Several frame rates are available, and each is associated with certain mediums. They are as follows:

✔ **24 fps (frames per second):** This rate is mainly used for films.

✔ **25 fps:** This is for audio, video, and film equipment used in Europe and other places that use the SECAM or PAL formats.

✔ **29.97 fps:** This is for color televisions used in the United States, Japan, and other places that employ the NTSC format.

✔ **30 fps:** This rate is used for black-and-white television in the United States (Europe's black-and-white TVs use the 25-fps rate).

If this isn't confusing enough, both the 29.97- and 30-fps rates also have either drop frame or nondrop frame formats. This gets pretty technical, but drop frame formats basically drop two frames every minute, except for the tenth minute, so that the timing data match the clock exactly. These are generally used for live video feeds.

MIDI Clock is different from MTC in that it tracks the time of a song in beats and measures rather than minutes and seconds. MIDI Clock messages are generally sent every $\frac{1}{24}$ of a beat, but you can set most sequencer programs to much higher resolutions than that. Cubase VST version 5 can be set as high as, get this, 1,920 PPQ (pulses per quarter note).

When you choose MIDI Clock, you need to choose between using tempo map or synch track, as follows:

✔ **Tempo map:** This is basically a layout of the tempos and time signatures used in a song. To use a tempo map to synchronize your SIAB system and sequencer, you need to create the map itself. Every system is a little different in this procedure so I don't go into detail here.

✔ **Synch track:** A synch track is a track (at least was a track on analog recorders) that follows along with the tempo and measures of a song. To use a synch track, you need to first record one. If you have a digital recorder, you most likely don't need to take up an actual track to do this.

So which do you choose? Unfortunately, that question doesn't have a clear answer. The equipment that you have dictates part of your answer. (For instance, the Roland VS-1680 SIAB system can send MIDI Clock and MTC messages, but it doesn't always effectively respond to those messages.) The goals you have for your music dictate the other part. If you're composing music for film or TV, your choice is clear (24 fps and 29.97 fps, respectively).

If your equipment and musical goals don't limit your choice, choose what you like. Just make sure that both machines have the same settings.

you to send machine control messages from the slave device to the master device. For example, in the setup shown earlier in Figure 12-3, you can set the sequencer to send MMC messages and the SIAB system to receive them. Your sequencer must be set as follows:

- ✔ MTC slave – External synch
- ✔ 24 fps
- ✔ MMC master

Your SIAB system in turn must be set as follows:

- ✔ MTC master – Internal synch
- ✔ 24 fps
- ✔ MMC slave

These settings enable you to use either device's transport functions to control the other. The MTC master sends the timing data, but each device sends control messages to the other. Check with your system's manuals to see whether you can do this with your gear.

Sequencing

Sequencing is the heart of most home recordists' MIDI studios because sequencing allows you to actually record your instrument's part and play it back. If you're like most people, the sequencing part of MIDI is what excites you the most. With sequencing, you can play as many instruments as your room can handle (or more, if you have long cords).

Sequencing is not unlike audio recording: You have the same transport functions (start, stop, record, rewind, and so on), and you have the ability to record each instrument on a separate track. This is where the similarities between audio tracks and MIDI tracks end, however. As I've mentioned before, MIDI sequencing deals with performance commands and not audio waveforms. This opens a few doors that can come in mighty handy in the following situations:

- ✔ If you aren't the greatest player in the world
- ✔ If you're not sure what key you want the song to be in
- ✔ If you don't know (or haven't decided) what sounds you want to use

With MIDI sequencing, you can make a whole host of changes to your performance after you've recorded it. You can change the placement or volume of individual notes, you can change the song's key, and you can change the instrumentation (for example, you can have a brass ensemble play a part that you originally wrote for the strings). One of the other great things about MIDI sequencing is that you can capture a performance that you don't have the chops (skills) to pull off live.

Recording MIDI data

You can record a MIDI track in one of the following ways:

✔ **Real-time recording:** Play the part as you would for a regular audio recording.

✔ **Step-time sequencing:** Manually input the music one note at a time. Step-time sequencing is a great tool if you don't have the skills to perform that part in real time.

The MIDI tracks in most sequencer software programs look virtually the same as the audio tracks except for a small icon. Logic, for instance, has an M icon, and in Cubase, you find a small musical note. Each icon is located to the left of the track name. You generally engage the track that you want to record to by clicking it once.

Preparing to record

Before you start to record a MIDI track, you need to make the following adjustments to your setup:

✔ **Make sure that your MIDI gear is synchronized.** For details on how to do this, check out the section "Synchronizing Your Devices," earlier in this chapter.

✔ **Set your levels and the patch (sound) that you want to hear.** Setting levels simply means setting the volume that you hear through your monitors at a comfortable level.

To choose the sound that you want to hear, you can select the sound in your synthesizer, in which case the sequencer recognizes this setting, or choose the sound within the sequencer program. This process is done differently for each type of sequencer, but most of them have a track menu located to the left of the screen that applies to the track you have engaged.

Figure 12-4 shows a basic track menu setup in a sequencer program. In this figure, the patch is set for program 58, bank 0 (short for Sound #58 in one of the sound module's banks of sounds). Most sound modules also give you the patch name, such as "program 1, bank 0, acoustic grand piano." (My ddrum4 doesn't show the patch name, so it's not included in the figure).

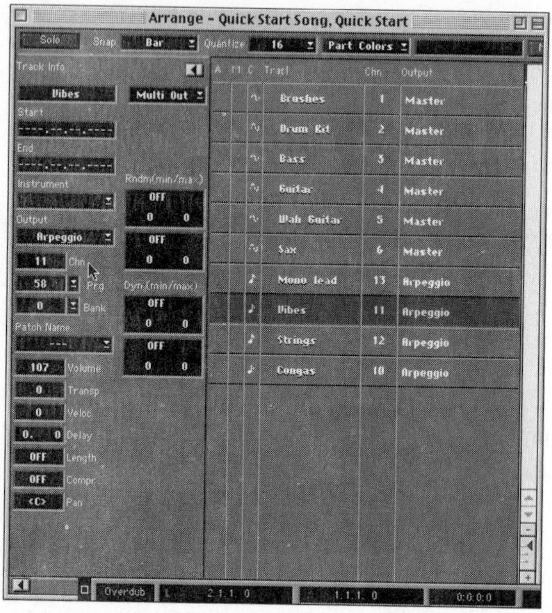

Figure 12-4:
The MIDI
track menu
shows you
the settings
for that
track,
including
the MIDI
patch
program
and bank
number.

[Screenshot: Arrange – Quick Start Song, Quick Start window showing track list with Brushes, Drum Kit, Bass, Guitar, Wah Guitar, Sax, Mono lead, Vibes, Strings, Congas and their channel and output settings]

✔ **Set your metronome to the tempo that you want to record to.** You do this by opening the Metronome Settings menu (which is often located on the Options menu). Choose the tempo and time signature for your song, and you're set to go.

Within the Metronome Settings menu, you can also choose the MIDI note that the metronome sounds on, whether you have a count in before the song actually starts (called a preroll), and more.

You don't need to set the tempo for a song ahead of time. You can always adjust this later. In fact, you can set the tempo slower than the final version so that you can play the part slower and get the notes right. This can be especially beneficial if the part is difficult or if you're not the greatest player in the world. Just be sure to set the tempo to its final speed before you start recording audio tracks because you can't change the tempo of the audio tracks later like you can with MIDI tracks.

Real-time recording

If you're recording in real time, just press the Record button and start playing. You can find the Record button on the Transport Bar if you use a computer-based software program (this can be found on the Windows menu in Logic, for example). On a Roland VS-1680, it's the red button on the lower left of the device. (Don't forget to wait until the preroll is finished if you have that function engaged.)

If your recorded performance is the way you want it, you can move on to another instrument's part. Just set up a new track to record the sound that you want on the MIDI channel that you prefer. If you don't like your performance, you have the following options:

- ✔ **Re-record your part from the beginning.**

- ✔ **Re-record only those sections that don't sound right.** Re-recording parts of a performance is generally referred to as punching in and out. This involves setting your recorder to just record a section of your performance, as described in Chapter 11.

- ✔ **Edit the performance.** I discuss the details of editing in the section "Editing your data," later in this chapter.

Step-time sequencing

Step-time recording involves entering your part one note at a time. This can take a long time to do, especially if it's a difficult part (one with lots of notes). But step-time recording may be your only option if you don't have the skills to play the part live.

Most sequencer programs include a step-time recording mode. Select this mode and then click the Record button. You enter your part by selecting the note value (eighth note or sixteenth note, for example) for the first note or chord. Then when you play the note on your keyboard, it is entered into the sequencer. Choose your next note, press the key(s) you want to record, and so on.

Some sequencers allow you to go into a score window and enter your notes that way. If you can read music, this can be much easier and faster than the traditional step-time mode. Just choose the note's duration from the menu bar and click the place where you want that note to be. After you get the hang of this method, step timing can be pretty quick. Check your sequencer program's manual for details.

Overdubbing

After you record some MIDI performances, you can easily add to or change them. The time-honored name for this kind of recording is *overdubbing*. Overdubbing MIDI performance data is similar to overdubbing your audio data. Most programs allow you to overdub in several ways: manually punching in and out, punching automatically, and loop punching. In addition, because MIDI is strictly performance information with no actual sound, most recording programs allow you to either replace or merge existing MIDI data when you overdub.

Using MIDI Merge/Replace

When you overdub to a MIDI track, many MIDI recording programs offer you the option to either replace existing material or add new data to it. For example, in Pro Tools, you make this selection by clicking the MIDI Merge/Replace button. This button is located in the Transport window, as shown in Figure 12-5. Here's how it works:

- ✔ When the Merge/Replace button is engaged (MIDI Merge mode), new material is merged with existing MIDI data on the record-enabled track(s).

- ✔ When the Merge/Replace button is disengaged (MIDI Replace mode), new MIDI data replaces existing information on the record-enabled track(s).

Figure 12-5:
Add new data in a sequencer program without erasing what's there.

To engage MIDI Merge in Pro Tools, follow these steps:

1. **Open the MIDI controls section of the Transport window by choosing Display⇨Transport Window Shows⇨MIDI Controls.**

   The Transport window expands to include the MIDI controls section.

2. **Click the MIDI Merge button.**

   The button becomes highlighted.

Most MIDI sequencers have a similar function, but by default, any overdubs you do are placed in a new sequence — leaving the original intact.

Punching in and out

If you like some of your initial take and want to record over only part of it, you can set points at which to start and stop recording within the session. This is called *punching in and out.*

As is the case with audio tracks, most programs allow you to punch into MIDI tracks in several ways. These include punching in and out *manually, automatically,* and *repeatedly* (looping). With the exception of being able to choose to merge your punched data with your original performance or being able to replace it, punching into and out of MIDI tracks is the same as punching into and out of audio tracks. I detail the exact procedures for performing these punches in Chapter 11.

Editing your data

The editing capabilities for MIDI tracks are quite extensive. Not only can you perform the typical cut, copy, and paste functions, but you can also *quantize* (adjust the timing of a note) and *transpose* (adjust the pitch of a note), which I cover in the sections to follow. Heck, you can even fix a single bad note if you want to.

In most newer sequencer programs, you have the following three ways of performing edits:

✔ **Piano-roll graphic window:** This is the most common way to edit MIDI performances. Look at Figure 12-6. In this window, the horizontal bars in the center are the MIDI notes recorded on the track. Each of these notes can be lengthened, shortened, and moved. Also, just above the note grid, a bar tells you the note's start time and length, pitch, velocity (volume — both on and off), and MIDI channel. Each of the parameters can be adjusted by typing a value. The top of this window contains navigation tools, more editing options, and quantization values (the note value used to adjust the timing of a performance). Just select the note and you can do any of these editing functions.

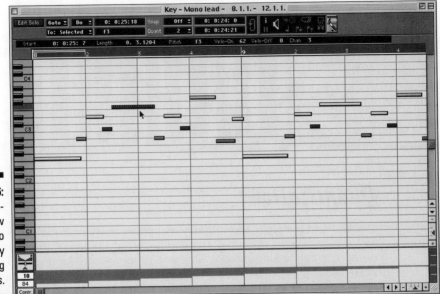

Figure 12-6:
The piano-roll window lets you do a variety of editing functions.

✔ **Score window:** If you read music, the score window may be your choice for editing. This window looks just like a piece of sheet music. Within this window, you can move notes around in much the same way as the piano-roll window. The only difference is that you get to see the musical score as you do it. Some sequencers allow you to print the score as well. This can be handy if you're composing music that you want other people to play.

✔ **Events list:** If you're a real computer geek (you know who you are), you may prefer the data-filled look and feel of the Events list editing menu. This menu shows you the list of MIDI events that make up your track. Look at Figure 12-7. This menu shows all the performance and MIDI commands for that track. The only thing you may not find in this menu, depending on the sequencer program that you have, is the actual note that you played, so you may not be able to change that data. But you can edit every other part of your performance.

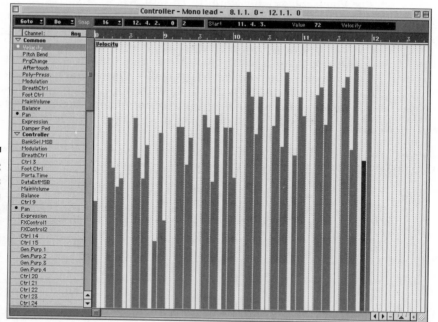

Figure 12-7:
The Events list menu shows you the MIDI control messages and allows you to edit them.

Quantization

Quantization is simply allowing the sequencer to fix your rhythmic timing. Say you recorded a drum pattern, and because you played it on your keyboard, the timing kinda stinks. The bass drum missed the downbeat, and the snare drum is inconsistent. Don't worry — you don't need to re-record your part. You can just move all those notes into their proper places — and you don't even have to touch each of those notes to do it. Just choose the quantization value and click a button.

The quantization value determines the subdivision to which the quantization feature moves the notes. For example, if you choose a quantization value of 16, all your notes are moved to the nearest sixteenth note. With most sequencers, you can choose a number of quantization values, including eighth notes, sixteenth notes, and thirty-second notes.

Most new quantizers also allow you to assign a percentage to the quantization value. For example, a setting of 50 percent moves the note halfway between where you played it and the next quantization point designated by your quantization value. The higher the number, the closer to the actual quantization point your note will go. This feature is essential in keeping quantized music from sounding stiff.

Double-check your track after you've quantized it because it may have moved a misplaced note in the wrong direction. This happens if your note is farther away from where you want it to be than it was to another quantization point. If a note has moved in the wrong direction, select that note and move it to where you want it.

Transposing

Imagine that you write a song that you plan to sing but then you meet someone with a great voice who wants to sing it. The only problem is that you already recorded all the parts and this great singer's voice is in a completely different range than yours. The song would sound so much better if it were raised a couple of keys. Well, if your recorded tracks are MIDI, you simply go to the Options menu, choose Transpose, and type in the change of key. Presto, your whole song has changed key, and you didn't have to re-record a single part! Try doing that with your audio tracks.

Saving Your Data

For the most part, saving data in your sequencer program is like saving data in any computer program. Yep, you need to click the Save button (or press ⌘-S if you have a Mac). Don't forget to save your work regularly, lest your computer crashes and you lose several hours' work.

The main thing to know about saving data in a sequencer program is that most programs have their own proprietary file format. You generally can't take a saved file from your program and play it on another one.

If you want to play your MIDI tracks on another sequencer program or make it available on the Internet for other people to play, make sure that you save your music as an SMF (Standard MIDI Format) file. Nearly all sequencer programs allow you to save in this format. Some even do this by default. Check your owner's manual to see how to do this. Then you can give your MIDI tracks to anyone who can play an SMF file, and if you recorded your stuff by using a GM standard, it sounds just how you intended it to sound, regardless of the listener's gear.

Transferring Data Using MIDI

Another great thing about MIDI is that you can use the cable and ports to send more than just MIDI performance information. Many manufacturers allow you to send sound patches through the MIDI connection by using system-exclusive messages. This can be a great tool. In fact, I own an electronic drum set whose sounds can be changed and updated by connecting a MIDI cable between the sound module (brain) and my computer. I can store gazillions of sounds on my computer without cluttering up (or overloading) my drum set's brain. But wait, it gets even better. This manufacturer makes new sounds available on its Web site to download for free! Yep, I can add new sounds to my drum set without having to buy anything. You gotta love it!

Performing a data transfer via your MIDI connection is easy. Just connect your device to the MIDI interface on your computer, open the data-transfer software provided by the manufacturer, and follow the directions.

Part V

Turning Your Tracks into a Finished Song

The 5th Wave   By Rich Tennant

MIXING THE FIRST "RUDE AUDIENCE" CD

"I laid down a general shuffling sound, overdubbed with periodic coughing, some muted talking files, and an awesome ringing cell phone loop."

In this part . . .

*P*art V helps you to take all your individual tracks and turn them into the best song possible. Chapter 13 explores the process of editing audio and MIDI data to help you clean up your recorded tracks or to create new arrangements of your songs. Chapter 14 demystifies mixing: the process of blending all your individual tracks into a cohesive whole. Chapter 15 explores how you can use signal processors to add interest and dimension to your music, and Chapter 16 introduces you to the most misunderstood part of the recording process: mastering. With mastering under your belt, you can add the final touch to your CD so that it can compete with the CDs you find at the music store. The final chapter in this section, 17, offers some ideas for getting your music out to your listeners, both on the Internet and with a finished, duplicated CD.

Chapter 13

Editing Your Performance

. . . .

. . . .

*E*ven after you put in all the time needed to get the best sound and performance, you most likely will want to make changes to your tracks. You may want to get rid of some noise or maybe clean up a few bad notes. Well, you can do this with editing. And if you have a digital hard-drive system, you can edit to your heart's content without sacrificing sound quality and without losing your original tracks.

In this chapter, you discover the joys of fixing a performance with editing. I cover the basics and try to help you find out whether your editing style is visual or auditory. You also explore the ways that you can use the editing capabilities of your digital system to create a performance that never happened by creating loops, assembling song sections, and making composites from virtual tracks.

The way you edit your tracks depends on your digital recording system. Some systems, such as computer-based DAWs (Digital Audio Workstations), use tools similar to those in word processing programs. Other systems, such as stand-alone systems and SIAB (studio-in-a-box) systems, base their editing methods on traditional audio approaches. I can't possibly cover all the variables that exist in the many types of systems, but what I can do is show you the basics so that you understand what possibilities exist. Hopefully you get enough of a glimpse into the world of audio editing that you can then apply these skills to the system that you own.

Some people never do any editing of a recorded performance except to get rid of unwanted noise. What gets to disk is what they use. I rarely do any editing except for making the occasional loop and/or getting rid of a stray bad note. You may be like I am and have little use for the amazing tools available in most digital systems' editing menus. That's okay; don't feel like you have to use every capability of your system. On the other hand, if editing fits your style, don't be afraid to pull out all the stops and get creative.

Understanding Digital Editing

In the old days of analog tape, you needed to break out the razor blade and adhesive tape to do audio editing. Cutting out a performance was exactly that — physically cutting the performance from the tape that contained the audio. The problem was that after you finished the cut and taped the open ends back together, you couldn't reassemble the original performance. (Well, I suppose you could try to peel that tape off the new joint and tape the part you cut out back in again.)

And it got even worse. If you wanted to edit a single track, you had to cut a little window in the tape where that part was, only in the track you were working on. You were left with a hole in the tape.

And then consider this: While you were cutting and taping the tape, you were touching it with your fingers and getting oils all over your precious tracks. The result: sound degradation. In all, analog tape editing was messy work that introduced unneeded stress on the tape (and perhaps the recordist) and degraded the sound of the music.

Lucky for you, there's a better way — digital editing. You can edit digitally by using your hard-drive recording system. Digital hard-drive recording allows you to do a staggering variety of things to your recorded tracks. You can cut, copy, delete, erase, insert, move, and paste your music, among other things. And the best part is that you can do any of these procedures and still change your mind when you're done.

This aspect of digital editing is called *nondestructive editing,* which means that your original recording is kept intact (the recorder often makes a copy of the original data before it makes the edits). On the other hand, the no-returns policy of analog editing is referred to as *destructive editing,* and after it's done, you're committed to the results, regardless of whether you like them.

Editing can be done in a variety of ways, and almost every recording system does it a little differently. In the following sections, I list many of the basic editing functions that a digital hard-drive system can perform.

Copy

The Copy command is universal in digital audio and does exactly what you think — it makes a copy of a selected performance. Here's how the different systems generally work:

✔ **Computer-based systems:** Copy can work much like the Copy function of your computer's word processing program. A copy of your selection is made and put into a clipboard section of your system. You can then take that copy and paste it somewhere else in the song.

✔ **Stand-alone or SIAB systems:** These systems don't necessarily place copied material on a clipboard. Instead, you're prompted to choose a place to paste your work before you make the copy.

Many systems also allow you to choose how many times you want to copy the part and choose whether you want to override the existing material where you copy it or insert the new material into that section instead. If you insert the copy, the existing material moves over and makes room for the copied section.

Cut/Delete/Erase

The Cut, Erase, and Delete commands all do the same thing to the selected section — it goes away. The difference is what happens to that material after it disappears and what happens to the remaining material on the track; Figure 13-1 illustrates these differences. Here's the lowdown on the commands:

✔ **Cut:** Lifts the selected audio section and puts it on a clipboard so that you can place it somewhere else. On some systems, such as Cubase VST, the rest of the audio track stays put, leaving an empty space where the cut section was. On other systems (Logic Audio, for example), the existing material is brought forward to fill the space left by the cut material, similar to the way that your word processing software deals with the Cut command. Some systems, such as Cakewalk, allow you to choose whether the existing material moves forward.

✔ **Delete:** Eliminates the selected material, keeping you from placing it anywhere else. Delete acts like an analog audio cut-and-tape procedure: The material following the deleted section is brought forward to fill the empty space. The Delete command is common among stand-alone recorders like the Akai DR-16Pro and among SIAB systems such as the Roland VS-1880.

Some computer-based systems, such as Pro Tools, have a Snap option that treats existing material the same way as Delete. The Snap option snaps existing material back to fill any space left by a cut section.

✔ **Erase:** Like Delete, Erase gets rid of the selected section and doesn't allow you to put the section anywhere else. Unlike Delete, Erase leaves a hole in the audio where the selected section used to be. The remaining audio stays put.

Most computer-based systems have a Silence procedure that acts just like Erase. When material is "silenced," an empty space is left where the material used to be.

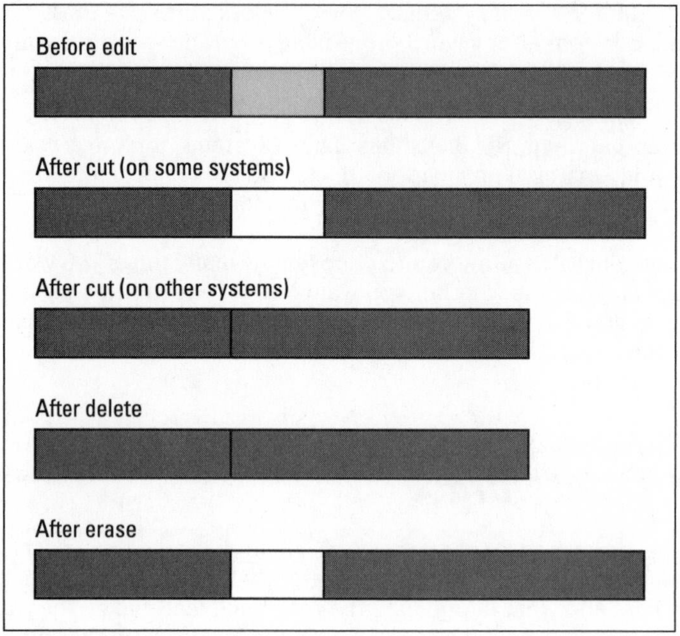

Before edit

After cut (on some systems)

After cut (on other systems)

After delete

After erase

Figure 13-1:
Cut, Delete,
and Erase
are each
treated
differently
in digital
recording
systems.

Insert

The Insert function is common among stand-alone and SIAB systems. It allows you to place a selected piece of music in a track (or multiple tracks) and moves the music that exists after the insert point so that there's room for the inserted material (see Figure 13-2). This is a handy feature that lets you add to a section without losing data.

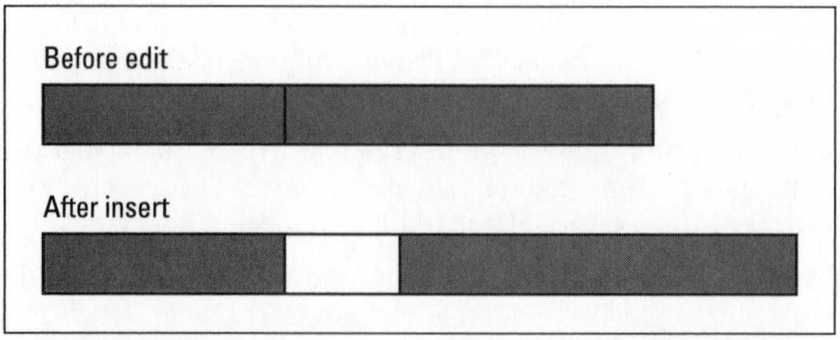

Figure 13-2:
Insert
pushes
existing
material
back to
make room
for the
inserted
music.

Before edit

After insert

For example, say you have a bridge section of a song that you wrote and recorded to be 8 bars long, but after you've finished the song, you want to add a guitar solo to the bridge and 8 bars just isn't long enough (you guitar monster, you!). You want the bridge to be 16 bars long instead. Well, rather than having to re-record the entire song with the new bridge section, you can copy the 8 bars that you have for the bridge and insert them at the end of the existing bridge section, making the bridge 16 bars long. This only takes a second to do, and you don't have to plug in any mics or play any instruments.

If you have a computer-based system that doesn't have an Insert function, just select all the music immediately after the current bridge section and move it over 8 bars by using your mouse. This leaves an 8-bar space that you can then fill using the procedure I described previously.

If you have a song with a lot of tempo changes and you use a *tempo map* (a function that allows you to set the tempo and time signature for each section of the song), make sure that you double-check your tempo map after you've made your edits because the tempo map won't adjust automatically. For example, if you add 8 bars to the bridge (like I describe in the earlier example), you need to add 8 bars to that section of the tempo map to make sure that the rest of the song remains accurate.

Paste

As obvious as this may sound, pasting is just placing your selected music somewhere. Like the Cut and Copy functions, this function is a staple for computer-based systems, but it isn't common among stand-alone or SIAB systems. In most cases, Paste overwrites the existing material where you put it, as shown in Figure 13-3, unless you have an Insert option and you use it. Some computer-based systems treat Paste like a word processing program does — the existing material moves over and makes room for the pasted section.

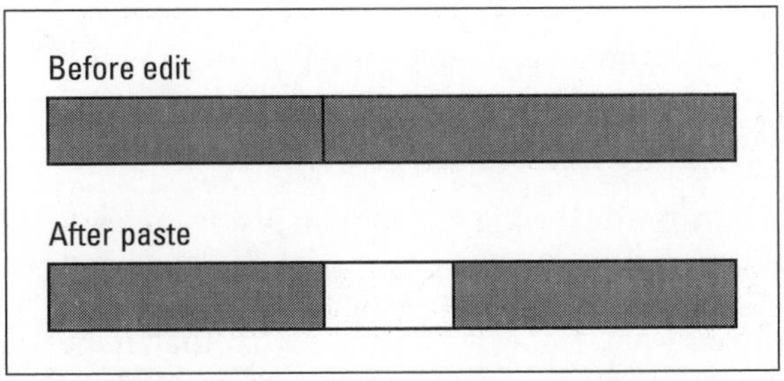

Figure 13-3:
Paste places your selection over existing material.

Before edit

After paste

Like all computer Paste functions, whatever you put on the clipboard stays there until you replace it with something else. So you can paste the same selection as many times as you like.

Move

Nearly all digital recording systems have some sort of Move function. In most cases, you can just choose the audio section that you want to move and choose a destination for it. If you don't have a Move function key, your system probably has the Cut, Copy, and Paste options that you can use the same way. Cut and Paste can move your music just as effectively as the Move function.

Moving audio data can be performed several ways depending on the system, but you probably move data by using a Move menu or by clicking and dragging. On the Move menu, you designate the section to be moved and where you want to move it to. This can be within a particular track or from one track to another. Within this menu, you may have the choice between overwriting the material at the destination point with your selection or moving the existing material to make space for the stuff that you moved. The latter is sometimes called a Move/Insert procedure.

If you have a system that uses a large video monitor, a mouse, and a keyboard, you may have the option to just click and drag the selection where you want it. In most cases, your moved selection overwrites the existing material in its new place, effectively erasing it (although it may still be hidden underneath — but you can't hear it when you play back the track). In other systems, the moved material is inserted in its new place, moving existing material in the process. Your system's owner's manual should spell out how this procedure is treated.

Export/Import

Exporting and importing involve moving music from one song file to another. Some systems enable you to import a single track from another song, whereas on other systems, you have to import everything in a song file.

If you can import only a whole song file but you just want a single track, just make a copy of the song that you want to import and erase everything you don't need from that song. Then when you import the song file, you import only the stuff that you want. Doing it this way rather than importing the whole song file and then erasing the unwanted stuff afterward is quicker because the computer doesn't have to import more than you need.

Undo

Undo is the most important key/function that you have in your digital system. It allows you to, well, undo what you just did. Without it, you may as well be trying to edit with analog tape, a razor blade, and adhesive tape.

How much you can undo depends on your system. Most systems give you at least 99 levels of undo — that is, you can make 99 consecutive edits and reverse them all (or just some of them). Some systems even go as far as giving you 999 undos. How's that for insurance? So edit at will, because you can always change your mind later.

On the other hand, some systems, such as older versions of Logic Audio, have only one level of undo. This isn't a deficit, however, because this program gives you the option of saving your selection before you make the edit. If you choose to do this before each edit, you are essentially allowed as many undos as you want, as long as you have the hard drive space to store all those copies of your audio track.

Some systems, such as the Roland V-Studios, have a Song Optimize function. Song Optimize enables you to save the song and throw away junk that you don't think you need, thus reducing the size of the song file. This is a nice feature except, after you optimize your song, you lose the ability to undo anything you did before you optimized. So, if you think that you may want to undo something you've done, don't click that Optimization button!

As you can see by all the different ways that various programs use and define editing procedures, you need to read your owner's manual and be familiar with your program to use these functions properly.

Finding the Section You Want to Edit

To use an editing function, you need to find the section of music that you want to change. It can be the whole song from one track, a short musical phrase from several tracks, or even a single note. The following sections deal with the two basic ways that you can find the beginning and end of the section that you want to edit. These are editing aurally and editing visually.

Each method has its advantages, and you'll probably prefer one method over the other for your working style. I'm from the old school and much prefer editing by listening to the section I work with. I trust my ears much more than my eyes. You may find that the opposite is true for you. But chances are that you'll use a little bit of both approaches for your music.

Editing aurally

The traditional way to perform an edit is to play the song on the tape deck until you reach the general area of the music that you want to edit. You then stop the tape and manually rock it back and forth against the play head to find the precise place to make the cut. You mark the back of the tape with a wax pencil and go looking for the next edit point. This process requires careful listening, and finding the exact spot to edit often takes quite a while.

For predigital people, such as myself, the manufacturers of digital systems make this process similar to editing analog tape (yeah). Finding an edit point aurally is often a two-step process: First you need to find and mark the general section that you want to edit using a marker (also called an *anchor point*), and then you need to identify the exact spot for your beginning and end points. You do this with the Scrub function, as detailed in the following steps:

1. **Listen to the song and place a marker (sometimes called an anchor point) on the fly as the section you want to edit passes.**

   Do this by clicking the appropriate Marker button (the Tap key on a Roland VS-1680, for instance). Mark both the beginning and end points as accurately as you can. Your markers will be a little off, but don't worry about that now. Your next step involves honing those points using the Scrub function.

2. **Use the Scrub function that's associated with your system to zero in on the spot you need.**

   The Scrub function works much like analog tape where you can "rock" the music back and forth (this is called *scrubbing*, hence the name) to find the precise spot that you're looking for. In some systems, such as the Akai DR-16, you can use the Jog wheel to scrub with. Start from the marker points that you set on the fly and dial the wheel back and forth until you find the exact spot to edit. This may take a while, so be patient. Do this for both the beginning and end points for your edit.

   Other systems, such as the Roland VS-1880, don't allow you to scrub like analog tape. Instead, the Scrub function uses a short loop — from 25 to 100 milliseconds — that you scrub with. The overall process of scrubbing is the same, except you have a couple more steps to follow. The Scrub feature on most digital recorders works pretty well; each just works a little differently and one approach may work better for you.

Not all digital recorders have a Scrub feature that works as well as the old analog tape rocking technique. So if being able to scrub is important to you, be sure to test this feature on the systems you're looking at before you buy.

If you have a computer-based system, you may find a scrub-type feature on the Tool palette. In Cubase, for instance, the Scrub tool uses an icon that looks like a small speaker. Look at your system to see whether you have this function.

Editing visually

Digital recording systems, especially those that use large video monitors, enable you to edit your music visually. This can be a great asset when you want to edit sounds down to the waveform level or if you don't want to hassle with aural searching.

In visual editing, you choose your edit points by viewing the audio waveform of a track on-screen. The audio waveform shows the amplitude (volume) of the sound that's recorded to disk. Check out Figure 13-4 for an example.

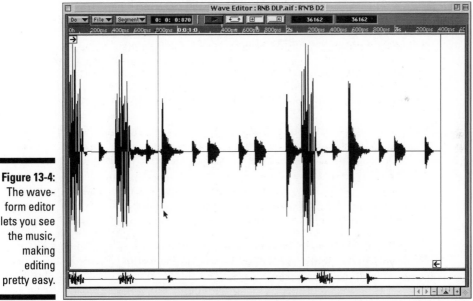

Figure 13-4: The waveform editor lets you see the music, making editing pretty easy.

You can use the waveform as a guide to show you where a particular sound is located. For example, if you pull up the waveform of a drum rhythm and set the track to play, you can see where the various sounds of the drum set (snare drum, kick drum, and so on) are located. Then just put a marker on the fly or stop the playback roughly where you want to be. As you get used to hearing the music and seeing the waveform pass by on your computer screen, you'll be able to tell by looking at a waveform where a sound starts and stops.

Take a look a Figure 13-4 again and find the cursor that's located just before the third large waveform. This is a snare drum note. You can select that section in the following ways (some systems offer you several ways, while others just have one):

✔ **Click and drag to create a box around the section you want to edit.** This is generally the easiest way to choose a section of audio.

✔ **Choose the numerical location points.** On SIAB systems, which typically don't have a cursor or mouse to work with, you can do this quickly by finding the point in the waveform and clicking a button (called the Now button in the Roland SIAB systems). The data is entered into the box, and you don't have to type the numbers.

✔ **Type the beginning and ending edit points in the appropriate dialog box.** This is an option if you have a computer-based system. If you have a keyboard and you're a fast typist, this may be the most efficient way for you to choose edit points.

On most systems, you can zoom in or out on the waveform graphic for a better look. You can often increase both the height (amplitude) and width (time frame) of the image of the waveform that you see.

With most instruments that have slow *attacks* — a slow initial sound, as with vocals or guitars — you can see the start of the sound by looking at the wave-form. The beginning in the rise of the waves matches the beginning of the sound. But on drums and other instruments with very fast attacks, the attack of the instrument happens before the rise in amplitude. In fact, if you look again at Figure 13-4, you can see a vertical dotted line just to the left of the snare drum's part in the waveform. This is where the attack starts for that drum sound. If you were to rely only on your eyes and choose the waveform part that you see, you would miss the initial point of the stick hitting the drum (and all the character that it contains). What you would hear is a mushy-sounding snare drum.

Even though you use the waveform screen to do editing, you still need to find the beginning of that sound by using the Scrub function (described in the preceding section). Just search the space before your drum note until you hear where the attack starts. It's usually about 40 to 50 milliseconds before the waveform jumps up.

Editing to Improve the Sound of a Performance

If you're going to be editing your music, you need to know a couple of useful skills. These include being able to edit individual notes and phrases, finding and replacing notes that are too loud or too soft, getting rid of noise and distortion, and correcting pitch problems.

Replacing a bad note

Replacing a bad note is one editing procedure that I use frequently. Here's an example: A few weeks ago, I played the drum part of a new song for the band I'm currently recording with. I really got into the groove — the feel was right, I made all the changes, and I even did some really cool fills and stuff. When I listened to the part after I finished recording, it sounded fine, so I went on to record some other parts. But when I listened to it again a week later, I heard one snare drum hit in which I caught the rim, and it sticks out in the mix like the proverbial sore thumb. I could just punch in a new snare drum note, but I'm lazy. Besides, I had already put away my mics, and there's no way I could set them up the way I did the day I recorded the drums, not to mention tuning the drums exactly the same way I had them that day.

Well, here's a time when I'm thanking my lucky stars that I have a digital system that allows me to make minute edits (just try slicing a single snare drum note out of an analog tape). Hopefully you won't have to do this procedure, but if you do, follow these steps:

1. **Copy the track that you want to fix to another track in your system.**

   This way, you can reference the original track.

2. **Place the copy on a track or virtual track that allows you to hear both the original and the copy at the same time.**

3. **Listen for a snare drum hit that you especially like and select it by using one of the techniques that I describe in the section "Editing aurally," earlier in this chapter.**

4. **Make a copy of the selection.**

5. **Find and mark the bad note.**

6. **Place the copy of the good note right where the bad note is.**

   The procedure for this varies depending on your system.

Make sure that the Insert function is turned off. Otherwise, you add an extra note and move the bad note over, along with the rest of the music from that track.

7. **After you have the good note in the place of the bad one, turn up the volume of both versions of your track and listen to them again.**

   You should hear an exact copy of the track, except for that one note. Listen carefully at the place of the replaced note for any timing problems. The two tracks should match perfectly. If they don't, just use the Undo function and try again. Also, check the rest of the song after that note to make sure that you didn't accidentally insert the note rather than replace it.

If your system doesn't allow you to make such a fine edit or if you can't successfully select a single note, you can replace a whole measure instead of just the single note. Just follow the same steps and use a larger phrase instead of the one note.

Evening out a performance

Evening out a performance means making adjustments to the levels of a note or phrase within the song. Sometimes it can also mean changing the emphasis of certain notes to change the meaning or "feel" of a part. This section covers these areas using two functions called Normalize and Quieten. It's not uncommon for a track to contain a stray note that is either much louder or much softer than the rest of the notes around it. In this case, you don't need to cut it out and replace it with another note, like I did in the example in the preceding section. Instead you can just make a change to the volume (or level) of that note, as follows:

  ✔ **To raise the volume of a note:** Select the note that you want to change and choose Edit➪Normalize. In most cases, Normalize allows you to choose the maximum dynamic level (in dB) that you want the section to be, the amount below clipping (0dB) that you want, or the minimum headroom you want to have left (also in dB). These last two options are essentially the same thing.

  ✔ **To lower the volume of a note:** Select the note that you want to change and choose Edit➪Quieten. This lowers the amplitude of the selected section by a predetermined amount. On some systems, you can choose this amount.

If you know where your levels are in decibels (dB), you can also choose Edit➪Normalize to reduce the level of a note. In the dialog box that appears, choose a value that's lower than the peak of your selected note. For example, if you have a drumbeat that is too loud — right at 0dB — and the surrounding notes are at –6dB, you can then choose 6dB for either the minimum headroom you want to have left or the amount below clipping. This drops your signal by 6dB — the level of the rest of the notes. If you don't know where your levels are in dB, you can experiment until you get the level where you want it. Using the Normalize function to reduce the volume of a note may be better than using the Quieten function if you want to control exactly how much quieter you want the note and your system doesn't allow you to set the value used by the Quieten function.

TIP

You're not limited to making adjustments to single notes. You can also use Quieten or Normalize to adjust the levels of short phrases or an entire track.

REMEMBER

Normalize and Quieten only adjust the levels of the section that you choose to work with. So when you use these functions, be aware of how your edits relate to the music in and around your edits. For example, if you normalize or quieten a section of the waveform, the softest notes increase in volume only by the level that the highest note increases. For example, Figure 13-5 shows a saxophone line before and after normalizing to maximum dB. The view on the left shows the levels before normalization. The one on the right is after the normalization procedure. The notes were raised a bit, and the overall dynamic range remains the same.

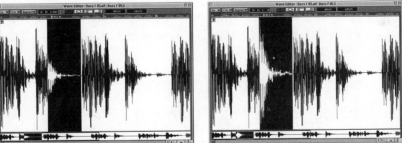

Figure 13-5:
Normalizing keeps the dynamic range of the original section.

Next, take a look at Figure 13-6. This shows what happens when you choose the quietest section to normalize. As you can see, the relationship between the various notes has changed dramatically. Played back, this passage now sounds unnatural, and the original performance is altered beyond recognition.

Figure 13-6:
Choosing
a quiet
section of a
song and
normalizing
it alters the
dynamic
range of
the music.

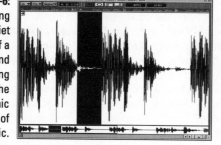

You can use normalization to change the emotional content of a piece of music — even its meaning — by changing where the emphasized (accented) notes are located. For example, take the phrase "I love your music" (a phrase that I hope you hear a lot). Depending on which word of the phrase is emphasized, you get a slightly different meaning:

I love your music.

I *love* your music.

I love *your* music.

I love your *music.*

These are slight variations but ones that can alter how the listener perceives something. In the same way, by changing the level of a note or phrase, you can change the emotion of the performance.

Getting rid of distortion

In Chapter 10, I am adamant about getting your levels set so that you don't get digital distortion. Even if you follow my advice and are extremely diligent in making sure that you didn't get any digital clipping, one note may have snuck through anyway. Well, it may not be the end of the world.

If you have a system that allows you to adjust the individual waves of a waveform, just reduce the level of the single clipped note. You do this by zooming in as close as you can to the distorted note and choosing only that one note to quieten. (Your system's manual should clearly explain this procedure.) If you can't adjust the waveform, you need to replace that note with a good, undistorted one (if you can find one) or reduce the level of that note until the distortion is hidden.

If this is the lead vocal, you probably don't have the option to reduce the level, and replacing a bad note in a vocal part generally sounds unnatural. If you can replace the section with another phrase from the song, this is your best bet. If you don't have that option and you can't re-record the part, you can mask the distortion by adding a little distortion as an effect to the entire vocal track — a procedure that's performed more often than you may expect.

Getting rid of noise

No matter what you do when recording, you're going to end up with extra noise, such as a chair squeak, a cough, or too much breath from the singer. To get rid of the noise, just select the noise and follow your system's procedures for erasing or silencing a selection. When you do this, be sure that you don't have a Snap function engaged; you don't want the material following the erasure to move.

Correcting pitch problems

It used to be that if you sang or played an out-of-tune note, you had to record it over again. If you're singing is mediocre (like mine on a good day), you could spend hours trying to get every note just right. And after all these hours of fixing out-of-tune notes, you're often left with a performance that lacks "feel" (emotional impact). Well, those days are behind you. You can now edit your sour notes using a pitch-correction program. You can find pitch correction on nearly all digital recording systems that have effects processors included in them (computer-based and SIAB systems in particular).

To correct pitch, choose the note or notes that you want to correct and then choose the pitch-correction option on your editing menu. In the dialog box that appears, choose the amount of change that you want. You may need to experiment a little to find just the right pitch.

Some devices, such as Antares Autotune, make the correction for you automatically. (Antares Autotune is available as both a stand-alone processor and as a plug-in for a computer-based system. You can find these components at most major musical instrument retailers.) And some pitch-correction programs, such as the one in Logic Audio, allow you to adjust not only the change in fundamental pitch but also the pitch change of that note's harmonics. This can produce a much more natural sound.

Unless you're going for a particular effect, be judicious in your use of pitch correction because it can suck the life out of a performance. Sometimes the slightly out-of-tune notes are what give a performance its character.

Pitch correction is often part of the system's editing functions, but it can be used as an effect as well. Check out Chapter 15 to find some ways that you can use pitch shifting to add depth to your music.

Creating a Performance That Never Happened

Editing can be much more than just fixing a bad note or phrase — editing can consist of assembling a performance that never really happened. In the following sections, I walk you through the often-timesaving process of putting together a song from small parts: one or two measure loops, single sections such as verses and choruses, and parts of separate performances from virtual tracks (called a *composite take*). Doing these procedures has some advantages for you as a recording engineer. For example:

- By creating loops, you don't have to play the same 1- or 2-bar phrase over and over again for the duration of the song.

- By assembling song parts, you can alter the song's structure any way that you want.

- By making composite takes, you can create a performance that you could never play in one pass.

Creating loops

Loops are repeated phrases within a song. Looping has been around since the beginning of multitrack recording. You used to have to make an actual loop of tape containing the music that you wanted to repeat — thus the name *loop* — and load the loop into an analog tape deck to play repeatedly. This tape deck was then connected to the multitrack deck, and the looped performance was recorded onto that deck.

Now all that looping can be done digitally. You can make loops of any instrument, but the most common ones involve drum rhythms. For example, each section of a song usually contains a short 1- or 2-bar rhythm that repeats many times. By using loops, you can just play the drum part once and make copies of it for the rest of the measures in that section. This saves you from having to play for the whole song. Looping can be a great feature if you play an instrument live and if keeping the part steady is fairly difficult.

Making loops is easy: Just select the section that you want and copy it to the end of your existing rhythm for as many times as necessary. Keep the following points in mind when looping, however:

- ✔ **Make sure that your beginning and end points are accurate.** If you choose beat 1 of the measure, choose beat 1 of the next measure (that is, if you want a 1-bar loop). If you're off just a little bit, this affects the feel and timing of the rhythm.

- ✔ **Choose a point in the rhythm with a sharp attack.** An example is the downbeat with the kick drum or the snare drum back beat on beat 2. This helps you find the exact beginning and ending points for your loop.

- ✔ **When you record the part, set a metronome (click track) in your system and play along to it.** This creates a clear point from which you can find your edit points.

- ✔ **Give your looped music a more human feel.** To do this, overdub fills and embellishments onto another track (Chapter 11 covers overdubbing in detail). Then either adjust the mix so that you mute the main groove when the fill happens or place your fill directly into the groove track (Chapter 14 has details on mixing). Some songs and styles of music can work well if you let the fills and the groove happen at the same time, so experiment and use the approach that you prefer.

Assembling a song

Okay, you've recorded all the parts for your new song and have the arrangement and structure the way that you thought you wanted it. But suddenly (or maybe not so suddenly), you wonder what the song would sound like if you started with the chorus instead of the first verse. (I know this isn't common, but go along with me here.) All you have to do is choose the chorus from all the tracks in the song and copy or move the tracks to the place where you want them to be.

Today, many musicians play just a portion of a song and assemble the song from there. For instance, except for the lead vocal, you can just record one verse and one chorus on each instrument. You then go into your editor palette and put the song together. This lets you alter the song's structure quickly and easily.

This procedure is pretty simple: Just choose your musical section and then cut, copy, or paste it to where you want it. If your system doesn't have the Cut and Paste functions, you can use the Copy and Move functions instead. (All of these functions are described earlier in the chapter.)

Making composites of your tracks

If you used your digital system to record several versions or takes of a part onto different tracks (also known as *virtual tracks* in some systems — tracks hidden behind a main track), you can use the editing function of your system to blend the best parts of each performance into one perfect track. Take, for example, a lead guitar part that may be used throughout the song to act as a counterpoint to the lead vocal. Now assume that you weren't sure when you recorded the part what you wanted to do for each phrase. In this case, you would have recorded several versions of this guitar part onto different tracks in your system (or onto several virtual tracks of one track). I explain this procedure in Chapter 15.

To make a composite track of the best parts of your various lead guitar takes, choose the parts that you want to use and move them all onto one more track (assuming that you have another empty track or virtual track to put them on). Keep in mind that you need to move each of the good parts one at a time because they're each on separate virtual tracks.

You can move your guitar parts in one of the following ways:

- Click and drag your selection to the new virtual track.
- Use the Move function in your recorder to simply move the part from one virtual track to another.
- Use the Cut and Paste functions to cut the part from one virtual track and paste it to another.

When you're done assembling all the parts of one track, such as the lead guitar track, you can make adjustments to volume differences between the various assembled pieces using the Normalize or Quieten functions (described earlier in the chapter in the section "Evening out a performance").

Discovering Other Ways to Use Editing

Aside from being able to fix problems in your tracks or to make changes to the structure of a song, you can use editing to make some of your other work easier. The following sections cover a couple of ways that the editing capabilities of your digital system can be used outside the box, so to speak.

Making adjustments to the length of a performance

Time compression and expansion allow you to make small adjustments to the length of a section of music. This can be useful if you're trying to match your music to a video or if you want to change the feel of a vocal performance. For example, you can slow the last word in a phrase to give it a more crooner-type sound, or you can match certain words to rhythmic accents in the music. You can also fix a poorly performed drum fill (one that speeds up or slows down).

To compress or expand a section, you use a function called — at least on some systems — Time Stretch. To use it, select the music that you want to edit and fill in the parameters in the Time Stretch dialog box. You see the Time Stretch dialog box from Cubase in Figure 13-7.

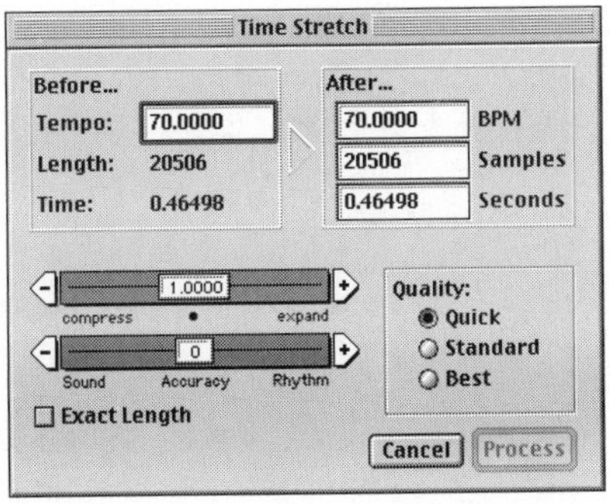

Figure 13-7:
The Time
Stretch
function
allows you
to make
adjustments
to a piece
of music's
length
of time.

Reversing a phrase

Being able to change the waveforms of your music can open a lot of possibilities for experimentation. I'm sure you've listened to a recording and been told that a subliminal message was hidden within the music. Of course, The Beatles were famous for putting reversed vocals in the back of the mix, and you can do this easily as well. Just record a vocal phrase like "Buy Jeff Strong's CDs," select it, and then choose Edit➪Reverse. Presto, you have a subliminal message (sit back and watch my CD sales go through the roof!).

Reversing a musical phrase can be used in many more ways than to peddle my sorry music, however. For example, you can add a reversed drumbeat or cymbal crash to add anticipation. This was overused in the '80s, but I think it can still be effective, depending on the style of music that you play.

To do this procedure, follow these steps:

1. **Select a drumbeat (be sure to get the initial attack) and copy it to an empty track.**

2. **Place the end of your selection where the drumbeat that you want to anticipate begins.**

3. **Choose Edit⇨Reverse to reverse the phrase.**

   If you play both tracks, you hear a reversed snare go right into a regular snare hit. Both attacks should happen at the same time. If they aren't exact, just move the reversed one over until the attacks are the same.

Chapter 14

Mixing Your Music

After you have all your tracks recorded, edited, and cleaned up as much as possible, it's time to turn all those individual parts into music. This is the act of *mixing*. Mixing involves setting levels, setting EQ (*equalization,* or adjusting the frequency response of your tracks), using stereo panning (placing your instruments from left to right in your mix), and adding effects so that your song tells the story that you want it to tell. How you mix your song has as much impact on the way it sounds as each of the individual parts that you've recorded — more so, in fact. Even minor adjustments in the relationship between the various instruments in your song can have dramatic impacts on how the song affects your listeners.

In this chapter, I introduce you to the process of mixing your music. You get a chance to take advantage of neat tools like the aforementioned EQ, effects, and stereo panning to make all your instruments fit in the mix. You discover how to reference your music to other people's recordings and how to train your ears so that your mix "translates" to different types of playback systems.

Mixing music is a subjective thing. How you have one instrument relate to another can be done in an almost infinite variety of ways. You may find that several mixes work equally well for your song. Allow yourself to experiment, and don't be afraid to record several different mixes.

Understanding Mixing

Think about all the time it took you to record all the tracks for your song. You spent countless hours setting up mics; getting good, "hot" (high, but not distorting) levels on your instruments; and making sure that each performance was as good as you could get it. You would think that most of your work is done. Well, on the one hand, it is — you no longer have to set up and play each instrument. On the other hand, you still have to make all the parts that you recorded fit together. This process can take as long as it took you to record all the tracks in the first place.

Your main tool during the mixing process is the mixer. Figure 14-1 shows a basic mixer setup in a software mixer program. The screen shot on the left shows the main mixer menu — with faders for each of your tracks. The screen shot on the right shows the channel strip section of the mixer. (For details on how the mixer functions, check out Chapter 4.)

Figure 14-1:
Left: The main mixer menu in a software mixer. Right: The channel strip section of the mixer.

Mixing involves making sure that each instrument can be heard in the *mix* — the recorded whole that's the result of blending all your recorded parts — without covering up something else or sounding out of place. You do this in the following ways:

- Choose the recorded parts that add to the emotional impact of the music and build intensity throughout the song. Also, don't use parts that are unnecessary or that clash with parts that have a greater impact.

- Set the levels (volume) of each of the instruments relative to one another so that nothing is buried so far back in the mix that you can't hear it and no instrument is so loud that it overpowers the other instruments.

✔ Adjust the *equalization* (EQ — frequency response) of each instrument so that each leaves room for the other instruments in the mix. This means getting rid of any frequencies of an instrument that clash with another or adding certain frequencies that define the sound of that instrument so that it can be heard clearly in the mix.

✔ Take advantage of stereo panning to put each instrument in its proper place in the stereo field — left or right — where it can either sound as natural as possible or can produce an effect that you want. Also, stereo panning allows you to make room for each instrument in the mix, especially those that have similar frequency ranges.

✔ Add effects, such as reverb or delay, to the instruments in the mix to either place them in front or in back relative to other instruments or to create a desired sound.

The mixing process is where you can get really creative in crafting your song. The stress of capturing great performances is over — you now have to massage all the parts of your song into a cohesive whole. Don't be afraid to try new things. Experiment with different EQ, panning, and effect settings. Take your time and have fun. The great thing about mixing is that you can make as many versions as you want and you can always go back and try again.

Getting Started Mixing Your Song

Before I start to mix a song, I do a few things to prepare myself for the process. My goal before I mix is to get in the headspace of mixing. This often means taking a step back from the song and approaching it as a listener rather than as the musician who recorded the tracks. Start the mixing process by following these steps:

1. **Determine the overall quality that you want from the song.**

   This can be defined as a musical style or a feeling. You probably don't need to think about this too hard because, when you started recording, you probably had a definite sound in mind. In fact, most composers hear a song in their heads before they even start recording.

2. **Listen to a song or two from a CD that has a similar sound or feel as the song you're trying to mix.**

   Listen on your studio monitors if you can and try to get a sense of the tonal and textural quality of these songs. Listen to them at fairly low volume and be careful not to tire your ears. All you're trying to do at this point is to get your ears familiar with the sound that you're trying to produce in your music.

3. **Set up a rough mix using no EQ or effects and listen through it once.**

   For this listening session, don't think like a producer; rather, try to put yourself in the mindset of the average listener. Listen to the various parts that you've recorded and see whether anything sticks out as being particularly good or bad. You're not listening for production quality. You're trying to determine whether some instruments, musical phrases, licks, melodies, or harmonies grab you as a listener.

4. **Get a piece of paper and a pen to jot down ideas as you work.**

   As you listen to the song, take notes on where certain instruments should be in the mix. For example, you may want the licks you played on the lead guitar throughout the song to be muted during the first verse. Or maybe you decide that the third rhythm-guitar part that you recorded would be best put way to the right side of the mix while the other two rhythm-guitar parts may be closer to the center. Write these ideas down so that you can try them later. You're likely to have a lot of ideas as you listen through the first few times.

After you follow these steps, go through the song and adjust the EQ, panning, and effect settings until you get all the instruments to fit nicely together. I outline these procedures in the following sections.

Exploring Equalization

The most useful tool that you have for mixing is equalization (EQ). Equalizers allow you to adjust the various frequencies of your instruments so that you have enough room for each of them in your stereo tracks. Three types of equalizers are used in a recording studio — *graphic, shelf,* and *parametric.* Each has its strengths and weaknesses, which I outline in the following sections.

Graphic

The graphic EQ has a prescribed number of frequencies that you can adjust. Graphic EQs generally have between 5 and 31 frequency bands, each affecting a small range of frequencies. (The manufacturer determines the range, which can't be adjusted.) Graphic EQs are useful for eliminating an offending frequency from the signal or for making other adjustments to the tonal quality of the source signal. You probably won't use a graphic EQ much in the mixing process because the parametric EQ can do what the graphic EQ can do — and a whole lot more.

Shelf

A shelf equalizer affects a range of frequencies above or below the target frequency. Shelf EQs are generally used to roll off the top or bottom end of the frequency spectrum. For example, you can set a shelf EQ to roll off the frequencies below 250 hertz (Hz) to reduce the amount of *rumble* (low-frequency noise) in a recording. You generally use the shelf EQ for the lowest and highest frequencies and the parametric EQ for any in-between frequencies when you mix.

Parametric

The parametric equalizer allows you to choose the frequency that you want to change as well as the range of frequencies around that frequency. With a parametric EQ, you dial in the frequency that you want to change and then you set the range (referred to as the *Q*) you want to affect.

The Q is a number that signifies the number of octaves that the EQ affects. Generally, you can adjust the Q setting to affect frequencies between ½ and 2 octaves wide. Not all parametric EQs use the same reference numbers for their Q settings. Some have ranges from 0.7 (2 octaves) to 2.8 (½ octave), while others use numbers from 0.5 to 16 without indicating what the numbers relate to in terms of octaves. The one constant among parametric EQs is that lower numbers affect larger ranges of frequencies than the higher numbers do.

The fact that each brand of parametric EQ uses slightly different numbers to reference its Q settings shouldn't matter much to you, because you choose your Q setting based on what you hear in the mix. Just as you can experiment with different frequencies to adjust in the mix, you can also try different Q settings to find the best possible frequency range to use.

The beauty of a parametric EQ is that you can take a small band (range) of frequencies and boost (increase) or cut (decrease) them. This capability enables you to get the various instruments in a mix to fit in with one another (called *carving out* frequencies). When you're mixing, the parametric EQ is the most useful one because you can adjust the frequency response of each instrument so that the other instruments can be heard clearly in the mix. The downside to parametric EQs is that some systems don't offer you many bands (sometimes just one with the addition of a couple of shelf EQs), so you have to make your EQ decisions based on the type and number of EQs you have to choose from.

Equalizing Your Tracks

Only so many frequencies are available for all the instruments in a mix, and if more than one instrument occupies a particular frequency range, they can get in each other's way and make the mix sound muddy. Your goals when equalizing (EQing) during the mixing process are to reduce those frequencies that add clutter and/or to enhance those that define an instrument's sound. To do this, make a little space for each instrument within the same general frequency range. You do this by EQing the individual tracks as you mix. The following sections explore this process in detail.

Dialing in EQ

Before you start EQing your tracks, you need to know how to find the frequencies you intend to adjust and how to make those adjustments. Figure 14-2 shows an EQ plug-in for Logic Audio. Although each EQ will look a little different, they all end up performing the same basic function. In this section, I walk you through Logic's Channel EQ.

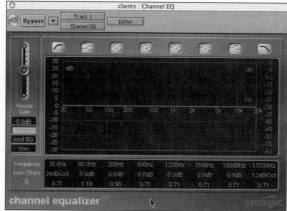

Figure 14-2:
The EQ section of a mixer's channel strip allows you to adjust the frequencies of your track.

Logic's Channel EQ is an 8-band EQ with four parametric bands, one high-shelf EQ, one low-shelf EQ, one high-pass filter, and one low-pass filter. As you can see in Figure 14-2, the EQ types are listed at the top of the graph, but the adjustments for these bands are located under the main graph.

TIP

Logic's EQ has a really great feature where you can see the frequency response of your track. This function is engaged by clicking the Analyzer button on the left side of the plug-in window. This is handy because, with the Analyzer button engaged, you can actually see the changes you're making to your track as you make them. This is also a potential problem because many people rely on their eyes instead of their ears. Be careful not to let what you see affect what you hear.

Using parametric EQ

To use the parametric EQ, click the Peak EQ button (it looks like a circle with a line coming from the left and right sides) in the EQ plug-in window you have open. You have three settings to adjust:

- ✔ **Gain:** This is the amount of *boost* (increase) or *cut* (decrease) that you apply to the signal. In Pro Tools, you can either type in the amount in the text box next to the Peak EQ button or use the slider to the right. In Logic, to get your boost (gain) amount, either you can point your mouse over the parameter and click and drag up or down, or you can click in the EQ graph above the parameter controls and drag up or down.

- ✔ **Freq:** This frequency is the center of the EQ. You select the range of frequencies above and below this point by using the Q setting (see next bullet). In Pro Tools, you can either type the frequency in the text box on the left or use the slider to make your adjustment. In Logic, to get the desired frequency, either you can point your mouse over the parameter and click and drag up or down, or you can click in the EQ graph above the parameter controls and drag left or right.

- ✔ **Q:** This is the range of frequencies that your EQ will affect. The higher the number, the narrower the range that gets EQed. In Pro Tools, you adjust this setting either by moving the slider or by clicking in the text box and typing a value between 0.33 and 12. In Logic, you can point your mouse over the parameter and click and drag up or down to get the Q value you want. Your settings can be anywhere from 0.10 to 100.

Using low-shelf/high-shelf EQ

To use low-shelf/high-shelf EQ, click the Low Shelf and High Shelf buttons in the EQ plug-in window. These buttons look like sideways tuning forks located second from the left and second from the right above the EQ graph in Figure 14-2. When you use low-shelf/high-shelf EQ, you have two parameters to adjust in Pro Tools and three on Logic:

- ✔ **Gain:** This is the amount of boost or cut that you apply to the signal. In Pro Tools, you can either type in the amount in the text box next to the shelf button or use the slider to the right. In Logic, to set the boost (gain), either you can point your mouse over the parameter and click and drag up or down, or you can click in the EQ graph above the parameter controls and drag up or down.

- ✔ **Freq:** This is the starting frequency for the shelf. In Pro Tools, you can either type in the frequency in the text box or use the slider to make your adjustment. In Logic, to set your desired frequency you can either point your mouse over the parameter and click and drag up or down or you can click in the EQ graph above the parameter controls and drag left or right.

✔ **Q:** This is the steepness of the shelf of your EQ in Logic. (Pro Tools doesn't have this option.) The higher the number, the steeper the shelf that's applied — meaning that the range of frequencies that are affected to get the gain change of the shelf is narrower. To adjust this parameter, you can point your mouse over the parameter and click and drag up or down to get the Q value you want. Your settings can be anywhere from .10 to 2.

Using low-pass/high-pass EQ

Here's where you tell your plug-in which frequencies to avoid in the course of adjusting the EQ. The low- and high-pass buttons are located at the far left and far right above the EQ graph in Figure 14-2.

To use the low- or high-pass filter, click the appropriate button in the EQ window. In Pro Tools, the only option to set is Freq, which is the frequency that the filter begins filtering. Any frequency below (high-pass) or above (low-pass) the setting is removed from the track. You can either type the frequency in the text box or use the slider to make your adjustment.

In Logic, you have the same three settings — frequency, gain/slope, and Q — as the rest of the EQ types. And as with the other EQ types, you adjust the settings by pointing your mouse over the column of the setting and clicking and dragging the parameter that you want to adjust. With the high-pass and low-pass EQ (filters), the gain/slope parameter adjusts the slope of the filter — how quickly it totally cuts off the frequency.

Deciding which frequencies to boost or cut

Here's a good trick to use when initially trying to decide which frequencies to boost or cut:

1. **Solo the track(s) you're working on by clicking the Solo button in the track's channel strip and set your parametric EQ to a narrow Q setting (a high number).**

2. **Next, turn the boost all the way up (turn the EQ knob all the way to the right) and** *sweep* **the frequency setting as you listen (to sweep, just dial the EQ knob's frequency dial to the left and right).**

3. **Notice those areas where the annoying or pleasing sounds are located.**

   This can help you better understand the frequencies that your instrument produces.

4. **After you find a frequency to adjust, experiment with the Q setting to find the range that produces the best sound and then adjust the amount of boost or cut to where it has the effect that you want.**

After you determine the frequencies that you want to work with, do your EQing to the individual track while the instrument is in the mix (not soloed). You're trying to make that instrument fit as well as possible with the rest of the instruments, and to do this, you need to know how your instrument sounds in relation to all the stuff (music) going on around it.

When making adjustments in EQ, your goal is to make all the tracks blend as well as possible. In some instances, this means making some radical EQ moves. Don't be afraid to do whatever it takes to make your mix sound good, even if this means having cuts or boosts as great as 12dB.

General guidelines

Although some instruments call for specific EQ guidelines, you should consider some general issues when EQing, regardless of the instrument involved. When it comes to the audible frequency spectrum (which is generally about 20 Hz to 20 kHz), certain frequencies always have certain characteristics. Table 14-1 describes these frequencies.

Table 14-1	EQ Frequency Sound Characteristics
Frequency	*Sound Characteristic*
20 to 100 Hz	Warms an instrument or adds boominess to it
100 to 200 Hz	Is muddy for some instruments but adds fullness to others
350 to 450 Hz	Sounds boxy
750 to 850 Hz	Adds depth or body
1 to 2 kHz	Adds attack or punch to some instruments and creates a nasally sound in others
2 to 5 kHz	Increases the presence of instruments
5 to 8 kHz	Sounds harsh in some instruments
8 kHz and above	Adds airiness or brightness to an instrument

You're generally better off cutting a frequency than boosting one. This thinking goes back to the early days of analog EQs, which often added noise when boosting a signal. This can still be a factor with some digital EQs, but it is much less of an issue. I still try to cut frequencies before I boost them just out of habit, and I recommend that you do the same (not out of habit, of course, but because if a noise difference exists between cutting and boosting, you may as well avoid it).

The exact frequencies that you end up cutting or boosting depend on the sound you're after, the tonal characteristic of the instrument, and the relationship between all the instruments in the song. In the following sections, I list a variety of frequencies to cut or boost for each instrument; Table 14-2 shows an overview. You may not want to follow all the suggestions. Just choose the ones that help you meet your goals.

Table 14-2	EQ Recommendations per Instrument		
Instrument	**Frequency**	**Adjustment (dB)**	**Purpose**
Vocals	150 Hz	+2 to 3	Adds fullness
	200 to 250 Hz	−2 to 3	Reduces muddiness
	3 kHz	+2 to 4	Adds clarity
	5 kHz	+1 to 2	Adds presence
	7.5 to 10 kHz	−2 to 3	Cuts sibilance
	10 kHz	+2 to 3	Adds air or brightness
Electric guitar	100 Hz	−2 to 3	Reduces muddiness
	150 to 250 Hz	+2	Adds warmth
	2.5 to 4 kHz	+2 to 3	Adds attack or punch
	5 kHz	+2 to 3	Adds bite
Acoustic guitar	80 Hz	−3	Reduces muddiness
	150 to 250 Hz	+2 to 3	Adds warmth
	800 to 1000 Hz	−2 to 3	Reduces boxiness
	3 to 5 kHz	+2 to 3	Adds attack or punch
	7 kHz	+2 to 3	Adds brightness
Bass guitar	100 to 200 Hz	+1 to 2	Adds fullness
	200 to 300 Hz	−3 to 4	Reduces muddiness
	500 to 1000 Hz	+2 to 3	Adds punch
	2.5 to 5 kHz	+2 to 3	Adds attack
Kick drum	80 to 100 Hz	+1 to 2	Adds body or depth
	400 to 600 Hz	−3 to 4	Reduces boxiness
	2.5 to 5 kHz	+1 to 2	Adds attack

Instrument	Frequency	Adjustment (dB)	Purpose
Snare drum	100 to 150 Hz	+1 to 2	Adds warmth
	250 Hz	+1 to 2	Adds depth or body
	800 to 1000 Hz	−2 to 3	Reduces boxiness
	3 to 5 kHz	+1 to 3	Adds attack
	8 to 10 kHz	+1 to 3	Adds crispness
Tom-toms	200 to 250 Hz	+1 to 2	Adds depth
	600 to 1000 Hz	−2 to 3	Reduces boxiness
	3 to 5 kHz	+1 to 2	Adds attack
	5 to 8 kHz	+1 to 2	Adds presence
Large tom-toms	40 to 125 Hz	+1 to 2	Adds richness
	400 to 800 Hz	−2 to 3	Reduces boxiness
	2.5 to 5 kHz	+2 to 3	Adds punch or attack
Hi-hats	10 kHz or higher	+3 to 4	Adds brightness or sheen
Cymbals	150 to 200 Hz	−1 to 2	Reduces rumbling
	1 to 2 kHz	−3 to 4	Reduces trashiness
	10 kHz or higher	+3 to 4	Adds brightness or sheen
Drum overheads	100 to 200 Hz	−2 to 3	Reduces muddiness
	400 to 1000 Hz	−2 to 3	Reduces boxiness
High percussion	500 Hz and below	−6 to 12	Cuts boxiness
	10 kHz or higher	+3 to 4	Adds brightness or sheen
Low percussion	250 Hz and below	−3 to 4	Reduces muddiness
	2.5 to 5 kHz	+2 to 3	Adds attack
	8 to 10 kHz	+2 to 3	Adds brightness
Piano	80 to 150 Hz	+2 to 3	Adds warmth
	200 to 400 Hz	−2 to 3	Reduces muddiness
	2.5 to 5 kHz	+2 to 3	Adds punch or attack

(continued)

Table 14-2 *(continued)*

Instrument	Frequency	Adjustment (dB)	Purpose
Horns	100 to 200 Hz	+1 to 2	Adds warmth
	200 to 800 Hz	−2 to 3	Reduces muddiness
	2.5 to 5 kHz	+2 to 3	Adds punch or attack
	7 to 9 kHz	+1 to 2	Adds breath

Vocals

For most popular music, the vocals are the most important instrument in the song. You need to hear them clearly, and they should contain the character of the singer's voice and style. One of the most common mistakes in mixing vocals is to make them too loud. The next most common mistake is to make them too quiet. (This is especially true if you're the singer and are even slightly self-conscious of your vocals skills.) You want the lead vocals to shine through, but you don't want them to overpower the other instruments. The best way to do this is to EQ the vocal tracks so that they can sit nicely in the mix and still be heard clearly. The following guidelines can help you do this.

Lead

You can use several techniques with the lead vocal, depending on the singer and the style of music. For the most part, I tend to cut a little around 200 Hz and add a couple dB at 3 kHz and again at 10 kHz. In general, try following these guidelines:

- To add fullness, try adding a few dB at 150 Hz.
- To get rid of muddiness, cut a few dB at 200–250 Hz.
- To add clarity, boost a little at 3 kHz.
- For more presence, add at 5 kHz.
- To add air or to brighten, boost at 10 kHz.
- To get rid of sibilance, cut a little between 7.5 and 10 kHz.

Backup

To keep backup vocals from competing with lead vocals, cut the backup vocals a little in the low end (below 250 Hz) and at the 2.5–3.5-kHz range. To add clarity, you can boost a little around 10 kHz without getting in the way of the lead vocal.

Guitar

For the most part, when it comes to guitars, you want to avoid getting a muddy sound, and you want to make sure that the attack comes through in the mix.

Electric

Electric guitars can often use a little cutting below 100 Hz to get rid of muddiness. A boost between 120 and 250 Hz adds warmth. A boost in the 2.5–4-kHz range brings out the attack of the guitar, and a boost at 5 kHz can add some bite to the guitar.

Acoustic

Acoustic guitars often do well with a little cut below 80 Hz and again around 800 Hz to 1 kHz. If you want a warmer tone and more body, you can try boosting a little at 150–250 Hz. Also try adding a few dB around 3–5 kHz if you want more attack or punch. A few dB added at 7 kHz can add a little more brightness to the instrument.

Bass

This instrument can get muddy pretty fast. The mud generally happens in the 200–300-Hz range, so I either leave that alone or cut just a little if the bass lacks definition. I rarely add frequencies below 100 Hz but boost some between 100 and 200 Hz if the instrument sounds flat or thin. Adding a little between 500 Hz and 1 kHz can increase the punch, and a boost between 2.5 and 5 kHz accentuates the attack, adding a little brightness to the bass.

With the bass guitar, one of the most important things is to make sure that it and the kick drum can both be heard. You need to adjust the frequencies of these two instruments to make room for both. For the most part, try cutting frequencies from the bass that you may add to the kick.

Drums

The guidelines for EQing the drums depend on whether you use live acoustic drums or a drum machine. (The drum machine probably requires less EQ because the sounds were already EQed when they were created.) Also, the type and placement of your mic or mics also affect how you EQ the drums. (You can find out more about mic placement in Chapters 8 and 9.)

Kick

You want the kick drum to blend in with the bass guitar. To do this, reduce the frequencies that the bass guitar takes up. For example, if I boost a few dB between 100 and 200 Hz for the bass guitar, I generally cut them in the kick drum (and maybe as high as 250 Hz). To bring out the bottom end of the kick, I sometimes add a couple of dB between 80 and 100 Hz. The kick drum can get boxy sounding (you know, like a cardboard box), so I often cut a little between 400 and 600 Hz as well to get rid of this boxiness. To bring out the click from the beater hitting the head, try adding a little between 2.5 and 5 kHz. This increases the attack of the drum and gives it more presence.

Snare

The snare drum drives the music, making it the most important drum in popular music. As such, it needs to really cut through the rest of the instruments. Although the adjustments that you make depend on the pitch and size of the drum and whether you used one mic or two during recording, you can usually boost a little at 100–150 Hz for added warmth. You can also try boosting at 250 Hz to add some depth and cutting at 800 Hz to 1 kHz if the drum sounds too boxy. A little boost at around 3 to 5 kHz increases the attack, and an increase in the 8–10-kHz range can add a crispness to the drum.

If you used two mics during recording, consider dropping a few dB on the top mic in both the 800-Hz to 1-kHz range and the 8- to 10-kHz range. Allow the bottom mic to create the crispness. I generally roll off the bottom end of the bottom mic below, say, 250 to 300 Hz. Depending on the music (R&B and pop, for instance), I may add a little sizzle to the bottom mic by boosting frequencies above 10 kHz with a shelf EQ.

For many recording engineers/producers, the snare drum sound is almost a signature. If you listen to different artists' songs from the same producer, you'll likely hear similarities in the songs' snare drum sound. Don't be afraid to take your time getting the snare drum to sound just right. After all, if you become a famous producer, you'll want people to recognize your snare drum sound too.

Tom-toms

Tom-toms come in a large range of sizes and pitches, but for mounted toms, you can boost a little around 200 to 250 Hz to add depth to the drum. A boost in the 3–5-kHz range can add more of the sticks' attack, and for some additional presence, try adding a little in the 5–8-kHz range. If the drums sound too boxy, try cutting a little in the 600-Hz to 1-kHz range.

For floor toms, you can try boosting the frequency range 40 to 125 Hz to add some richness and fullness. You may also find that cutting 400–800 Hz can get rid of any boxy sound that the drum may have. To add more attack, boost the 2.5- to 5-kHz range.

Hi-hats

Most of the time, the hi-hats are pretty well represented in the rest of the mics in the drum set, but depending on which mics are picking up the hi-hats, you can use the hi-hat mic to bring out their sheen or brightness. To do this, try boosting the frequencies above 10 kHz with a shelf EQ. You may also find that cutting frequencies below 200 Hz eliminates any rumble created by other drums that the hi-hat mic picked up.

Cymbals

With the cymbals, I usually cut anything below 150–200 Hz with a shelf EQ to get rid of rumbling that these mics may pick up. I also drop a few dB at 1–2 kHz if the cymbals sound kind of trashy or clanky. Adding a shelf EQ above 10 kHz can add a nice sheen to the mix.

Overhead mics

If you used overhead mics to pick up both the drums and the cymbals, be careful about cutting too much low end — this can just suck the life out of your drums. Also, if the drums coming through the overhead mics sound boxy or muddy, work with the 100–200-Hz frequencies for the muddiness and 400-Hz to 1-kHz frequencies for the boxiness.

Percussion

High-pitched percussion instruments, such as shakers, sound good when the higher frequencies are boosted a little bit — over 10 kHz, for instance. This adds some brightness and softness to their sound. You can also roll off many of the lower frequencies, below 500 Hz, to eliminate any boxiness that may be present from miking too closely (see Chapter 8 for more on mic placement).

Lower-pitched percussion instruments, such as maracas, can also have the lower frequencies cut a little — use 250 Hz and lower. Try boosting frequencies between 2.5 and 5 kHz to add more of the instrument's attack. To brighten them up, add a little bit in the 8–10-kHz range.

Piano

For pianos, you often want to make sure that the instrument has a nice attack as well as a warm-bodied tone. You can add attack in the 2.5–5-kHz range, and warmth can be added in the 80–150-Hz range. If your piano sounds boomy or muddy, try cutting a little between 200 and 400 Hz.

Horns

You find a variety of horns, from tubas to soprano saxophones, so to offer blanket recommendations for all of them would be ridiculous (although I'm no stranger to ridiculous). So with this thought in mind, I often start the EQ process for these instruments by looking at the 100–200-Hz range to add warmth to thin-sounding instruments. Next, I approach the 400–800-Hz range to get rid of any muddiness that occurs unless it's a really low horn like a tuba. In this case, I often look for the muddiness a little lower — say, in the 200–400-Hz range. To add some more attack to a horn, you can tweak the 2.5–5-kHz range a bit, and to add some of the breath of the instrument, look toward the 7–9-kHz range.

Using the Stereo Field

When you're at a live concert and you close your eyes, you can hear where each instrument is coming from on-stage. You can hear that certain instruments are on the left side of the stage, others are on the right, and still others seem to come from the center. You can also generally discern whether an instrument is at the front or the back of the stage. Put all these sounds together, and you have a *stereo field*.

The stereo field consists of placement from left to right and front to back. When you mix a song, you can set your instruments wherever you want them on the "stage" that's created by your listeners' speakers. You can do this with *panning*, which sets your instruments from left to right, and you can use *effects*, such as reverb and delay, to place your instruments from front to back in your mix. When you mix your song, try to visualize where on-stage each instrument may be placed.

Some people choose to set the panning and depth of their instruments to sound as natural as possible, while others use these settings to create otherworldly sounds. There is no right or wrong setting when panning and adding effects to simulate depth — just what works for your goals. Don't be afraid to get creative and try unusual things.

Left or right

You adjust each instrument's position from left to right in a mix with the *panning knob*. The panning knob is generally located just above each channel's fader. This can either be a knob that you turn left or right or a slider that you move to the left or right. Panning for most songs is pretty straightforward, and I outline some settings in the following list:

- **Lead vocals:** Lead vocals are usually panned directly in the center.

- **Backup vocals:** Because backup vocals are often recorded in stereo, they are panned hard left and hard right. If you recorded only one track of backup vocals, you can make a duplicate of the track and pan one to each side, just as you can with stereo tracks.

  In addition to tracks panned to each side, some mixing engineers also have a third backup vocal track that's panned in the center to add more depth. Your choice of doing this depends on how you recorded your backup vocals and how many tracks you have available for them.

- **Guitar:** Lead guitar is often panned to the center (or just slightly off-center if the sound in the center of the stereo field is too cluttered). Rhythm guitar, on the other hand, is generally placed somewhere just off-center. It doesn't matter which side you place it, but it's usually the opposite side from other background instruments, such as an additional rhythm guitar, synthesizers, organs, or pianos.

- **Bass:** Most of the time, the bass guitar is panned in the center, but it's not uncommon for mixing engineers to create a second track for the bass and pan one to the far left and the other to the far right. This gives the bass a sense of spaciousness and allows more room for both the bass guitar and kick drum in the mix.

- **Drums:** As a general rule, I (and most other people) pan the drums so that they appear in the stereo field much like they would on-stage (but this doesn't mean you have to, too). The snare drum and kick drum are typically panned right up the center, and the tom-toms are panned from right to left slightly. Hi-hat cymbals often go just to the right of center, the ride cymbal just left of center, and crash cymbals sit from left to right, much like the tom-toms.

- **Percussion:** Percussion instruments tend to be panned just off to the left or right of center. If I have a shaker or triangle part that plays throughout the song, for instance, I pan it to the right an equal distance from center as the hi-hat is to the left. This way, you hear the hi-hat and percussion parts playing off one another in the mix.

- **Piano/synthesizers/organs:** These instruments are usually placed just off-center. If your song has rhythm guitar parts, the piano or organ usually goes to the opposite side. Synthesizers can be panned all over the place. In fact, it's not uncommon for the synths to be actively panned throughout the song (that is, they move from place to place).

Some mixing engineers like to keep their instruments toward the center of the mix, while other engineers prefer spreading things way out with instruments on either end of the spectrum. There's no right or wrong way to pan instruments. In fact, no one says that you have to leave any of your instruments in the same place throughout the entire song.

Front or back

As you probably discovered when you were placing your mics to record an instrument, the quality of sound changes when you place a mic closer to or farther away from the instrument. The closer you place a mic to the instrument, the less room ambience you pick up, thus making the instrument sound close to you, or "in your face." In contrast, the farther from the instrument you place your mic, the more room sound you hear. As a result, your instrument sounds far away.

If you've ever stood in a large room and talked to someone, you have seen (well, heard, actually) how this relationship works. When your friend stands close to you, you can hear him clearly. You hear very little of the reflections of his voice from around the room. As he moves farther away from you, the room's reflections play an increasing role in the way that you hear him. By the time your friend is at the other side of the room, you hear not only his voice but also the room in which you are talking with him. In fact, if the room is large enough, your friend probably sounds as if he were a mile away from you, and all the reflections from his voice bouncing around the room may make it difficult to understand what he says.

You can easily simulate this effect by using your reverb or delay effects processors. In fact, this is often the purpose of reverb and delay in the mixing process. With them, you can effectively place your instruments almost anywhere that you want them, from front to back, in your mix.

 The less reverb or delay that you use in conjunction with your instrument, the closer it appears on the recording, whereas the more effect you add to an instrument, the farther away it seems from you.

The type of reverb or delay setting that you use has an impact on how close or far away a sound appears as well. For example, a longer reverb decay or delay sounds farther away than a shorter one. In Chapter 15, I go into detail about the various effects processors to help you understand how best to use them. I also present settings that you can use to create natural-sounding reverb and delay on your tracks, as well as some unusual settings that you can use for special effects.

Adjusting Levels: Enhancing the Emotion of the Song

After you have a rough mix and have your EQ and panning settings where you want them, your next step is to determine which parts of which tracks are used when — and sometimes, whether a part or track is used at all. If you're like most musician/producers, you try to get all the wonderful instrumental and vocal parts you recorded as loud as possible in the mix so that each can be heard clearly all the time. After all, you didn't go through all the time and effort to record all those great tracks just to hide them in the mix — or worse yet, mute them — right?

Well, I feel your pain. But when you get to the mixing point of a song, it's time to take off your musician's hat and put on the one that says *producer*. A producer's job is to weed through all the parts of a song, choose those that add to its impact, and dump those that are superfluous or just add clutter. Your goal is to assemble the tracks that tell the story that you want to tell and that carry the greatest emotional impact for the listener.

This can be the toughest part of mixing your own songs because you aren't likely to be totally objective when it comes to determining what to use. Try not to get stressed out. You aren't erasing any of your tracks, so you can always do another mix later if you just have to hear the part that you muted before.

One of the great joys when listening to music (for me, anyway) is hearing a song that carries me away and pulls me into the emotional journey that the songwriter had in mind. If the song is done well, I'm sucked right into the song, and by the end, all I want to do is rewind it and listen to it again.

What is it about certain songs that can draw you in and get you to feel the emotion of the performers? Well, aside from a good melody and some great performances, it's the way that the arrangement builds throughout the song to create tension, release that tension, and build it again. A good song builds intensity so that the listener feels pulled into the emotions of the song.

Generally, a song starts out quietly, becomes a little louder during the first chorus, and then drops in level for the second verse (not as quiet as the first, though). The second chorus is often louder and fuller than the first chorus, and is often followed by a bridge section that is even fuller yet (or at least different in arrangement than the second chorus). The loud bridge section may be followed by a third verse, where the volume drops a little. Then a super-heated chorus generally follows the last verse and keeps building intensity until the song ends.

You have two tools at your disposal when crafting your song to build and release intensity. They are dynamics and instrumental content (the arrangement).

Dynamics

Dynamics are simply how loud or soft something is. Listen to a classic blues tune (or even some classical music), and you can hear sections where the song is almost deafeningly silent and other sections where you think the band is going to step out of the speakers and into your room. This is an effective and powerful use of dynamics. The problem is that this seems to be a lost art, at least in popular music.

It used to be that a song could have very quiet parts and really loud ones. Unfortunately, a lot of modern CDs have only one level — loud. This often isn't the fault of the musicians or even the band's producer. The radio stations and record-company bean counters have fueled this trend because they want to make sure that a band's music is as loud as (or louder than) other CDs on the market. (You can read more about this trend in Chapter 16.)

Try recording a song with a lot of dynamic changes. I know this bucks the trend, but who knows, you may end up with a song that carries a ton of emotional impact. Also, as you mix your song, incorporate dynamic variation by dropping the levels of background instruments during the verses and bringing them up during the chorus and bridge sections of the song. You can always eliminate your dynamic variation by squashing your mix with compression during the mastering process.

The biggest mistake that most people make when they mix their own music is to try to get their song to be as loud as commercial CDs. This is the mastering engineer's job, however, not yours, so don't worry about it. Get your song to sound good with a balance between high and low frequencies and loud and soft sections. Let the mastering engineer make your music as loud as it can be. He or she definitely has gear that is better designed to raise the volume of a recording without making it sound squashed or harsh.

The arrangement

Building intensity with the arrangement involves varying the amount of sound in each section. A verse with just lead vocal, drums, bass, and an instrument playing the basic chords of the song is going to have less intensity (not to mention volume) than a chorus with a wash of guitars, backup vocals, drums, percussion, organ, and so on. Most songs that build intensity effectively start with fewer instruments than they end with.

When you mix your song, think about how you can use the instruments to add to the emotional content of your lyrics. For example, if you have a guitar lick that you played at every break in the vocal line, think about using it less to leave space for lower levels at certain points in your song. If you do this, each lick can provide more impact for the listener and bring more to the song's emotion.

Automation, or Riding the Faders

When you have the levels of each instrument set so that you can hear each of them when the song plays, you would think that you can pretty much leave the levels that way during the whole song. Well, you can, but that often limits the amount of dynamics that you get in your mix.

Rarely do you set the levels of each instrument at the beginning of the song and not move the various instrument levels up and down throughout the song. For example, you may find that you want the rhythm guitar parts louder during the chorus, or maybe you have a short guitar lick in the second verse that you want to bring up a little in the mix.

To adjust levels during the song, you used to need several hands (or at least one more person to help), and you jumped from one fader to another and constantly made changes to the effect settings while you recorded the final mix. One mistake and you had to start recording over again. This is no longer the case for most digital recorders because most of them have an automix feature. Automix enables you to record the fader moves and effects changes that happen throughout the mix so that you don't have to actually move the faders when you record to two tracks.

Depending on your system, you have one of two types of automation features (or both): *real-time automation* and *scene* or *snapshot automation*.

Real-time automation

Real-time automation is also referred to as *dynamic automated mixing*. This feature allows you to record the fader, panning, effects settings, and other things in real time to each track as the song plays. The advantage of this type of automation is that you can seamlessly get volume changes, and you can record these changes while the song plays. The disadvantage of real-time automation is that it takes you a while to do, especially if you have a lot of tracks to automate. Real-time automation can also take up a lot of hard-drive space and can tax your processor if you have a complicated mix with lots of tracks, effects, and mixer-setting changes.

Snapshot automation

Snapshot automation involves saving the mixer data at intervals rather than throughout the entire song. To do snapshot automation, just set your mixer (levels, EQ, effects, and so on) the way you want it for a particular section in your song (the verse, for instance) and take a "snapshot" of it. Whenever you make a mixer move, you take another snapshot, and so on. Snapshot automation can be useful if you have a song without a ton of complex mixer changes. The advantage of snapshot automation is that it takes up a lot less hard-drive space and requires less processor power. The disadvantage is that it can take much longer to automate the song (you have to program each instance into the mixer), and any complex mixer moves, such as fade-ins and fade-outs, may not sound as smooth.

If you're going to mix your music and have more than eight tracks, get a system that enables you to do automated mixing (I say eight tracks because, for the most part, you can handle mixing up to eight tracks the old-fashioned way). Research the automation features of the system that interests you before you buy it. For example, a given system may offer real-time automation, but it may tax the system's processor and add to your song's file size so quickly that using it becomes more hassle than it's worth. Likewise, some systems (the Roland VS-1680, for example) don't allow you to change the effects patch during automation. The more you know about your mixing needs, the better you can tell what automation approach will work for you.

Tuning Your Ears

To create a mix that sounds good, the most critical tools you need are your ears, because your ability to hear the music clearly and accurately is essential. To maximize this ability, you need a decent set of studio monitors and a good idea of how other people's music sounds on your speakers. You also need to make sure that you don't mix when your ears are tired. The following sections explore these areas.

Listening critically

One of the best ways to find out how to mix music is to listen to music that you like and listen for the way that it's mixed. Put on a CD of something similar to your music (or music that has a sound that you like) and ask yourself the following questions:

- ✔ **What is the overall tonal quality or texture of the song?** Notice how the frequencies of all the instruments cover the hearing spectrum. Does the song sound smooth or harsh, full or thin? Try to determine what you like about the overall production.

- ✔ **How does the song's arrangement contribute to its overall feel?** Listen for licks or phrases that add to the arrangement. Notice whether the song seems to get fuller as it goes on.

- ✔ **Where are the instruments in the stereo field?** Notice where each instrument is, from left to right and front to back, in the mix. Listen to see whether the instruments stay in one place throughout the song or whether they move around.

- ✔ **What effects are being used on each instrument?** Listen for reverb and delay lengths as well as the effect level compared to the dry (unaffected) signal.

- ✔ **What tonal quality does each instrument have?** Try to determine the frequencies from each instrument that seem dominant. Pay particular attention to the way the drums sound, especially the snare drum.

Even if you're not mixing one of your songs, it's a good idea to occasionally sit down and listen to music on your monitors to get used to listening to music critically. Also, the more good music you hear on your monitors, the easier it is for you to know when your music sounds good on them, too.

A good mix should sound good on a variety of systems, not just through the speakers in your studio. Before you decide that a mix is done, copy it to a CD and play it in your car, your friend's stereo, and a boom box. In fact, try to listen to your music on as many different kinds of systems as you can. As you listen, notice whether the bass disappears or becomes too loud or whether the treble becomes thin or harsh. Basically, you're trying to determine where you need to make adjustments in your mix so that it sounds good *everywhere*.

Unless you spent a lot of time and money getting your mixing room to sound great, you have to compensate when you mix to get your music to sound good on other people's systems. If your room or speakers enhance the bass in your song, the song will sound thin on other people's systems. On the other hand, if your system lacks bass, your mixes will be boomy when you listen to them somewhere else.

Choosing reference CDs

A reference CD can be any music that you like or that helps you to hear your music more clearly. For the most part, choose reference CDs that have a good balance between high and low frequencies and that sound good to your ear. That said, some CDs are mixed really well, which can help you get to know your monitors and train your ears to hear the subtleties of a mix. I name a few CDs in the following list. (Disclaimer: I try to cover a variety of music styles in this list, but I can't cover them all without a list that's pages long.)

- Steely Dan, *Two Against Nature*
- Peter Gabriel, *So*
- Sarah McLachlan, *Surfacing*
- No Doubt, *Return of Saturn*
- Los Lobos, *Kiko*
- Marilyn Manson, *Mechanical Animals*
- Depeche Mode, *Ultra*
- Bonnie Raitt, *Fundamental*
- Macy Gray, *Oh How Life Is*
- Pearl Jam, *Yield*
- Metallica, *S&M*
- Dr. Dre, *2001*

All commercial CDs have been mastered. This is going to affect the sound of them a little — most importantly, they will be louder than your music. If you toggle back and forth between your mix and a reference CD, adjust the relative levels so that each sounds equally as loud coming through your speakers because the louder song always sounds "better." And remember: Don't try to match the volume of your mix to a reference CD.

Dealing with ear fatigue

If you've ever had a chance to mix a song, you've probably found that you often do a better mix early in the process, and the longer you work on the song, the worse the mix gets. In most cases, this is because your ears get tired, and when they do, hearing accurately becomes harder. To tame ear fatigue, try the following tips:

- **Don't mix at the end of the day, especially after doing other recording.** Save your mixing for first thing in the morning, when your ears have had a chance to rest.

- **Keep the volume low.** I know you'll be tempted to crank the volume on your song as you work on it, but doing so only tires your ears prematurely and can cause damage, especially if you have monitors that can get really loud.

- **Take an occasional break.** Just 10 or 15 minutes of silence can allow you to work for another hour or so. Also, don't be afraid to walk away from a mix for a day or more.

- **Try not to mix under a deadline.** This suggestion fits with the preceding one. If you're under a deadline, you can't give yourself the time you may need to rest and reassess your mix before it goes to print.

Making several versions

One great thing about digital recording is that it costs you nothing to make several versions of a mix. All you need is a little (or a lot of) hard-drive space. Because you can make as many variations on your song's mix as your hard drive allows, you can really experiment by trying new effects settings or trying active panning in your song. You may end up with something exciting. At the very least, you end up discovering more about your gear. That's always a good thing.

Print (record) a mix early on. Most of the time, your best mixes happen early in the mixing process. Print (or save) the first good mix that you make before you try making creative ones. This way, if you get burned out or run out of time, you have a decent mix to fall back on.

Chapter 15

Dialing in Signal Processors

*U*nless you record your songs using a live band in a perfect acoustic environment, your music will sound a little flat without the addition of some type of effects. Effects allow you to make your music sound like you recorded it in just about any environment possible. You can make your drums sound as if they were recorded in a cathedral or your vocals sound as if you were singing underwater. Effects also have the ability to make you sound better than you actually did. For example, you can add harmony parts to your lead or backup vocals, or you can make your guitar sound like you played it through a number of great amplifiers.

In this chapter, you discover many of the most common signal processors used in recording studios. (*Signal processors* are the neat hardware behind all the effects you can achieve in a recording studio.) You discern the difference between insert (line) and send/return effects, dynamics processors, and effects processors. You also get a chance to explore ways of using these processors, with recommendations for using reverb, delay, chorus, pitch shifting, compression, noise gates, and expanders.

All effects have presets. *Presets* are factory settings that enable you to dive right into using the effects processor without having to know how each parameter works. Presets are a good place to start when you're not really sure how to get the sound that you want. Most presets are named, and the name may give you a hint about where you may use it. For example, a reverb with a preset called *vocal plate* lets you know that it may be worth trying on vocals. After you choose a preset, don't be afraid to tweak it a little to get the sound you're after. Most decent effects processors allow you to save any changes that you make to the preset.

The best way to discover how to use effects on your music is to experiment. The more you play around with the different settings, the more familiar you'll become with how each effect operates. Then you can get creative and come up with the best ways of using effects for your music.

The *Bypass* button on your effects processor is your friend. With a press of this button, you can quickly turn off the effect to your signal. Use it to check your effect settings against your original signal. Sometimes you'll like the original sound better.

Connecting Effects

For an effects processor to work on your sound source, you need to connect the processor properly. Regardless of the type of signal processor or recording system you're using, you have the option of connecting your processor directly into the channel strip (called a *line* or *insert* effect) or routing it through your aux bus (a *send/return* effect).

Insert

Insert (line) effects are placed in the signal path so that all the instrument's sound passes through the effect, as shown in Figure 15-1. Line effects alter the entire signal of the instrument and don't allow you to mix the amount of effect that you have with the original dry (unaffected) signal at the mixer. (Some insert effects allow you to adjust the balance of dry and affected signal using a Mix dial.) Line effects are generally dynamics processors like compression or gates, which are great for evening out signal levels and getting rid of noise on your tracks, but they can also be the useful new effects, such as amp or microphone simulators, that are available to the home recordist.

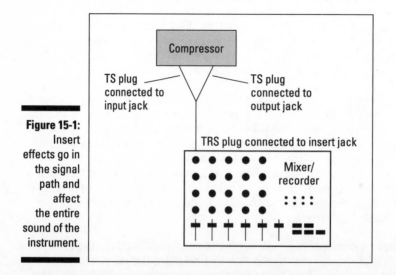

Figure 15-1:
Insert effects go in the signal path and affect the entire sound of the instrument.

Send/return

Send/return effects, such as reverb, delay, chorus, and flange, allow you to mix both the affected and unaffected sound separately. The send/return effect is connected to the aux bus in your mixer (through the aux jack), as shown in Figure 15-2, and as a result, you can adjust both the dry signal and the affected signal separately. This enables you to do the following things that you can't do with a line effect:

✔ Run as many instruments through the same processor as you want. For example, you can have your snare drum, kick drum, bass guitar, and backup vocals all run through the same reverb.

✔ Have as much or as little of the affected sound in your music as you want. This can be an advantage if you want just a little reverb on your vocal track, for instance.

✔ Pan the dry signal to one side of the mix and the affected signal to the other side. This can add depth to an instrument and can be used for a variety of cool effects.

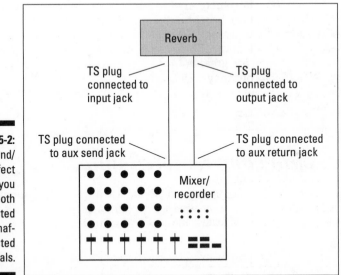

Figure 15-2:
A send/
return effect
allows you
to have both
affected
and unaf-
fected
signals.

Dynamics Processors

Dynamics processors allow you to control the dynamic range of a signal. The *dynamic range* is the difference between the softest and loudest signals that a sound source produces. This range is listed in decibels (dB). The larger the dynamic range, the more variation between the softest and loudest notes.

The three types of dynamics processors are *compressor/limiters, gates,* and *expanders.* The following sections give you the lowdown on each item, but suffice it to say that, with the help of dynamics processors, you can do a number of important things to your music. You can add punch or smooth out an instrument's sound, you can eliminate noise from a track, or you can even out an erratic performance.

Figure 15-3 shows the dynamics processors section of a popular computer-based recording program. Although each dynamics process works a little differently, they all use some of the same controls. In this figure, you use the sliders in the middle of the window to control the different parameters for the processor. The upper section's level meters show you how much processing of the dynamic range that you're doing.

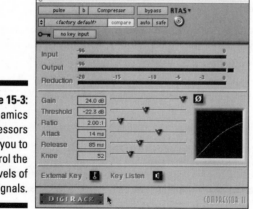

Figure 15-3:
Dynamics
processors
allow you to
control the
levels of
your signals.

Introducing compressors/limiters

The compressor's job is to compress the dynamic range of the sound being affected. The compressor not only limits how loud a note can be, but it also reduces the difference between the loudest and softest notes (it compresses the dynamic range).

The limiter works much like the compressor except it limits the highest level of a sound source. Any signal above the threshold is chopped off rather than compressed, as with the compressor.

Compressor/limiters are used for the following three main purposes (although other purposes certainly exist as well):

✔ **To keep transients from creating digital distortion during tracking:** This is common with drums that have a very fast attack (initial signal) that can easily overload the recorder (or converters or preamps).

✔ **To even out a performance that shows a high degree of unwanted dynamic variation:** You do this during either the mixing or tracking stage. An example is a singer who has poor mic control (moves constantly in front of the mic), and as a result, some recorded passages become loud while others are very quiet.

✔ **To raise the overall apparent level of the music during mastering:** For example, listen to a CD recorded ten years ago and one from the last year or so, and you'll notice that the newer CD sounds louder than the older one.

I cover purpose 1 in Chapter 7, and I explore purpose 3 in Chapter 16. So that leaves purpose 2 to explore with sample settings later in this chapter.

In Chapter 7, I explain the purpose of the various parameters of a compressor, but to keep you from having to flip through the book to find that information, I present those parameters here as well:

✔ **Threshold:** The threshold setting dictates the level that the compressor starts to act on the signal. This is listed in dB (decibels). This setting is often listed as dB below peak (0dB). In other words, a setting of –6dB means that the compressor starts to act when the signal is 6 decibels below its calibrated 0dB mark. (In digital systems, 0dB is the highest level a signal can go before clipping.)

✔ **Ratio:** The ratio is the amount that the compressor affects the signal. The ratio, such as 2:1 for instance, means that for every decibel that the signal goes over the threshold setting, the signal is reduced by a factor of 2. In other words, if a signal goes 1dB over the threshold setting, its output from the compressor is only ½dB louder. With ratios above 10:1, your compressor starts to act like a limiter.

✔ **Attack:** The attack knob controls how soon the compressor kicks in. The attack is defined in milliseconds (ms), and the lower the number, the faster the attack.

✔ **Release:** The release parameter controls how long the compressor continues affecting the signal after it has dropped back below the threshold setting. Like the attack, the release is defined in milliseconds. The lower the number, the faster the release time.

✔ **Gain:** The gain knob allows you to adjust the level (volume) of the signal going out of the compressor. This is listed in decibels. Because adding compression generally reduces the overall level of the sound, you use this control to raise the level back to where it was going in.

✔ **Hard knee or soft knee:** Most compressors give you the option of choosing between a *hard knee* and a *soft knee* (or they do it for you based on the setting that you've chosen). Hard knee and soft knee refer to how the compressor behaves as the input signal passes the threshold. They are defined as follows:

- **Hard knee** applies the compression at an even rate regardless of the level present over the threshold. So if you choose a compression setting of 4:1, the compressor applies this ratio for any signal over the threshold limit. Hard knee compression is used for instruments like drums, where you need to clamp down on any transients quickly.

- **Soft knee,** by contrast, applies the compression at a varying rate, depending on the amount the signal is over the threshold setting. A soft knee setting gradually increases the ratio of the compression as the signal crosses the threshold until it hits the level that you set. Soft knee compression is used on vocals and other instruments where the signal doesn't have fast peaks.

Some two-channel compressors have a link function that allows you to connect the two separate channels and control them from one set of controls. Having the two channels linked ensures that you end up with the same settings on both channels. This is useful when you want to compress a stereo signal.

Some compressors have a *sidechain jack* located on the back panel. This jack allows you to insert an equalizer into the signal path of the compressor (you use a Y cord). The sidechain option is used to "de-ess" vocals (get rid of the nasty *s* sounds of sibilance).

Multiband compression

Multiband compressors allow you to designate the frequency range that you want to compress. Most multiband compressors have three or four bands. The four-band versions have low, low-mid, high-mid, and high band versions. The three-band versions have low, mid, and high band versions. You often get to choose where your frequency ranges are.

Multiband compressors are used most often during the mastering process, but they can be handy on individual tracks as well. The main advantage of these types of compressors is that you can compress a specific frequency range without affecting the sound of the rest of the track. This can be helpful if you have an instrument that's either buried or is overpowering a mix. You just add a little (or a lot) of compression to the bass, for example, to bring it up in the mix, without affecting the higher-frequency instruments.

Getting started using compression

The compressor is one of the most useful — and one of the most abused — pieces of gear in the recording studio. The most difficult part of using compression is that every instrument reacts differently to the same settings. So, instead of presenting specific settings for you to use, I offer you some guidelines and ideas for using the compressor effectively. (You can find sample settings and more ideas in the "Sampling some compression settings" section, later in this chapter.)

The following steps show you one good way to get familiar with the compressor:

1. **Dial in a high setting (an 8:1 to a 10:1 ratio), and set the threshold all the way up by turning the dial fully to the right.**

2. **Slowly turn down the threshold, watch the meters, and listen carefully.**

   As you dial the threshold down, notice where the meters are when you start hearing a change in the sound of the track. Also notice what happens to the sound when you have the threshold really low and the meters are peaked (the sound is very different from where you started).

3. **Slowly dial the threshold back up again, and notice how the sound changes back again.**

After you get used to how the sound changes as you adjust the threshold, try using different attack and release settings and do this procedure again. The more you experiment and critically listen to the changes made by the different compressor settings, the better you'll be able to understand how to get the sound that you want. The following guidelines can also help you get the sound you want:

✔ **Try to avoid using compression on your 2-track mix while you mix your music.** This is the job for the mastering phase of your project. If you compress your stereo tracks during mixdown, you limit what can be done to your music in the mastering stage. This is true even if you master it yourself and think you know what you want during mixdown.

✔ **If you hear noise when you use your compressor, you've set it too high.** You're compressing the loud portions enough to make the level of the softest sections of the music (including any noise) much louder in comparison. To get rid of the noise, turn down the ratio or the threshold settings.

✔ **To increase the punch of a track, make sure that the attack setting isn't too quick.** Otherwise, you lose the initial transient and the punch of a track.

> ✔ **To smooth out a track, use a short attack setting and a quick release time.** This evens out the difference in level between the initial transient and the body of the instrument and results in a smoother sound.
>
> ✔ **When using limiting to raise the volume of a track or mix, only limit 2 to 3dB at a time.** This way, the limiter doesn't alter the sound of your signal; it just reduces the highest peaks and raises the volume.

Less is more when using compression. Resist the temptation to dial too much in — it just squashes your music. On the other hand, if that's an effect that you're going for, don't be afraid to experiment.

Sampling some compression settings

Because compressors are used and abused so frequently, I thought it may be helpful for you to have some basic settings to get you started. This will hopefully save you the headache of ruining a few tracks before you get the hang of this powerful tool.

Lead vocals

Some recording engineers think compression is a must for vocals. It evens out the often erratic levels that a singer can produce and tames transients that can cause digital distortion. You can use compression on vocals to just even out the performance and to create an effect.

If you use a compressor to even out a vocal performance, you don't want to hear the compressor working. Instead, you just want to catch the occasional extremely loud transient that would cause clipping. A good compression setting has a fast attack to catch the stray transient, a quick release so that the compression doesn't color the sound of the singer, and a low ratio so that when the compressor does go on, it smoothes out the vocals without squashing them. Typical settings may look like this:

> **Threshold:** –8dB
>
> **Ratio:** 1.5:1 to 2:1
>
> **Attack:** <1 ms
>
> **Release:** About 40 ms
>
> **Gain:** Adjust so that the output level matches the input level. You don't need much added gain.

If you want to use a compressor that pumps and breathes — that is, one that you can really hear working — or if you want to bring the vocals way up front in the mix, try using the following settings. These settings put the vocals "in your face," as recording engineers say:

Threshold: −2dB

Ratio: 4:1 to 6:1

Attack: <1 ms

Release: About 40 ms

Gain: Adjust so that the output level matches the input level. You need to add a fair amount of gain at this setting.

As you can see, the two parameters that you adjust the most are the threshold and ratio. Experiment with these settings and check the effects of them by toggling between the affected and unaffected sound (use the Bypass switch on your compressor).

Backup vocals

What about compressor settings for backup vocals, you may ask? I recommend a setting that's midway between the invisible compressions and the pumping and breathing compressions that I describe in the previous section. Such a setting brings your background vocals forward slightly. Your settings may look like this:

Threshold: −4dB

Ratio: 2:1 to 3:1

Attack: <1 ms

Release: About 40 ms

Gain: Adjust so that the output level matches the input level. You don't need to add too much gain.

Electric guitar

Generally, electric guitar sounds are pretty compressed. You don't need additional compression when you track the guitar unless you use a clean (undistorted) setting on your guitar. If you want to use a little compression to bring the guitar forward and give it some punch, try these settings:

Threshold: −1dB

Ratio: 2:1 to 3:1

Attack: 25 to 30 ms

Release: About 200 ms

Gain: Adjust so that the output level matches the input level. You don't need much added gain.

The slow attack is what gives the guitar a bit of punch. If you want less punchiness, just shorten the attack slightly. Be careful though, because if you shorten it too much, you end up with a mushy sound. (Sorry . . . ahem . . . the guitar has no definition.)

Electric bass

Another way to get a handle on the potential muddiness of the amplified bass guitar is to use a little compression. Compression can also help control uneven levels that result from overzealous or inexperienced bass players. Try these settings for a start:

Threshold: –4dB

Ratio: 2.5:1 to 3:1

Attack: 40 to 50 ms

Release: About 180 ms

Gain: Adjust so that the output level matches the input level. You don't need much added gain.

When using compression on bass, make sure that your attack setting isn't too short or the sound becomes muddy.

Strummed or picked acoustic stringed instruments

You don't generally need a lot of compression on acoustic stringed instruments, especially if you want a natural sound. You can use the compressor to even out the resonance of the instrument to keep the main character of the instrument from getting lost in a mix and to avoid a muddy sound. These are good settings for strummed or picked acoustic instruments:

Threshold: –6dB

Ratio: 3:1 to 4:1

Attack: Around 150 ms

Release: About 400 ms

Gain: Adjust so that the output level matches the input level. You don't need much added gain.

The release is set very high because of the amount of sustain that these acoustic instruments can have. If you play an instrument with less sustain, like a banjo, you may find that a shorter attack and release work just fine. In this case, try the following settings:

Threshold: –6dB

Ratio: 2.5:1 to 3:1

Attack: 40 to 50 ms

Release: About 180 ms

Gain: Adjust so that the output level matches the input level. You don't need much, if any, added gain.

Horns

It's rare that I use a compressor on horns. The only time I may use one is if an unnatural variation exists in levels due to poor playing (although I usually prefer to ride the faders to even the levels instead of trying to fix the problem with compression). Still, if I were to use a compressor, I would start with these settings:

Threshold: –8dB

Ratio: 2.5:1 to 3:1

Attack: Around 100 ms

Release: About 300 ms

Gain: Adjust so that the output level matches the input level. You don't need much added gain.

Piano

As with other acoustic instruments, I don't often use compression on a piano unless I'm going for a specific effect or I want to even out an erratic performance. Settings for effect can run the gamut; just dial in some settings and see what you get. Using compression to even an erratic piano performance takes a little more finesse. In this case, start with these mild settings:

Threshold: –10dB

Ratio: 1.5:1 to 2:1

Attack: 100 to 105 ms

Release: About 115 ms

Gain: Adjust so that the output level matches the input level. You don't need much, if any, added gain.

Classical strings

For the most part, adding compression to string instruments played with a bow isn't necessary. However, you will find that using a compressor on a plucked acoustic bass and fiddle can bring them out in a mix.

A starting point for compressor settings for a fiddle would be as follows:

Threshold: –4dB

Ratio: 2:1 to 3:1

Attack: 40 to 50 ms

Release: About 100 ms

Gain: Adjust so that the output level matches the input level. You don't need much, if any, added gain.

Try these settings for the acoustic bass:

Threshold: –6dB

Ratio: 5:1 to 8:1

Attack: 40 to 50 ms

Release: About 200 ms

Gain: Adjust so that the output level matches the input level. You need a bit of added gain here.

Kick drum

The kick drum responds well to a compressor when tracking. For the most part, you can get by with settings that allow the initial attack to get through and that tame the boom a little. Sample settings would look like this:

Threshold: –6dB

Ratio: 4:1 to 6:1

Attack: 40 to 50 ms

Release: 200 to 300 ms

Gain: Adjust so that the output level matches the input level. You don't need much added gain.

Snare drum

Adding compression to the snare drum is crucial if you want a tight, punchy sound. You have a lot of choices with the snare. The following settings are common and versatile:

Threshold: −4dB

Ratio: 4:1 to 6:1

Attack: 5 to 10 ms

Release: 125 to 175 ms

Gain: Adjust so that the output level matches the input level. You don't need much added gain.

Hand drums

Compression is usually a good idea with hand drums because the drum can produce unpredictable transients. For most hand drums, start with the following settings:

Threshold: −6dB

Ratio: 3:1 to 6:1

Attack: 10 to 25 ms

Release: 100 to 300 ms

Gain: Adjust so that the output level matches the input level. You don't need much added gain.

Percussion

Because percussion instruments have high sound levels and are prone to extreme transients, I often like to use a little compression just to keep these transients from eating up headroom in the mix. Here are good starting points:

Threshold: −10dB

Ratio: 3:1 to 6:1

Attack: 10 to 20 ms

Release: About 50 ms

Gain: Adjust so that the output level matches the input level. You need a bit of added gain here.

Introducing gates

A *gate* is basically the opposite of the limiter. Rather than limiting how loud a note can get, the gate limits how soft a note can get. The gate filters out sound below the threshold while allowing notes above it to be passed through unaffected.

Gates are useful to filter out unwanted noise that may be present in the recording environment. A classic place to use gates is when you record drums. You can set the gate to filter any sound (other drums for instance) except for the sounds resulting from the hits to the particular drum that you have miked.

The following settings are similar to the ones for compressors/limiters:

- **Threshold:** The threshold sets the level (in dB) at which the gate opens (stops filtering the signal). The gate allows all signals above the threshold setting to be passed through unaffected, whereas signals below the threshold setting are reduced by the amount set by the range control.

- **Attack:** Like with the compressor/limiter, the attack time sets the rate at which the gate opens (in milliseconds). Fast attacks work well for instruments with, well, fast attacks, such as drums, whereas slow attacks are better suited for instruments with slow attacks, like vocals.

  For the most part, try to match the gate's attack time with that of the instrument you're gating. If you don't do this well, you may hear a click when the signal crosses the gate's threshold. This is generally a result of having the attack set too slow for the instrument. Adjust the attack time until this click goes away.

- **Hold:** The hold setting controls the amount of time that the gate stays open after the signal drops below the threshold. After the hold time is reached, the gate closes abruptly. This parameter is listed in milliseconds (ms). The hold parameter allows you to get the gated drum sound that was so popular in the 1980s (Phil Collins, anyone?).

- **Release:** The release setting dictates the rate at which the gate closes after the signal hits the threshold (listed in milliseconds). Unlike the hold feature, the release setting doesn't close abruptly; rather, it slowly closes (according to the release setting). This produces a more natural sound. You should set the release time so that it matches the natural decay time of the instrument. Otherwise, you can get a clipped-off sound. (If you want the clipped-off sound, use the Hold feature.)

- **Range:** The range is similar to the ratio setting on the compressor except you choose the amount (in dB) that you want the signal to be attenuated (reduced) by the gate. For example, a setting of 40dB drops signals below the threshold setting by 40 decibels.

Getting started using gates

Noise gates can be extremely useful in getting rid of unwanted noise. The most common use for a gate is to eliminate bleeding from drum mics. For example, you may get bleed from your snare drum into your tom-toms mics. When using noise gates, keep the following tips in mind:

✔ When the threshold is reached, the gate allows the signal through. If your background noise is high enough, when the gate opens, you still hear not only the intended sound but also the background noise. This can be a problem if you're using gates to eliminate the noise of your hard drive fan or other room noise. Your best bet is to use acoustic panels to eliminate the noise rather to use than gates.

✔ When gating drums, be sure to set the attack very fast. Otherwise, the initial transient is lost, and you end up with mushy-sounding drums.

✔ Take your time setting the release time of the gate so that it sounds natural and doesn't clip the end of your instrument's sound.

✔ Only set the range high enough to mask unwanted noise. If you set it too high, the sound becomes unnatural because the natural resonance of the instrument may be filtered out.

Introducing expanders

The *expander* is to the gate what a compressor is to a limiter — instead of reducing the volume of notes below the set threshold by a specified amount, the expander reduces them by a ratio. In other words, with the gate, you set a certain amount, in dB, that a signal is reduced, and with the expander, you reduce the signal by setting a ratio. The ratio changes the signal gradually, making the affected signals sound more natural.

You use an expander when you want to subtly reduce noise from a track, rather than just filtering it out completely. A classic example is when dealing with the breath sounds from a singer. If you use a gate, you get an unnatural-sounding track because the breaths are filtered out completely. However, you can set the expander to reduce the breath sounds just enough to be not so noticeable, but you can leave a little of the sound in so that the singer sounds normal. (Everyone has to breathe, right?)

Again, the following settings sound familiar from my previous discussion of compressors and gates:

✔ **Threshold:** The threshold in an expander works the same way as with the gate — anything below the threshold is affected and signals above the threshold pass unaffected.

✔ **Ratio:** The ratio dictates how much the signal is attenuated by the expander. When using a ratio of 2:1, for instance, the expander reduces signals below the threshold by a factor of 2. In this case, a signal that is 10dB below the threshold is reduced to 20dB below it; likewise, a signal that's 2dB below the threshold would be reduced to 4dB below it.

Getting started using an expander

Because the expander works much like a gate, you can use the same basic starting points. Choose the gate or expander based on the type of overall attenuation of the signal you want. For example, the expander is a good choice if you have an instrument that contains sounds that are too loud but you don't want to get rid of them completely (you just want to reduce them a little).

A vocalist's breath is the perfect situation for using an expander over a gate. In this case, you can set the expander's threshold just below the singer's softest note and start with a low ratio (1.5:1 or 2:1, for instance). See whether the breath sounds improve, and if they don't, slowly dial up the ratio until you get the effect that you want. Be careful not to overdo it though. If the breath sound drops too far away from the vocal, the vocal sounds unnatural.

If you use a high ratio in your expander (6:1 or above), the effect you get is similar in sound to that of the gate, only you end up having less control of the sound because you don't have the hold or release parameters to adjust. So, if you have to use a high ratio on a signal, a gate may be a better choice for that situation.

Effects Processors

Effects processors can be used as either send/return or insert effects. In both cases, you can work with both the dry (unaffected) signal and the wet (affected) signal separately. If you use the effect in a send/return routing, you can adjust the wet and dry signals with the Aux Send and Aux Return knobs. If you use the effect in a line configuration, the effect has a Mix parameter on it, where you can adjust the wet/dry balance. Because most people record in a studio with a fairly dead environment, acoustically speaking, effects are necessary to make the music sound more natural. The purpose of effects processors is to mimic real-world situations or to add a supernatural feel to the music.

You have quite a few choices in effects processors, and many more show up every year. The most common effects processors are reverb, delay, chorus, flange, and pitch shifting, all of which I detail in the following sections.

Introducing reverb

Reverb is undoubtedly the most commonly used effects processor. Reverb is a natural characteristic of any enclosed room and is the result of sound waves bouncing off the walls, floor, and ceiling. A small room produces reflections that start quickly and end soon, whereas larger rooms, halls, or cathedrals have slower start times and the reflections last longer.

This room effect enables you to place your track from front to back in the mix. You do this by varying how much of the affected signal you include with the unaffected one. For example, mixing a lot of reverb with the dry signal gives the impression of being farther away, so your instrument sounds like it's in back in the mix.

You can adjust several parameters when using reverb, which gives you a lot of flexibility. Check out Figure 15-4. This shows what the reverb processor looks like in a popular computer-based system.

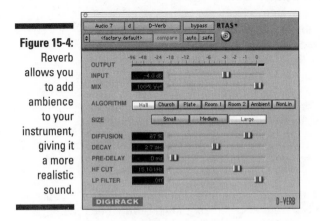

Figure 15-4: Reverb allows you to add ambience to your instrument, giving it a more realistic sound.

The following list explains how the parameters, most of which you can see in Figure 15-4, affect the sound of the reverb:

- ✔ **Algorithm:** Whether you use a reverb patch within your recording system or a separate outboard reverb unit, you can choose the type of reverb that you want to use. You have the option of a room, hall, or plate (a type of reverb that uses a metal plate to create its sound). In addition, you can choose the size of the room (in this case small, medium, and large).

- ✔ **Decay:** The *decay* is the length of time that the reverb lasts. Larger or more reflective rooms produce a longer decay.

- ✔ **Predelay:** A sound reaches your ears before the sound's reverb does, and the *predelay* is the amount of time from the sound's beginning and the start of the reverb, which is described in milliseconds (ms). Because reverb is made up of reflections of sound within a room, the sound takes time to bounce around the room and reach your ears. By then, you've already heard the sound because it came directly to you. Predelay helps to define the initial sound signal by separating it from the reverb. This parameter is essential in making your reverb sound natural.

  A small room has a shorter predelay than a large room. Predelay times generally range between 10 and 50 ms.

✔ **Density:** The density parameter (not shown in the reverb plug-in in Figure 15-4) controls the level of the early reflections (the first few milliseconds of the reverb sound). Because the early reflections take less time to reach your ear than the main body of the reverb, you hear a thinner reverb sound to begin with, followed by the main reverb. The density parameter enables you to simulate different room sizes because the main section of a reverb takes longer to reach you in a larger room. The higher the density setting, the larger the apparent room size. Not all reverbs have this setting.

Some reverb processors don't have a density setting (as is the case for the processor shown in Figure 15-4). In such a case, this parameter is usually factory set and varies based on the type and size of room parameters that you choose.

✔ **Diffusion:** Diffusion affects the density of the reflections in the main section of the reverb sound. A higher diffusion setting results in a thicker sound. Think of the diffusion parameter as a way to simulate how reflective the room is. More reflective rooms produce a much higher diffusion. To simulate a less reflective room, use lower diffusion settings.

Like the density setting, some reverbs don't have a diffusion parameter; instead, it's factory set and depends on the room type/size parameter that you choose.

✔ **Hi Cut and Low Cut filters:** These filters allow you to control the rate at which the high and low frequencies decay. Most of the time the high frequencies decay faster, so being able to control this effect can result in a more natural-sounding reverb.

Getting started using reverb

Reverb is like garlic: The more you use, the less you can taste it. Just as the new chef puts garlic in everything (and lots of it), many budding sound engineers make the same mistake with reverb. Go easy. *Remember:* Less is more.

Here are some other points to keep in mind:

✔ **Mixes often sound better when you use reverb on only a few instruments instead of them all.** For example, it's common for just the snare drum of the drum set to have reverb on it. The rest of the drums and cymbals remain dry (unaffected).

✔ **Think about how you want each instrument to sit in the mix when you choose reverb.** Make sure that the type and amount of reverb fit the song and the rest of the instruments.

✔ **Try putting the dry sound on one side of the stereo field and the reverb on the other.** For example, if you have a rhythm guitar part that you set at 30 degrees off to the right of the stereo field, set the reverb 30 degrees off to the left. This can produce a nice effect.

✔ **To keep the vocals up front in the mix, use a short reverb setting.** A vocal plate is a great choice because the decay is fast. This adds a fair amount of the reverb to the vocal without making it sit way back in the mix.

✔ **Experiment with room types, sizes, and decay times.** Sometimes a long decay on a small-room reverb sounds better than a short decay on a large-room or hall reverb.

Introducing delay

Along with reverb, delay is a natural part of sound that bounces around a room. When you speak (or sing or play) in a room, you often hear not only reverb but also a distinct echo. This echo may be short or long depending on the size of the room. The original sound may bounce back to you as a single echo or as multiple, progressively quieter delays.

Several types of delay effects exist, including a slap-back echo, tape delay, and multiple delays, and each of them is designed to add dimension to your instrument. To create these various effects, you adjust several parameters, as the following list and Figure 15-5 make clear. Different delay processors have different parameters, but the three most universal and useful parameters are time, feedback, and mix/effect level, as follows:

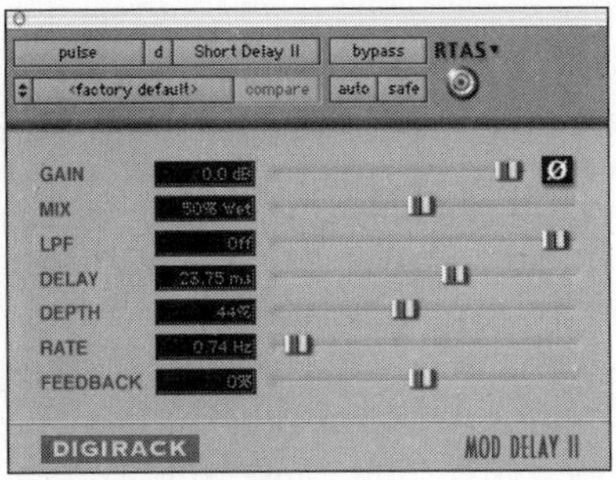

Figure 15-5:
A delay effect processor allows you to create various echoes.

✔ **Gain:** This lets you set the signal level going into the delay.

✔ **Mix:** This parameter controls the output level of the effect. The higher you set this parameter, the louder the delayed signal is relative to the original signal.

✔ **LPF:** The low-pass filter (LPF) lets you filter out some of the high frequencies from the delay.

- **Delay:** This parameter controls the amount of time between the initial signal and the repeated sound. The time is listed in milliseconds (ms) and can be as short as a few milliseconds or as long as several seconds.

- **Depth:** This parameter lets you add modulation to the delay so that you can create a chorus effect. (See the "Getting started chorusing" section, later in this chapter, for more on chorus and flange effects). The higher the level on this setting, the greater the modulation.

- **Rate:** This setting lets you adjust the amount of time that the modulation takes to go one time through its cycle.

- **Feedback:** The Feedback parameter controls how many times the echo repeats. A low setting makes the echo happen just once, and higher settings produce more echoes.

Getting started using delay

Delay is used a lot in contemporary music, and many times you don't hear it unless you listen carefully. Other times, it is prominent in the mix, like the snare drum in some reggae music. Here are ways that you can use delay in your music:

- **Use delay as a slap-back echo on vocals.** A *slap-back echo* consists of one to three repeats spaced very closely together, which fattens the sound of the vocals. You generally want to set your time parameter between 90 and 120 milliseconds. Set the level so that you barely hear the first echo when your vocal is in the mix and adjust it from there until you like the sound. In pop music, a slap-back echo and a vocal plate reverb are commonly used on lead vocals (it was really common in the 1950s).

- **Use the tempo match feature to have your delay echo in time with the music.** This can add some depth to the mix without creating a muddy or cluttered sound. Be careful, because if you use this too much, it can make your music sound annoyingly repetitive.

- **To create special effects with delay, try using the pan or shift controls to move your instruments in the mix.** This can be a lot of fun on background instruments, such as rhythm guitar and synthesizers.

Introducing pitch shifting

Pitch shifting allows you to change the pitch of a recorded instrument. This gives you a number of different options when you mix. For example, you can run your backup vocals through a pitch-shifting device to make them sound fuller. Or you can create backup vocals from the lead vocal track by *multing* (making a copy and putting it on another track or two) the lead vocal and subjecting it to a pitch shifter.

Using a pitch shifter is pretty easy: Open the program and choose how much you want to change the pitch either up or down. To use the pitch shifter to fill out a vocal, just change the pitch (up or down — it doesn't matter) a few semitones until you like the sound. You can either create a subtle effect that sounds like two or more people trying to sing the same pitch, or you can create harmonies by changing the pitch one or more steps.

Chorus

Chorus takes the original sound and creates a copy that is slightly out of tune with the original. Unlike the pitch shifter — an effect that remains constant — the chorus's shifted pitch varies over time. This variance is called *modulation,* and the result is an effect that can add interest and variety to an instrument. Chorus is used extensively to add fullness to a sound, particularly guitars and vocals.

Most chorus effects give you several parameters with which to work, as the following list makes clear:

- ✔ **Rate:** The rate dictates how fast the modulation happens. This parameter is described as a frequency (usually 0.1 to 10 Hz). The frequency actually doesn't refer to a pitch; rather, it describes how many times per second (Hz) the oscillation happens. The oscillation is controlled by the depth parameter.

- ✔ **Depth:** The depth parameter controls the amount of pitch modulation that's produced by the chorus. The settings are often arbitrary (you can get a range of 1 to 100). This range relates to a percentage of the maximum depth to which the particular chorus can go, rather than an actual level.

- ✔ **Predelay:** The predelay setting affects how far out of time the chorus's sound is in relation to the original. This setting is listed in milliseconds, and the lower the number, the closer the chorused sound is to the original in time.

- ✔ **Feedback:** The feedback control sends the affected sound from the chorus back in again. This allows you to extend the amount of chorusing that the effect creates. This setting can also be called *stages* in some systems.

- ✔ **Effect Level:** This could also be called *mix* in some systems. The effect level controls how much effect is sent to the aux return bus. This allows you to adjust how affected the sound becomes.

Getting started chorusing

If reverb is like garlic, chorus is like cayenne pepper. You may get away with adding a little too much garlic in your food, but if you add too much cayenne, you run the risk of making your food inedible. Such is the case with the chorus effect. Used sparingly, chorus can add a lot to your music, but if it's overdone, it can wreak havoc on a good song. Here are some tips for using this effect:

- ✔ To fill out a vocal track, try setting the rate at 2 Hz, the depth at about 20 to 30, and the predelay at 10 to 20 ms. Keep the feedback level low.

- ✔ Use a chorus on backup vocals to make them fuller and allow you to use fewer tracks.

- ✔ Pan the chorus to one side of the mix and the dry (unaffected) signal to the other. This can be especially interesting on guitars and synthesizer patches.

Along with chorus, your system may have other modulating effects, such as flange and phase shifting. These two effects work much like chorus, except they alter the original signal in time (flange) and in sound-wave position (phase shifting) rather than pitch. The parameters you have for such effects are similar to those that you find for chorus effects. You can use the flange and phase shifters in many of the same applications as the chorus if you're going for a different effect.

Simulating Effects

Recently, effects have emerged that allow you to alter your original signal so that it sounds like it was recorded using a different technique or source. These are simulator effects, and the two most common are microphone and amplifier simulators (modelers). Both of these effects are intended to be line effects, but on some systems, you can use them as send/return effects to create interesting, well, effects.

Microphone simulator

As its name suggests, the mic simulator alters your signal to make it sound like it was recorded through a different microphone than the one you used (obviously). The great thing about the mic simulator effect is that you can have a bunch of microphone sounds available to you without buying a bunch of expensive mics.

The only real drawback to mic simulator programs is that they don't sound exactly like the mics that they're trying to model. I mean, making a $100 dynamic mic sound like a $3,000 large-diaphragm condenser mic is pretty hard, no matter how much computer processing you do. But this is no big deal, because all you're trying to do with a mic simulator is to expand the options that you have with a given mic. So even though the modeler can't exactly match the bigger-buck mic, it can provide a pretty decent sound for your inexpensive mic.

The other possible drawback to using a mic simulator program is that the mic that you used to record the part in the first place may have an impact on how well the simulator sounds. Most mic simulator programs designate which mic was used to model the initial sound and which mic the simulator is trying to sound like. For example, in the Roland V-Studios, as you scroll through the various mic simulator patches (effects), you see them listed with one mic name followed by another ("SM57 – U87," for instance). If you want to get a sound like the second mic listed, you need to use the first mic listed.

If you use a different mic than the one listed first, you get a different sound, but this isn't necessarily a bad thing; it's just different.

Amp simulator

The amp simulator effect allows you to essentially have access to a whole roomful of top-notch amps without having to buy, maintain, or store them. One of the great things about amp simulators is that they allow you to plug your guitar directly into your mixer (or direct box), and you can eliminate a lot of noise that miking your guitar amp can cause. You also get to choose the sound that you ultimately want after you've recorded your part. This gives you more flexibility during mixdown.

The downside to amp simulators, as with mic simulators, is that they may not sound exactly like the amp they're trying to model, but this shouldn't matter as long as you get the sound that you want. Another downside is that amp simulators use processing power, and if you have a ton of tracks with a bunch of effects and other plug-ins, you may find your computer getting bogged down a bit. The remedy for this is to print (record) the effect onto a separate track before you mix the song. This frees power for other uses.

Chapter 16

Mastering Your Music

*Y*ou've spent a lot of time getting all your tracks recorded using the best mics that you can afford (mics you've carefully set up following the guidelines in Chapter 9, I hope!). You adjusted your levels just right, EQed, panned, and added effects to each instrument with great care so that they fit perfectly in the mix. Now you have awesome-sounding music. So all that's left is to burn a CD, create cool cover artwork, and make some copies — and you're ready to go platinum, right?

Well, you could do that, but you would be missing one of the most important steps in getting your music to sound its very best. This is the mastering process. Mastering can turn your already-good music into a truly great CD. The only problem is that most people have no idea what mastering is. It's been presented as some mysterious voodoo that only people who belong to some secret society and have access to a magical pile of gear can do.

This isn't the case. Mastering is, in fact, a pretty simple process that involves pieces of equipment that you've already used. Mastering does require specialized skills, but you don't need to go through strange initiation rites to understand them. All it takes is an idea of what to do, decent ears (you've got a couple of those, right?), and a dose of patience while you work your way through the process.

In this chapter, you get a chance to understand the "magic" that is mastering. You discover what's involved in mastering your music. You explore ways to master your music yourself and discern when it may be best to find a professional to do the job for you. You also discover how to burn your mastered music to CD and to make copies of your finished music.

Demystifying Mastering

The mastering process of recording involves preparing your music for dupli-cation. Several steps are involved in taking your songs from individual, mixed tunes to part of a whole album. First, you need to optimize the dynamics and tonal balance of each song, and then you need to process the songs so that they are matched in volume to each other. These steps usually involve doing some EQing, compressing, limiting, and sometimes expanding to the songs.

You also need to sequence your music so that you have the songs in the best possible order and you have the appropriate amount of time between each song. Your last step is to put your mastered music onto a format that enables you to duplicate it. (This is usually a CD. I describe this process in detail in the "Getting into CD Burning" section, later in this chapter.)

Processing

No matter how well you recorded and mixed your music, you still need to do some processing during the mastering stage. This usually consists of adjust-ing levels with compression, limiting, and EQing and using additional pro-cessing if necessary.

The purpose of the processing stage is to balance the overall tonal character-istics of each song and optimize the dynamics of each song so that the songs are at their best overall volume. You can achieve these goals by using the fol-lowing tools:

- **Compression:** Some music sounds best when it's smooth, and other music is much better when it has a punchy quality to it. Judicious use of com-pression can produce either of these effects. (I give you some sugges-tions for compressor settings in the section "Optimizing dynamics," later this chapter.) A good mastering engineer knows when and how to make music punchy or smooth. (Sorry, you can't have both at the same time.)

  Adding compression to the mastering process is an art. Too much or the wrong type of compression makes your music sound flat. Too little, and your music may sound weak.

- **Limiters:** If any instruments are too loud in comparison to the rest of the mix, a limiter can tame them so that the difference between the song's peak level and average level is optimal. This difference varies depending on the style of music, but it should never be less than 6dB and is usually between 12dB and 18dB.

- **EQ:** Because you recorded and mixed each of your songs individually over a period of time (often a *long* period of time), each song probably sounds a little different. Some may be brighter than others, some may be heavier on bass, but one thing's for sure — each has a different tonal quality.

For your compilation of songs to work as a unit, the songs' tonal quality needs to be somewhat consistent. The songs don't have to all sound the same, but they do need to work well together. The mastering engineer uses multiband EQs on each song to make them work as separate songs and gel as a complete artistic statement.

Sequencing

Sequencing involves putting your songs in the order that you want and setting the blank space between each song so that the CD flows well from one song to another. Because a CD is supposed to represent a cohesive body of work, this is one of the most important aspects of mastering.

Leveling

A crucial aspect of mastering a CD is getting the levels of all the songs to be the same. After all, you don't want your listener to have to adjust the volume of his stereo from one song to another. Having consistent levels from song to song helps with the cohesiveness and flow of a CD. This is done with simple gain adjustments, compressors, and/or limiters.

Getting Ready to Master

When mastering your music, you can save yourself a ton of time and energy if you keep a few things in mind during the mixing stage. When you're wearing your Mixing Master hat, the following reminders can make the mastering process go a bit more smoothly:

- ✔ **Check your levels.** Listen to your mix quietly and you can tell whether one instrument stands out too much in the mix. Also, burn a CD of your mixed song to test on other systems (your car, a boom box, or your friend's stereo system). Listen carefully. If the bass drum is even slightly too loud, it eats up the headroom of the rest of the instruments, and you can't get the volume of the song very high.

- ✔ **Check your EQ.** Even though the mastering engineer EQs the entire song, make sure that you spend the time getting each instrument EQed as best as you can in the mix. If you don't get your EQ just right during the mixing process and the bass guitar sound, for example, is muddy and needs to be EQed during mastering, you lose some of the low end on all the instruments. This makes your mix sound thin. If your bass is EQed properly in the first place, you don't have to make this adjustment to the entire mix.

✔ **Test your mix in mono (turn off the stereo panning on your master bus).** This helps you hear whether any instrument's volume or tonal characteristics are seriously out of balance with others. I never consider a mix finished until I monitor it in mono.

✔ **Apply compression to your mix before you record the 2-track mix just to see what your music sounds like compressed.** Don't record the compression, though. Leave that for the mastering engineer. By testing your mix with some compression, you may hear whether certain instruments are too loud in the mix because this becomes more apparent when the mix is compressed.

✔ **Listen for phase holes.** *Phase holes* occur when you record an instrument (for example, piano or back-up vocals) in stereo and the two tracks are out of phase. To listen for phase holes, pay attention to how the instrument sounds in the stereo field. You have a phase hole if you hear sound coming only from the far right and far left and nothing seems to be coming from the center of the stereo field. If you have this problem, just reverse the phase on one of the two channels for that instrument.

Even though a lot can be done to your music in the mastering stage, don't rely on mastering to fix problems in your mix. Get your music to sound as good as you can during mixing. If you do this, the mastering engineer has an easier job and can make your music sound even better. If you don't, you're stuck with a bunch of compromises in the mastering stage.

Paying a Pro or Doing It Yourself

Whether to master your music yourself or to hire a professional may be one of your toughest music-making decisions. If you master your music yourself, you can have complete control from start to finish and save yourself some bucks. On the other hand, if you hand your mixed music to a skilled professional, you have the added benefit of another person's ears and advice, and you can end up with a finished product that far exceeds your expectations.

So how do you choose? Well, your first consideration is probably based on economics — do you have the money to spend on professional help (for your music, that is)? Mastering can cost from a couple hundred to thousands of dollars. A midline mastering engineer often charges around $500 to master your CD (about ten songs). This may seem like a lot of money, but if you find the right engineer for your music, it can make the difference between a decent CD and a truly world-class one.

Another consideration for hiring out your mastering is how well you know your equipment and how capable it is of performing the mastering procedure. To do mastering, you need at least one good (well, preferably great) multiband compressor, a limiter, and a great multiband parametric EQ. You also need to have a CD burner of some sort and the software to create a Red Book CD master (more about this in the section "Recording Your Music to CD-R," later in this chapter).

Before you decide, take a look at other benefits of hiring a skilled professional to do your mastering:

✔ **You get a meticulously tuned room and top-notch monitors.** This enables you to hear what your music actually sounds like.

✔ **The professional has equipment that's specifically designed to handle the process of mastering.** The EQs, compressors, and other gear that the mastering house uses can tweak your music so that it can sound its best.

✔ **You get a fresh set of professional ears that may be able to hear things in your mix that need fixing.** You may be so close to the project that you have a hard time hearing your mix objectively. You may not even know what adjustments to make to your music so that it sounds its best.

Hiring a Professional Mastering Engineer

If you decide to use a professional mastering engineer, the following tips can help you choose one for your project:

✔ **Ask around for referrals.** If you know local bands or musicians whose music you like and whose CD sounds great, ask them who mastered their music. Call local studios and find out who they recommend for mastering in your area. Also check out Brad Blackwood's forum at ProSoundWeb.com (recforums.prosoundweb.com/index.php/f/31/0) and Recording.org's mastering forum (www.recording.org/forum-20.html).

✔ **Listen to other recordings that the mastering house has done in a style of music similar to yours.** You're entrusting your artistic vision to someone else, and you need to be sure that this person is the right person for the job. If you like what the prospective mastering engineer has done on other people's music, you'll probably like what he does with yours. On the other hand, if he has never worked with music similar to yours or if you don't like the way he mastered someone else's music, he's probably not the right person for the job.

✔ **Clarify the fee for your project before you start working together.** Most mastering engineers charge by the hour and can give you a pretty good estimate of how many hours they will need to do the job. You'll also be expected to pay for materials (reference CDs, for example).

✔ **If you don't like the way the engineer mastered your music, you'll probably be charged the hourly rate to redo it.** Some engineers may redo your project for free, but don't count on it. Be sure to discuss this possibility before you start the project so that you're not met with an unwanted surprise.

Many mastering engineers can do a demo of one or two of your songs so that you can hear what kind of job they can do to your music before you hire them. Ask whether the mastering engineer you're interested in offers this service. This can save both you and the engineer a lot of time and energy if he or she isn't right for the job. It can also help you determine whether your mixed music is ready for mastering or whether you need to go back and make adjustments.

After you choose the mastering engineer that you think will work well for you and your music, you can make the process much easier and less stressful for both you and the engineer if you follow these guidelines:

✔ **Discuss your expectations and desires.** This is the best way to ensure that your mastered music turns out the way you want. People who are unhappy with the job that the mastering engineer does usually aren't clear about what they want or don't understand what is possible in the mastering process.

✔ **Take a few CDs whose sound you like with you to the mastering session.** Talk with the engineer about how you can get your music to sound similar. A skilled engineer can let you know right away whether the sound you want is possible.

✔ **Try to be present at the mastering session.** Many people send their music to a mastering engineer and expect him or her to do the job without their presence in the studio. Try to go to the studio, but if you can't, be sure that the engineer clearly understands your desires and expectations.

If you're in the studio during the mastering process and things aren't going the way you want, talk with the engineer and try to get things on track again. If you're unable to communicate with the engineer, stop the session, have him burn a *ref* (reference copy), pay for the time that you've used, and listen to the ref at home. If you don't like what you hear at home, you may be better off going somewhere else with your music.

If you're at the mastering session and the mastering engineer insists on working on your music while listening at really loud levels (although occasional checks at high volumes are okay), grab your mix CD and run, don't walk, from the session. This is a true sign of an inexperienced (or incompetent) mastering engineer. Mastering needs to be done at low to moderate levels because the tonal balance of music changes at high volumes.

Mastering Your Music Yourself

If you decide that you just have to do the mastering yourself, or at least you want to try it once before you decide to spend the money on a pro, following some guidelines can increase your chances of mastering success. I describe them in this section.

In other chapters, I present some specific techniques and settings to get you started. Unfortunately, I can't do that when it comes to mastering. There are just too many variables and too many ways to mess up your music when trying to master it. What I can (and do) help you with in the upcoming sections is walk you through the process of mastering and show you the tools to use for each step. When reading these sections, keep the following points in mind:

- ✔ **Less is more when mastering.** Do as little as possible to your music. If you find that you have to make a lot of adjustments, you may want to go back to the mixing process and try again. When you master your music, you only need to optimize the dynamics and tonal balance of each song, get the levels between the songs even, and sequence your songs.

- ✔ **Mastering is all about compromise.** Each adjustment you make to your mixed music affects all the instruments. If you use EQ to get rid of muddiness on the bass guitar, you affect not only the bass guitar but also every other instrument in the mix.

- ✔ **Don't try to master a song right after you mix it.** Give yourself time and space from that song before you do anything. In fact, I recommend that you take a few days away from any of the songs for your album between the mixing and mastering stages. A little time to reflect and rest your ears can do wonders for your ability to hear what your music needs.

- ✔ **You can only master music if your monitors and monitoring environment are great.** Without a good reference for how your music sounds, trying to EQ or dynamically process your music does no good. The music may sound good through your speakers but probably doesn't through others'. Before you master, make your room sound as good as you can and get to know the strengths and weaknesses of your monitoring environment by listening to a ton of commercial CDs that have a sound that you're trying to emulate.

Optimizing dynamics

Okay, this is where the magic in mastering happens. This is where you can make your music shine or where you can royally mess it up. (How's that for adding a little pressure?) Before you get tense (okay, breathe), remember that you can always go back and try again. Oh, did I mention that you should make backup copies of your individual tracks and your final mix? Well, if you haven't already done the backing-up business, now would be a good time to do that. I'll wait.

Are you done? Okay, now to the job at hand — getting your music to be as loud as possible. (I'm just kidding; see the sidebar "Turn it up!") Seriously, optimizing the dynamics of your songs doesn't mean getting it as loud as you can, but rather getting it to have life and emotion. And, yes, this also means getting it to be loud enough to sound good.

The style of your music and the arrangements that you use determine how you optimize the dynamics of your music. For example, classical music has a much broader dynamic range than rock music, and the infamous "wall of sound" type of arrangement has a narrower dynamic range than a song with sparse verses and thicker choruses.

When you're optimizing the dynamics of your music, be sensitive to the song and try not to get sucked into the idea that you need to get the most volume out of your music. I know I'm beating this volume thing into the ground, but you would be surprised how seductive it is to try to get just a few more dB out of the song (no, wait; you'll soon find out).

You have two main tools to use when you work on the dynamics during mastering — a compressor and a limiter — and each has its purpose. For the most part, if you're trying to add punch or smoothness to your music, a compressor does the job nicely. On the other hand, if you're trying to squeeze a little more volume out of a song and you don't want to change the song's sound quality, a limiter is your best choice.

Here are suggestions that can help you to use compression and limiting (also covered in Chapter 15) most effectively during mastering:

- **Use a mild compression ratio (between 1.1:1 and 2:1) to keep from overcompressing your music.**

- **Apply only 1–2dB of compression or limiting at one time.** If you need more than that, chain more than one compressor together and use these small amounts on each. If you compress or limit more than 1 or 2dB at a time, you end up with *artifacts* (audible changes to your music caused by the compressor or limiter).

✔ **Work with your attack and release times.** An attack that's too short takes the punch out of your music by cutting off the initial transients. Likewise, a release time that's too long doesn't recover quickly enough, and the dynamics of the vocals disappear. In contrast, if the release time is too short, you hear distortion.

✔ **Set the threshold so that your compressor's meters dance (bounce) to the rhythm of the music.** Only the loudest notes (snare drum or lead vocal accents, for example) should trigger the meters and then only by 1 or 2 dB.

✔ **Use a multiband compressor to bring out individual instruments in the mix.** For example, if the bass drum seems to be getting lost, you can apply mild compression to the lower frequencies (around 80 to 100 Hz). This brings the instrument forward in the mix slightly.

✔ **When you're not sure that what you're doing sounds better, don't use the processor.** Any dynamics processing is going to affect the quality of your song's sound to some extent. If adding this processing doesn't improve the overall sound, you're better off not using it.

A song without a significant difference between its softest and loudest notes quickly becomes tiring to listen to. Always keep the difference between the average level and the peak level greater than 6dB. In fact, try to have a peak-to-average ratio of 12 to 18dB if you can. Your music will have a lot more life in it and sound much more interesting.

You can get a good idea of the peak-to-average ratio of your song by watching your meters and noticing where they max out and where they seem to stay most often. Some systems allow you to switch your meters between Peak and Average settings. (To find out whether your system has this option, check your owner's manual, which should be clear about your metering options.) Play the song and make note of the highest peaks using the Peak metering setting. Then listen to your song again using the Average setting on your meters and make a note of this level. When you're done, compare the two. More scientific ways to do this exist, but this technique gives you a good idea of your peak-to-average ratio.

When you're testing your compression or limiter settings (you do this by comparing the processed and unprocessed versions), be sure to have the volume of both versions exactly the same. Any difference in volume defeats the purpose of side-by-side comparison because people almost always prefer the louder version, regardless of whether it sounds better.

Perfecting tonal balance

The *tonal balance* of a song is how the various frequencies of the music relate to one another. You're not concerned with how each instrument sounds in the mix (that's the job for the mixing stage); instead, you're looking for an overall balance of frequencies within the hearing spectrum.

Turn it up!

Everyone wants his or her music to be as loud as possible. Louder sounds better. In fact, test after test has shown that when people listen to two versions of a song, they nearly always prefer the louder one (regardless of whether it actually sounds better). Musicians, producers, and engineers seem to be in a competition to see who can make the loudest CD. If you compare a CD made about ten years ago with one made this year, you'll notice that the newer one is much louder. Give them both a good listen though. Does the louder one really sound better?

You can test this by setting both CDs to play at the same volume and then switching back and forth. (You need to turn the volume up a bit on the older CD to match the volume of the newer one.)

One way to do this is to record both songs into your DAW and set the levels of each so that they're the same. At the same volume, which song sounds better to you? I'm willing to bet that nine out of ten times, you'll prefer the older song. This is because older recordings have more dynamic range than newer ones. The variety is pleasing to listen to, whereas the song with only a small dynamic range quickly becomes tiring.

Do yourself and your listeners a favor, and resist the temptation to compress the dynamic variability out of your music. Your mix will be much easier to listen to and have a lot more life and excitement. You can always turn the volume up on your stereo if it's not loud enough, but you can't add dynamic range after you've squashed it out.

For the most part, a tonal balance consists of an even distribution of frequencies from 20Hz–10 kHz with a slight drop-off (1–2dB) from 10–20 kHz or higher. That's great, you say, but what does that sound like? Well, listen to a number of great CDs, and you'll hear it.

When you master your music, you want to constantly compare the sound of your song to that of other CDs whose sound you like. In Chapter 14, I list a variety of excellent reference CDs for mixing. These CDs work just as well for mastering, so check them out.

When you adjust the overall tonal balance of your songs, listen carefully for frequencies that seem too loud or too soft. You can find these frequencies by listening to the instruments in the mix or by using a parametric EQ and sweeping the frequency spectrum. To do this, set your Q fairly wide (0.6, for instance) and turn the gain knob all the way up. Start with the lowest frequency and slowly raise the frequency as the song plays. Adjust annoying frequencies by cutting them by a couple of dB to see whether your overall mix improves.

Follow these general EQ guidelines:

- **If your mix sounds muddy, add high frequencies (above 10 kHz) or cut low ones (200–400 Hz).** Likewise, if your mix is too bright (common with digital recording), try reducing the frequencies above 10 kHz by using a shelf EQ or a Baxandall curve.

To use a Baxandall curve, use a parametric EQ and set the threshold at 20 kHz with a Q setting of about 1. This gradually cuts frequencies above around 10 kHz. You can adjust the Q to reach as far down as you want. Your EQ graph shows you what's happening.

✔ **Use the same EQ adjustments for both the right and left channels.** This keeps the stereo balance intact and doesn't alter the relative phase between the channels. For example, if you add some bass frequencies (100 Hz, for example) to the one channel and not the other, you may hear a wavering or pulsating sound around this frequency that goes back and forth between the speakers.

✔ **If you used a multiband compressor on specific frequencies, you may need to make some EQ adjustments to them.** Compression tends to mess with the frequency response.

✔ **If you need to adjust the EQ of certain instruments in the mix (the snare drum is buried, for example), note the overall effects of your adjustments on the rest of the mix.** If your adjustments aren't fixing the problem, go back to the mixing process and make your adjustments there. You'll be glad you took the time to do this.

Any adjustments you make to the EQ during mastering impact more than just those frequencies; the adjustments alter the entire frequency spectrum and the relationship between all the instruments. So listen carefully as you make adjustments, and back off the additional EQ if you don't like what you hear.

Some people check the tonal balance of their songs against that of their favorite CDs. You do this by recording a song into your mastering program and taking a look at its frequency response by using a spectral analyzer. (Some programs have a built-in spectral analyzer, but you can also buy one as a plug-in for many systems.) Then do an analysis of your song and compare it to the spectral analysis of a CD you like. This technique seems to work for many people (not me though; I like using my ears instead — but alas, I'm old-fashioned).

Sequencing your songs

Sequencing your songs consists of choosing the order of the songs on the CD as well as the amount of silence between each song. When you wrote and recorded your songs, you probably had an idea about the order in which you wanted them to appear on your CD. If you don't know how you want to arrange your songs, here are some things to consider:

✔ Consider each song's tempo in the sequencing equation. Some CDs work well if songs with a similar tempo are placed together, while others work best when contrasting songs follow one another.

> ✔ Think about a song's lyrics and how they relate to the lyrics from the other songs on your CD. If you want to tell your listener a story, consider how the order of the songs can best tell that story.
>
> ✔ Think about the chords that you used in each song and how they relate to another song that you may want to place before or after it in the sequence. The ending chord of one song can conflict with the beginning chord of another.

Aside from having to decide how your songs are ordered on your CD, you also have to think about how much time you put between each song in order to create the most impact. Many people assume that you use a set amount of time between all the songs on each CD. This isn't the case. You can put any amount of silence between each song that you feel is appropriate to set the mood that you want. Sometimes you may want just a second or two; other times four or five seconds is more appropriate.

For example, if you have a mellow ballad followed by an upbeat song, you may want to leave a little more time between these two songs so that the listener is prepared for the faster song (try leaving a space that's 4 to 6 beats long at the slower song's tempo, for instance). Or, if you want two tunes to flow together, you can leave less time in between them. Use your ears and think about how you want your listener to respond when going from one song to another.

Balancing levels

For a truly professional-sounding CD, you want all your songs to be at nearly the same relative level so that your listeners (I hope you have more than one) don't have to adjust the volume on their stereos from song to song.

Balancing the levels of your songs to one another is pretty easy. In fact, in most cases, you have very little to do after you EQ and optimize the dynamics of each song. You balance the levels from one song to the next by playing one song, then the next, and listening for significant volume differences. (Didn't I say that it was easy?) You can also look at your master bus meters to see whether each song is at the same level, but your ears are a much better judge.

If you notice any differences, just raise (or better yet, lower) the levels until they are all roughly the same. Don't get too finicky. Some variation from song to song is okay. In fact, minor differences can help to make your CD more interesting to listen to. When you're balancing levels, just make sure that any differences aren't enough to make the listener run to his or her stereo to adjust the volume knob. If one or two songs seem to be much lower in volume than the rest, you may want to go back to the volume-optimizing stage and raise those songs up a bit to make them more consistent with the rest of the songs on the CD. This way, you don't lower the volume of the entire CD based on one or two quiet songs.

Preparing for CD

After you have all your songs optimized, balanced, and sequenced, it's time for the final step. This last step involves saving your music in a format that enables you to duplicate the music. Generally, duplication plants can take your mastered music in several formats, but the most popular and easiest is a Red Book audio CD-R. If you go to a professional mastering house, whoever you work with will put your mastered music on the format that they prefer (or you can ask for the format of your choice). If you're mastering your music yourself, you're most likely doing this with a hard-drive recording system, so you'll use a CD-R to make a Red Book CD master.

To make a CD master, you need to get your music files to a 16-bit, 44.1-kHz format. If you're using any of the newer hard-drive recording systems, you probably recorded at a higher resolution and possibly higher sampling rate than this. (You would have set these parameters when you set up your song. If you can't remember, check your owner's manual to find out how to determine a song's settings.) If this is the case, you need to translate your music from the higher rates to the CD rates. This is called *dithering*.

Don't worry; dithering is easy to do — a heckuva lot easier than the recording, mixing, and mastering steps you've done so far. In fact, you just set your mastering software to dither for you, and you're set. Before you take your master to be duplicated, be sure to listen to the dithered and undithered versions to make sure that they sound the same (or close enough, because you lose some audio quality when you dither down).

Getting into CD Burning

Today, one of the coolest things about audio recording is that you can create music in your home and put it on the same medium that the biggest record companies use. When I first started as a recording engineer, the best you could do was put your music on a cassette for other people to listen to. Pressing vinyl was expensive. But now anyone with a computer, a CD burner, and a few inexpensive CD-Rs can put his or her music on the same format as all the best albums in the record store. You gotta love it!

You probably have a computer with a CD-R or CD-RW drive. If so, you also have software that you can use to burn your CDs. Most CD-burning software works fine for putting your mastered music onto CDs. If you don't already have a burner and want to add one to your existing computer, check the system requirements for the burner that interests you to make sure that your system is capable of using it. For audio CDs, you can use just about any CD burner on the market (as long as it's compatible with your system, of course).

If you have an SIAB (studio-in-a-box) system or a stand-alone system, you can burn CDs in one of these three ways:

- **Connect your recorder to a computer and transfer your music files to your computer to burn your CDs.**

- **Get a CD burner that's designed to work with your recorder.** All SIAB systems have a CD recorder option. This option is mounted inside the box (a Yamaha AW4416, for instance) or connects to the SCSI port of the recorder (Roland systems).

- **Get a stand-alone CD-burning system.** Stand-alone CD recorders come in a variety of types, from real-time recorders that function like a cassette recorder to hard-drive-based recorders, such as the Alesis Masterlink.

Regardless of the CD burner you get, make sure that you can create a Red Book CD. I know that this sounds mysterious, but all the Red Book term means is that the CD is an audio CD, not a CD-ROM. Red Book is a standard that dictates that the data is in an audio CD format. This ensures that your CD can play on all audio CD players. Your CD burner clearly states whether it can burn audio, or Red Book, CDs.

Purchasing CD-Rs

A staggering variety of CD-Rs are available. You have green, blue, gold, even black CDs, and you have data and music CDs. So which ones are best? Well, that depends.

Unless you have a consumer CD recorder from a few years ago, you can record your CD onto any data CD-R. You can find these just about anywhere, and they can cost as little as $0.10 to $0.15 apiece if you buy in bulk. If you have an older consumer CD recorder, you have to use music CD-Rs. These CD-Rs have a code in them that allows older consumer recorders to actually record. These CD-Rs cost a lot more, not because they capture music any better, but because a royalty, which is about a dollar and goes to the recording industry, is figured into the price of the CD (don't get me started).

So, if you have a recent CD-R recorder connected to your computer or SIAB system, or if you have a professional-grade CD burner, you can get by just fine using run-of-the-mill data CD-Rs.

As far as which of the countless CD-R brands to use, they're all pretty much the same. I always go with the least expensive. The worst thing that can happen is that an error occurs and you have to record again. Keep in mind that some CD-Rs work better on some recorders, and the only way to find out is to try them. When you find a brand that works, try to stick with it.

Recording Your Music to CD-R

Burning a CD is easy. Just open your CD-burning software and follow the prompts. A few things, however, can be helpful to know to get the best sound and to create a CD that you can duplicate. I cover these topics in the following sections.

Using different CD recorders

If you're using a computer-based system, burning a CD is as simple as opening your software and following the program's directions for making a CD. If you have an SIAB system, you follow similar procedures, but your UI (user interface) is going to be much different. If you use a stand-alone burner, things are going to be even more different.

Some systems, such as computer-based programs, allow you to dither your mix separately, before you burn your CD. (Dithering is described in the section "Preparing for CD," earlier in this chapter.) I highly recommend this approach because it gives you a chance to hear the dithered music before you commit it to disc. If your system doesn't support this approach (SIAB system users, take note), make sure that you compare your disc with the original mix file. (Actually, you should always check your burned CD to make sure that it plays properly and sounds good.) You'll hear a slight difference in sound, but that's what happens when you go from the 24-bit to the 16-bit format.

Computer-based systems

If you have a CD burner program, such as Toast, Jam, or CD Creator, burning your CD is easy. One of the advantages of burning a CD by using one of these programs is that you have quite a bit of flexibility in organizing your songs and placing space between them.

You generally just click the Add Track button on the main screen and select the track you want to add. You are also prompted to choose any silence that you want to place before the track as well as PQ subcode information. (A *PQ subcode* is additional information added to the CD data that includes start and stop times for each track, among other things.) When you have all your tracks assembled, you can burn your CD. Pretty simple, huh?

SIAB systems

Studio-in-a-box systems often contain a CD burner as one of their options. This can be convenient because you can do everything in the SIAB system, including preparing your master CD for mass production. On most SIAB systems, making a CD is pretty easy; the only problem is that you often end up having to do things differently than with a computer-based or stand-alone system.

For one thing, you can't dither your file and check it before you record the CD. The dithering is done during the burning process. This isn't a big deal because you're going to double-check your finished CD before you send it out or sell it, anyway, right?

One thing that you often need to do, however, is assemble and sequence your songs before you enter the CD-burning program. This can be a lot more work than doing it in a computer-based system, as the following steps show. Here I list the procedure for assembling, sequencing, and burning a CD in a Roland SIAB system (other SIAB systems have similar procedures), just to give you an idea of the process involved (which can go pretty quickly after you get the hang of it):

1. **Create a new "song."**

   This opens a new file for you to put all your mastered songs into. You end up with a "song" that consists of all the songs on your CD.

2. **One by one, import your mastered tracks into the new "song" (follow the track import procedures for this).**

   You get to the track import menu by pressing Shift+Track. Next, press Page once to bring up the Track Import function. Press F5 and follow the prompts to import a track.

   The assembly process works best if you work out the order of the songs beforehand and import each song in succession.

3. **Place the amount of space you want to have between songs, well, between the songs. Use the Track Insert function to insert the space.**

   You access the Track Insert function by pressing Shift+Track. Next, press F5 and follow the prompts to insert space in a track.

4. **Place markers for the beginning of each track.**

   You do this by pressing Shift+Tap (VS-1680) or Play+Tap (VS-880, 890).

5. **Open the CD write menu and choose the "song" file that contains the sequenced songs and tracks on which you imported these songs.**

6. **Choose Disc at Once mode and 2x write.**

7. **Press Enter.**

Stand-alone CD burners

A variety of stand-alone CD burners are available, and they all work differently. Some record the CD the same way that a cassette player records — you connect the input of the CD recorder to the output of the device that contains your music and press the Record button on the CD recorder while pressing the Play button on the device with the music. The CD is recorded in real time. Other stand-alone CD burners, such as the Alesis Masterlink (the CD-burning standard for many pro studios), work more like computer software programs than cassette recorders.

With the Masterlink, you need to first copy the music files from your recorder's hard drive to the Masterlink's hard drive. From there, you can edit, sequence, and even dynamically process each song before you burn all the songs to a CD-R. When you're happy with the order of the songs and the spacing between them, you can then burn your CD.

If you want to do dynamic processing to your music in the Masterlink, be sure to send your files to the machine undithered. You can dither in the Masterlink after you make your changes. This improves the sound of your final CD. If you're only sequencing your songs, you can send the files dithered if you want.

Burning for mass production

If you intend to send your CD-R to a duplication or replication company to have it mass produced, keep the following suggestions in mind:

- ✔ **Check for physical defects to the CD-R before you try to burn to it.** Scratches, fingerprints, smudges, and other imperfections on the mirror side (bottom) of the CD-R can cause errors in the data. Be sure to use a clean and unblemished CD-R for burning your master.

- ✔ **Always write your master CD by using the Disc at Once mode.** This allows the CD to be read as a Red Book audio CD. Your other option when recording a CD is to use Track at Once. Track at Once burns one song (track) at a time and produces more errors than Disc at Once, which burns the entire CD at one time. Because of the errors present on CDs that are burned using Track at Once, a mass producer's equipment can't read — and therefore summarily rejects — CDs that people produce with this method. (In fact, many older CD players for homes and cars can't read these CDs either.) So be sure that you use Disc at Once whenever you make a CD of your mastered music.

✔ **If you can, use an error-detection software program to check for errors in your recorded CD.** If you don't have access to an error-detection program, check the back of the CD for any blemishes (just like you did before recording onto it).

✔ **Listen carefully to your entire CD after it's been recorded.** Compare it with your original file and make sure that the CD is perfect. Also, spend time reevaluating the order of the songs. Make sure that they flow well together.

✔ **Use a felt-tip marker to label your finished CD master, not a ballpoint pen or an adhesive label (paper or plastic).** A ballpoint pen can damage the surface of the CD. Adhesive labels can slow the rotational speed of the CD and can cause errors in the duplication or replication process. They have also been known to come off inside a duplication machine, clogging the works (and irritating your duplication technician).

✔ **Label the CD master with the name of your album and all your contact info.** Use a felt-tip marker, of course, and write on the top (nonmirror side) of the disc. Your contact information should include your name (or your band's name), your phone number, and the date the master was made.

✔ **Make three CD-Rs of your mastered music.** Keep one copy safe in your studio and send two to the duplication or replication company. This ensures that, if one of the two CDs that you send for mass production has an error, you don't waste time sending the company a replacement.

✔ **Prepare a PQ subcode log.** PQ subcodes are additional information written on the CD that provides time code information, such as track numbers and start and stop times of each track. If your CD burner software doesn't support PQ subcodes, make a list of the start and stop time of each track (referenced from the start of the CD) on a separate piece of paper — as well as the track number and length of each track — and send it along with your CD masters. If your software program can generate a PQ subcode log, print it and send it with your CD master.

If you're burning a CD for a major record label, first of all, congratulations, and second, you need to supply ISRC codes with your CD. ISRC stands for *International Standard Recording Code,* and it contains information about the CD, such as the owner of the song, country of origin, year of release, and serial number. You enter ISRC codes into a dialog box on most CD-burning programs, and the information is placed within the PQ subcodes.

Protecting your rights

Before you put your music out into the world, get it copyrighted. Getting a copyright on your music is easy and relatively inexpensive, so there's no reason not to do it. Just fill out an SR (sound recording) form and send it to the U.S. Copyright Office at the Library of Congress. You can find the SR form at `www.loc.gov/copyright/forms`, or you can call the Copyright Office at 202-707-9100 and ask to have it mailed to you. Choose (or ask for) the *Form SR with Instructions*. The current cost for filing the form is $30, but double-check this fee before you send in your form, because the fee has been known to go up (hey, it's the government). You can fill out one form for each CD, so the cost per song isn't very high.

The form is pretty easy to fill out, but if you find that you have difficulty, you can call an information specialist to help you out. The number is 202-707-3000. Be prepared to wait on hold for a little while (again, it's the government).

Send your completed form, the fee, and a copy of your CD to the address listed on the form. You'll receive a certificate in the mail, but you can consider your music copyrighted as soon as you mail the form (as long as you sent it to the correct address). If you're especially protective of your music (paranoid?), you can wait until your check clears your bank. At this point, you can be almost certain that your form is being processed. If you can't sleep at night unless your music is copyrighted, it's best to wait until your certificate arrives in the mail before you start selling or distributing your CD. (This is a good reason to file for your copyright early.)

Making Multiple Copies

When you have a CD that you want to copy, you can either make the copies yourself or hire someone to make the copies for you. If you do them yourself, you have to burn CDs one at a time, just like the first one. This can cost little but takes a lot of time (as you undoubtedly found out when you burned your first CD).

Doing it yourself

Well, you've done everything else yourself, so why not add the copying process to the list? If you have more time than money and only need a few CDs, making them yourself may be a good option.

To make saleable CDs yourself, you need not only the CD burner but also a graphics design software program and a printer to print the CD labels and cover material (the CD sleeve and tray card). Even with this equipment, your package won't look as professional as the package that a CD duplication or replication company can create, but what you create is probably good enough for you to sell a few copies to your friends and acquaintances.

Having someone else do it

Depending on how many copies you want, you can either have them duplicated or replicated. Either process can provide you with a professional-quality product that you can sell alongside major releases. Your choice between duplication and replication depends on how many copies you plan to have made.

Duplication

Duplication involves making copies of your master CD-R the same way you made the CD-R in the first place. The only difference is that duplication companies use CD burners that enable them to make more than one copy at a time. Duplication is great if you want to make a small number of copies — from 50 to 300. CD-duplication companies often provide one-color printing on the CD and either a vinyl sleeve or a jewel case to hold the CD. Some companies can prepare retail-ready packages, which look like other commercial CDs and include CDs with printing on them, jewel cases with color-printed inserts, and shrink-wrap. You can expect to pay $3 to $5 for each CD, depending on the quantity that you order.

An advantage to having your CDs duplicated is that they can usually be done quickly. Many duplication companies can provide you with a finished product in as little as a few days (although seven days seems to be the average). The disadvantage is that you usually pay considerably more for each CD than if you do it yourself or go the replication route.

To have your CDs duplicated, you need to provide a CD-R master, that is, a CD-R that was recorded as an audio CD. If you want the duplication company to create retail-ready packages, you also need to provide artwork that's laid out to the company's specifications.

If you're interested in going the duplication route, here are a few resources to get you started. You can also do an Internet search for more places by using the search term *CD duplication.*

- **Master Mind CD Duplication,** 26 Route 13, Brookline, NH 03030; phone: 877-8MASTER; Web site: www.mastermindcdduplication.com

- **CD Works,** 1266 Soldiers Field Road, Boston, MA 02135-1003; phone: 800-CDWORKS; Web site: www.cdworks.com

✔ **The CD Marksman,** 2105 S. McClintock Drive, Tempe, AZ 85282; phone: 877-890-5470; Web site: www.cdmarksman.com

Most of the companies that I list in the following section also provide duplication services for smaller quantities.

Replication

Replication is used for making commercial CDs and involves burning a *glass master* — the master disc from which all your CD copies will be made — from your master CD-R. The glass master is then used to transfer the data onto CD media. Replication is designed for larger runs of 500 or more copies. Quantities less than 300 aren't cost effective because the glass master often costs between $100 and $200, and the film needed to print the CD and sleeve and tray card can cost several hundred dollars more.

CD replication usually comes with printing on the CD in one to four colors and a tray card and sleeve that are often printed in four colors. Most CD replication companies have retail-ready CD package deals that cover everything from the layout of your artwork (some do and some don't, so be sure to ask first) to printed CDs, jewel boxes, and shrink-wrap. You can expect to pay between $1,200 and $2,000 for 500 to 1,000 copies from most manufacturers.

If you want to go the replication route, you need to provide the replication company with a master audio CD, artwork set to the company's specifications, and a completed order form. Oh, and you probably need to pay half the money for the job up front before the work can start (bummer).

After people at the manufacturing company receive your order form, the CD, and artwork, they make a reference CD and proofs of your finished printed material. Be sure to look over the art proofs carefully and listen to every second of the reference CD. Any mistakes that you don't catch are your problem, so take your time and compare the reference CD very closely with the master recording. (You did make a copy of your master CD before you sent it out, right?) The master and the reference CD should be identical.

Having your CD replicated is a stressful thing. You're spending a ton of money and getting quite a few copies that you'll need to be proud enough of to go out in the world and sell them. So choosing a CD-replication company is an important task. Quite a few companies are out there, so choose the place that makes you feel the most comfortable and that makes a high-quality product. Following is a list of the larger CD-replication companies. For more possibilities, input the terms *CD replication* or *CD duplication* in your favorite Internet search engine.

✔ **Disc Masters,** 2460 West Main Street, Suite D300, Saint Charles, IL 60175; phone: 888-430-DISC; Web site: www.discmasters.com.

✔ **Oasis CD Duplication,** 12625 Lee Hwy, P.O. Box 214, Sperryville, VA 22740; phone: 888-296-2747; Web site: www.oasiscd.com.

> ✔ **Groove House,** 5029 Serrania Ave., Woodland Hills, CA 91364; phone: 888-476-6838; Web site: `www.groovehouse.com`.
>
> ✔ **DiscMakers,** phone: 866-707-0012; Web site: `www.discmakers.com/music`. This company has six locations in the United States and one in Puerto Rico.

Many CD-replication companies can provide you with great resources, information, and even opportunities for promoting your work. Take advantage of these opportunities if you can, but don't choose a company based on its promotional promises. Choose a company because of its customer service, price, and the quality of its product.

Be sure to ask for referrals — or at least a list of satisfied clients — before you choose a duplication or replication company. As always, your best bet when entrusting someone with your precious music is to ask friends for recommendations. Also, take timing estimates with a grain of salt — I've had a couple of occasions where a company promised to finish my CDs by a certain date and the company missed its date. So leave plenty of time between when you print your CDs and when you need them.

UPC bar codes

If you make a CD that you intend to sell through major retailers, such as music stores or Internet retailers, you need a UPC bar code. A *UPC bar code* is a string of numbers that identify your product. Every CD has its own unique bar code. You can get a bar code in one of two ways: register with and pay $750 to the Universal Code Council (UCC) or pay $0 to $50 to a CD replicator or distributor.

Unless you intend to release more than 35 CDs, your best bet is to buy a bar code from a replicator or distributor, who can provide bar codes for a small (or no) fee with your CD order. Here are additional places where you can get a UPC bar code:

✔ **Discmakers:** `www.discmakers.com/music`

✔ **Oasis CD Duplication:** `www.oasiscd.com`

✔ **CD Baby:** `www.cdbaby.com`

✔ **Ampcast:** `www.ampcast.com`

Chapter 17

Getting Your Music Out to Listeners

· ·

In This Chapter

▶ Getting started promoting your music

▶ Formatting your music for the Internet

▶ Finding a Web host site

▶ Using the Internet to promote your music

· ·

Congratulations, you have a CD to sell. The hard . . . oops, I'm sorry . . . the *easy* part is behind you. I'm sure that you don't want to be stuck with boxes of expensive coasters, so now you have to work on getting people interested in buying your music. You've just gone from being a musician-composer-engineer-producer to being all those plus a record company owner-businessperson (exactly how hyphenated can a person get, anyway?).

Your friends and some acquaintances will probably buy a few copies, but after you've sold a CD to all of them, you need to get your music to the broader world. This can be tricky. After all, you're now competing with the big boys and, face it, you don't have nearly the resources that they do. Traditional channels of distribution and marketing are pretty much out of the question for you. So, to succeed in selling your music, you need to try some alternative approaches.

In this chapter, you explore a variety of ways to get your music out to the masses. From basic promotional ideas to Internet distribution, this chapter covers a lot of ground. You discover how to find Web hosting sites, how to encode your music for Internet distribution, and how to make a few bucks from music downloads.

Promoting Your Music

I'm no marketing guru, but I have managed to create a nice niche for myself and my music. So trust me; you can do the same. All it takes is a little imagination and a lot of hard work. In the following list, I present a few ideas that have worked for me and other enterprising, independent artists:

- **Take yourself seriously.** What I mean by this is take the job of promoting and selling your music seriously — treat it as a business. Getting people to notice and buy your music is a lot of work, but it doesn't have to be a drag (if it is, you're better off getting someone else to do it for you).

- **Get organized.** Get your new business off on the right foot by developing a habit of keeping track of your sales and developing a contact list. One of the best investments that you can make is to get a contact management database (Act! is a good one) to keep track of promotion contacts (newspapers, radio stations, and clubs), CD sales, and fans. Also, do yourself a big favor and keep meticulous records of your income and expenses; you'll be grateful that you did when tax time comes.

- **Create a mailing list.** This is one of the most cost-effective and powerful ways that you can start to develop a following. Make a sign-up sheet for your mailing list available at every public appearance. (Ask people to include not only their postal mail address but also their e-mail address.) Then enter those names into your database. You can then either send out snail mailings or e-mail notices whenever you play or do anything worth mentioning.

- **Get out and be seen.** This one is pretty straightforward. Get out in the world and let people know about your music. This can mean playing gigs or talking about your music. I have a good friend who releases an album each year. He prints a thousand copies, which he sells at his gigs, and every year he sells out. (Hey, that's an extra ten grand a year after expenses — not bad.) He also uses his albums as his calling card to get more gigs.

- **Look beyond the music store.** It's nearly impossible to compete with the major labels in the music store. Unless you live in a small town or know of a music shop that has a section devoted to local bands and can sell your CDs, you need to think of other places to put your music. For example, another friend of mine has his CD at quite a few of the local businesses in his neighborhood around the holidays. Everything, from the local pack-and-ship to the video store, has a countertop display with his CD. He creates a small poster that fits on the counter describing him and his music. He sells quite a few CDs and gets a handful more gigs each year this way.

✔ **Capitalize on your style.** Another one of my friends composes folksy, New Age music, and he managed to get his CDs into a handful of New Age, gift-type shops. He often puts them in the stores on consignment and checks each store once a week to refill the countertop display and collect money that the store took in (minus the store's cut, of course). Going into the stores every week helps him to develop a connection with the store owners, many of who have arranged for him to do performances in their stores, increasing exposure and sales.

✔ **Try something different.** Years ago, I teamed up with a local author and played at her book signings. (This is before I wrote books myself.) She read a passage from her book, and then I played for a few minutes. I always ended up selling a few dozen CDs at these events.

✔ **Don't be stingy.** Give away your CD. I usually count on giving away about 10 to 15 percent of the CDs that I print. These can be for reviews, to try to get gigs, or for any purpose that may spread the word about your music. Giving out your CD as a promotional tool is an inexpensive way to let people know what you're doing.

I'm sure you can come up with dozens more ways to promote and sell your music. Think outside the box and use your imagination. Don't be shy. Do whatever you can to get your music out into the world.

Exploiting the Internet

The tried-and-true approach to playing live and getting exposure still holds today, but now the Internet has opened some new doors — doors that can lead you to national and international exposure from your computer room. You just have to get your music on the Internet and promote it well (easier said than done, I know). You can then make money from your music while you sleep (or at least make your music available while you sleep).

"How do I do this?" you may ask. Well, that's the purpose of the remaining sections of this chapter. Here you explore the ways that you can use the Internet to promote and sell your music. You discover how to put up music files so that your potential customers can either download your music or listen to it online. You find out about some of the best ways to have your music hosted online, and you take a look at promotional ideas to get you started.

Understanding MP3

I'm sure you've heard about MP3s. In fact, I'm willing to bet that you've already downloaded a few MP3s from the Internet and experienced firsthand the immediacy that MP3s offer. You go to a Web site and choose a song to download. After just a short while, you have a copy on your hard drive that you can listen to anytime you want. You can even put that song on a CD or portable player and take it with you.

With all this convenience and immediacy comes a downside. That MP3 song doesn't sound as good as one that was mastered to a CD. For most people, this is a small price to pay for the ability to download a song for free. After all, most people play their music on less-then-stellar stereos (Walkmans and boom boxes come to mind). If you're one of the lucky few with a stellar (or more-than-stellar) stereo system, you're going to hear the difference, which may prompt the following question: "Why doesn't a song in MP3 format sound as good as one mastered to a CD?" The answer: data compression.

MP3 is a process that compresses your music so that it takes up less hard-drive space. Data compression is necessary for MP3s to work. A regular CD music file can take up 30–40MB (about 10MB per minute). That same song can take up only 3–4MB in MP3 format. This is important because, if you're going to do any promoting of your music on the Internet, a 30–40MB file is way too big to download or to stream on the Web. For example, dialup users with a 28-Kbps modem would have to wait over 4 hours to download a 40MB file! I don't know about you, but I don't know anyone who is willing to wait that long to hear a piece of music.

Although compression causes your MP3 to lose fidelity as well as megabytes, I think this loss of quality is an advantage. Because your MP3 doesn't sound as good as your mastered CD, you give listeners just a taste of your music. By giving people this taste, along with the opportunity to purchase a CD, you help them to decide whether they want to buy the high-quality version.

Engine

When you convert a song on your mastered CD to an MP3 file, the *engine* is the encoding algorithm (technical term: number cruncher) that is used to convert your file. Not all engines make your song sound the same. Some engines make your song sound much better than others, and you may get a better-quality sound from an engine if you adjust the bit rate and/or recording mode. Some MP3 encoders allow you to choose the engine that you want to use, as shown in Figure 17-1, while others don't.

The standard and arguably best encoding engine is the Fraunhofer algorithm, although LAME is gaining in popularity. The encoding engine that you choose depends on the results that you get. You need to try a few engines to decide what works best for your music and your situation.

What do you mean *near-CD quality?*

You may have heard the term *near-CD quality* when referring to MP3 sound. This is a marketing term that means, "It doesn't sound as good as a CD, but we'll make it sound like it's pretty darn close and maybe the buyer won't notice." If you sense a note of cynicism in my writing, you're right. Don't delude yourself into believing that the song you start with is going to sound the same after MP3 conversion.

The difference between a song on a CD and a song that's near-CD quality is like the difference between playing a CD in your car and then hearing the same song on the radio. You lose some high end and the bass is thinner. You may even lose the stereo image, depending on the conversion mode you choose, and you definitely lose some of the dynamic range. Overall, the song has a little less life to it.

This is not a huge difference for most people, but is noticeable nonetheless. The good news is that most people don't seem to care (or are at least willing to accept it).

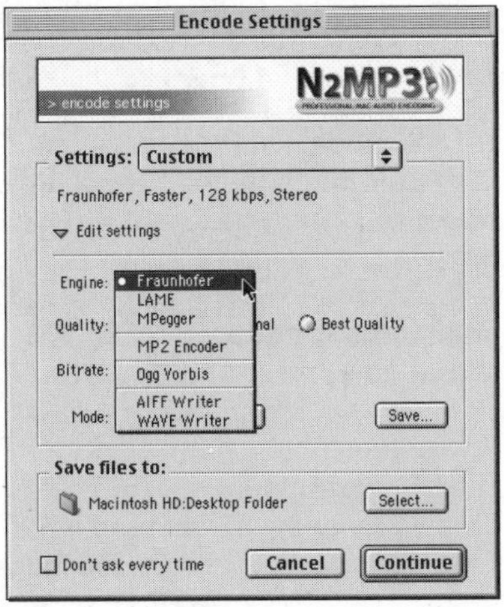

Figure 17-1:
MP3
encoders
use a
variety of
engines to
convert your
music.

Bit rate

The *bit rate* determines the quality of your encoded music. When you encode your music, you have to choose your file's bit rate, as shown in Figure 17-2. Bit rates range from 20 to 320 Kbps (kilobits per second). The higher the bit rate, the better the sound quality. The downside is that higher bit rates create larger files. When you convert your music to MP3 format, you're constantly balancing quality with file size.

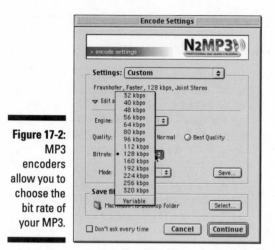

Figure 17-2:
MP3
encoders
allow you to
choose the
bit rate of
your MP3.

The bit rate that you ultimately choose depends on how you plan to use your MP3 file. For example, if you want to put your music on an MP3 host site (an Internet site that makes people's MP3 music available for download), you most likely need to choose the 128-Kbps rate because this is what many host sites require for Download or Hi-Fi mode. On the other hand, if you want to stream audio on the Web, you're better off choosing a much lower rate (between 20 and 24 Kbps). Otherwise, your song may pause while it's playing (for people with dialup modems anyway).

Variable bit rate (VBR) is an option that many encoders offer. VBR allows the encoder to change the bit rate as it compresses the file. The advantage to this approach is that sections with fewer instruments or less data can be compressed further than sections with more critical information. The result is often a better-sounding MP3 file that takes up less space. The only draw-back — and it's a big one — is that few MP3 players can read a file created with VBR. So, you're probably better off not using this approach for your Web-based files.

If you're making MP3s to listen to through your own player and it supports VBR playback, using VBR keeps your files smaller. If you do choose VBR, you are prompted to choose an average bit rate or a minimum and maximum bit rate. Try them both and choose the one that sounds best to you.

Mode

Modes essentially refer to whether your file is in stereo or mono, only your choices include more than just plain stereo and mono. You have the option to choose mono, stereo, joint stereo, or sometimes, force stereo (also known as dual mono), as shown in Figure 17-3. Again, choose the mode based on your music and how you prefer to balance quality with file size.

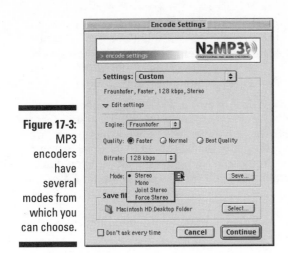

Figure 17-3:
MP3
encoders
have
several
modes from
which you
can choose.

Here's a look at the various modes and how they relate to quality and file size:

✔ **Mono:** Mono takes up little room because all the stereo data from your CD is contained on one track. The sound quality can be good, depending on the bit rate that you choose, but you lose all stereo-imaging data. Choose mono mode if the loss of the stereo image won't adversely affect your song or if the overall sound quality is more important to you than the stereo information.

✔ **Stereo:** Stereo mode consists of two mono tracks. With stereo mode, you retain all your stereo information. The drawback is that your two tracks are at half the bit rate as the mono one that uses the same bit-rate setting. For example, if you encode in stereo at 128 Kbps, each of your tracks is only encoded at 64 Kbps. So, if you want each track to be at 128 Kbps, you need to encode at 256 Kbps. This creates a file that's twice as large as the mono file at 128 Kbps and has the same sound quality.

Stereo mode is a good choice if you have a song with complex stereo panning effects that you just can't live without and you don't mind a sound quality that's slightly lower.

✔ **Joint Stereo:** Joint stereo mode is a cross between mono and stereo. This mode consists of creating one track of audio information and one track of information that tells the player to send certain sounds through one speaker or the other (called *steering* data). You get most of the stereo information with only a slightly larger file size than with mono mode.

For most songs, the difference between regular stereo and joint stereo is indistinguishable as far as the stereo image goes, but you end up with a higher-quality recording because the higher bit rate is used. You may find that this option works better for you than the regular stereo mode. Experiment and see whether you can hear a difference.

✔ **Force Stereo:** Force stereo (or dual mono) mode is essentially the same as the mono mode — one track of audio data is recorded and the stereo panning information is lost. The only difference between mono and force stereo is that force stereo makes sure that the mono data is sent through both speakers of the player. You choose force stereo mode if you don't mind your music being in mono but you want to ensure that it plays through both speakers.

Creating MP3 Files

To create MP3 files, you need MP3 encoding software and a CD or audio file of your music (well, you need a computer, too). To create an MP3 file of your music, just choose the song to convert and let the encoder do the rest. Certain variables can make your MP3s sound their best — such as which encoder you use and what parameters you choose. I cover these variables in the following sections.

Choosing encoding software

You have a lot of MP3 encoding software choices. Some software encodes from various file formats as well as from CD, whereas others don't encode directly from a CD. Not being able to encode directly from CD isn't necessarily a bad thing, however, because the process of lifting music from a CD (also known as *ripping*) can cause audible artifacts (noise, clicks and pops, and so on). If you encode from a WAV or an AIFF file, you can first make sure that the sound going into the encoding process is as good as possible.

If you get an encoder that doesn't encode from CD and you use a stand-alone or SIAB system that doesn't support file importing (or you don't have your recorder connected to a computer), you need CD ripping (copying) software as well.

A couple of popular MP3 programs that both encode and rip are as follows:

✔ **Musicmatch Jukebox (**www.musicmatch.com**):** You can download the basic version for free, which allows you to play, rip, burn, and convert MP3s and audio CDs.

✔ **N2MP3 (**www.proteron.com**):** This is a Mac-only program, but Proteron has a Windows version called EasyMP3. You can download trial versions of these programs for free that allow you to encode MP3s. The trial versions allow you to encode only 20 MP3s at full length (a maximum of one minute after that), and they put a voice clip at the beginning that says, "Encoded by N2MP3" that you can't get rid of. (Of course, if you buy the program, these limitations disappear.)

A lot of MP3 encoders are available, so if you're looking for a little more variety, check out these sites:

✔ **Shareware.com (**www.shareware.com**):** This site contains shareware of all sorts, from games to word processing software to MP3 encoders. From the main page, just type **MP3** into the keyword search function and choose the computer platform that you use (Mac or PC). You can find a bunch of matches from your search.

✔ **mp3software.com (**www.mp3software.com**):** This site claims to have the most complete list of MP3-related software products available for download. You can find freeware and shareware versions in this site.

✔ **MP3 for the Mac (**www.mp3-mac.com/Pages/Encoders.html**):** This site contains tons of software programs (some free, some not) for Macintosh computer users. You may find one or more programs that meet your needs.

If you record using a computer-based system and you use one of the more full-featured popular programs such as Pro Tools or Logic Audio, you can probably create MP3 files without getting additional software. Most decent programs offer this capability.

Encoding your music

The actual encoding process is pretty simple. Just open your MP3 encoding software and choose the parameters that you want for your file. I can't list step-by-step details here — every encoding program is a little bit different — but keep the following points in mind when you encode your music:

✔ **To ensure that you get the best sound quality possible, encode your MP3s from a WAV or AIFF file instead of directly from your CD.** The process of ripping a song from a CD can create problems in sound quality. So, by converting your CD to WAV or AIFF files first, you get a chance to hear your ripped song and to correct problems that ripping may have caused before your music goes to MP3.

✔ **Import your WAV or AIFF file into a sound editor.** Sound editor programs, such as Sound Forge XP, work fine. (You can find sound editors on the Web sites that I list in the preceding section.) When you have your file in the editor, use the Maximizer plug-in to raise the overall level of your song. You lose some dynamics, but they don't come through with the MP3 file anyway. If you recorded your music in your computer, you can use the recording software instead of a separate sound editor to do this procedure.

✔ **Choose the mono or joint stereo modes for a better sound.** The regular stereo option has a lower resolution (bit rate) and doesn't sound as good given the same file size. Choosing the force stereo is fine if your encoder supports it.

✔ **If you want to put your music on the Web, choose the 128-Kbps bit rate for downloading and a rate between 20 and 24 Kbps for streaming audio.** (I know I said this earlier in this chapter, but it's worth repeating.) If your encoder doesn't allow such a low bit rate (many of the newer encoders don't), choose the lowest option available. This is often 32 Kbps.

✔ **Experiment with different modes and encoding engines.** Some sound better than others on certain types of music.

Hosting Your Music

When you have your music in MP3 format, it's time to get it out into the world. This involves either putting it on your own Web site or someone else's. The following sections explore the pros and cons of — as well as the process involved in — both of these options. Chances are you'll end up choosing a combination approach if you're serious about selling your music online.

Choosing a host site

An *Internet host site* is a Web site that allows you to add your music to its list of available music downloads. Putting your MP3s on a host site can give you exposure that you wouldn't otherwise be able to get. You can not only direct people to the site to listen to your music, but you can also benefit from traffic that the site itself, other musicians, and the site's fans generate. For some of the larger sites, that can be a lot of potential listeners. Although MP3 host sites are constantly changing, a few have managed to hang around for a while.

Internet music host sites are always coming and going. To find out what sites are currently available and what they offer, check out `compo10.com/Music Hosts.htm`. This site has a comprehensive list that's updated regularly.

Be sure to read and understand the contracts (often called agreements) that each of these sites requires you to agree to. Make sure that you don't sign away your rights to your music. If you're not sure that you like a particular agreement, don't sign up for the service. You can find plenty of other places to put your music on the Internet.

Ampcast

`www.ampcast.com/artists/signup.php`

Ampcast has been around since 1998 and, as its Web site duly states, "is dedicated to introducing and exposing new musicians and bands as well as providing a forum for the promotion of more established musical artists." To join Ampcast, you pay a $75 annual fee. For this, you can put your music and pictures on its site and get 5 cents for each *unique* download, that is, the first download of a song by each person (so you can't have a friend download your song a hundred times and get paid for each one).

Ampcast also has a one-off CD program where it creates a CD of your music for you and makes the CD available on its site. The amount you get from each CD sale depends on the price you set, but it can range from $1 to $3 or more. The good thing is that you don't have to have a CD to sell one on this site — Ampcast creates it for you.

IUMA

`www.iuma.com/ArtistsOnly/`

IUMA is the oldest MP3 host site, having been around since 1993, and Vitaminic.com recently bought it. IUMA's Web site blurb states that it is "the one place to post your music where actual musicians are watching out for you — not weasels watching the numbers. You have your own URL with your band name first. And a custom Web page where you can post all your band info and MP3s, sell CDs, create message boards, fan lists, and of course, get e-mail from your fans — all Free."

You don't get paid for downloads from IUMA, but the fact that it costs you nothing to join easily offsets any disadvantage this may cause. Most bands don't earn their fees from downloads anyway. IUMA doesn't actually sell CDs on its site, but it enables you to put links from its site to where you sell your CDs.

Music.download.com

`www.music.download.com`

Music.download.com is run by CNET and, as a result of its Internet presence, it's one of the most visited music sites online. Music.download.com is free to put your music on, and the listener can download your music for free. This, of course, means that you can't make money from your music on this site unless a listener follows a link to a separate site where your music can be purchased. Still, with the exposure that this site can provide, you can hopefully get some people to go to another site where you have your music for sale, such as your own site. Check out the section "Setting up your own site," later in this chapter.

Vitaminic.com

`www.vitaminic.com`

Vitaminic is a European company that operates ten different sites. The address listed here takes you to the English-language site, where you can join for free and get exposure through all the sites. Vitaminic claims to have 10 million hits per month from 2 million unique users. Vitaminic doesn't pay you for downloads, but it does offer to sell your music from its site. Vitaminic creates CDs on demand and pays you half of the proceeds from your sales.

Setting up your own site

Even if you put your music on an MP3 site, you should consider creating your own Web site as well. With your own site, you can provide a lot more information for visitors. You can also offer more products that may make you more money than your CDs — T-shirts for instance.

Having your own Web site is not without challenges. For example, you have to design and maintain the site, which can take a lot of time. You also have to pay for things like hosting (granted, you can find places to host your site for free). If you intend to sell products on your site, you need to provide online ordering, which often involves setting up a merchant account with a credit card company. In all, having a Web site can be time consuming and expensive, so be prepared to do a fair amount of work if you really plan on making money from your Web site.

If maintaining a full e-commerce Web site sounds like too much for you, you can still make money from the Internet using your Web site to promote your band, especially if you get creative. In fact, with just a few simple steps, you can have a Web site without the expense or the hassle (at least less hassle)

and still provide your visitors with a great Web experience. Here are a few suggestions:

✔ Create links from your site to your MP3 host site. This keeps you from having to put MP3s or streaming audio on your Web site, and your visitors can still hear your music.

✔ Get your CD on Amazon.com (`www.amazon.com`) or CD Baby (`www.cd baby.com`) and link your visitors to those sites to buy your CD. You don't get as much money in your pocket, but these other sites take care of all the ordering hassle for you. (You find out how to sell your music through CD Baby and Amazon.com in the section "Selling Your CDs," later in this chapter.)

Designing your site

Your first step in getting a Web site up and going is to design it. When you design your Web site, keep the following points in mind:

✔ **Make your site easy to navigate.** Make sure that your visitors know where they are on your site at all times. It's often a good idea to have a menu bar on each page so that they can at least get back to the home page without having to search for it.

✔ **Make sure that your site loads quickly.** Most people still use dialup modems (often 28-Kbps), and sites with a ton of big graphics or streaming videos take forever to download. Most people don't have the patience to wait. Think lean and mean. Your visitors will appreciate it more than a fancy slow-to-load page.

✔ **Make ordering your CD (or other stuff) easy.** Put a Buy My CD icon on every page.

✔ **Double-check all your links.** Nothing is worse for a Web surfer than a bunch of links that don't work. If you have links on your site, double-check that each one works. And if you have links to other people's sites, check the links occasionally to make sure that the page you're linking to still exists.

✔ **Test your site.** Before you sign off on your site design, check it from a slow modem. You instantly get a sense of whether your site is dialup friendly. If it's slow to load or confusing, keep working on it until it works. You may also want to check your site using different Internet browsers and screen resolutions to make sure that your site still looks good.

✔ **Make your site your browser's home page.** I had a site down for weeks because I didn't have it set as my default site in my browser. I never found out until I got a call from a friend who told me it was down.

For more tips and tricks on creating a great Web site, check out *Creating Web Pages All-in-One Desk Reference For Dummies* (Wiley).

Putting up your site

After you design your site, you need to find an ISP (Internet service provider) to host it. Most ISPs allow you to put up a personal Web page for free, but if you want to do any business from it, you generally need to pay to have your site hosted. The exception is Geocities (geocities.yahoo.com/home), which lets you put up a site for free. Geocities also has an inexpensive domain-hosting option ($8.95 per month), where you can have your name as your URL (www.jeffstrong.com, for instance).

This leads me to the whole domain name thing, that is, a Web address that contains your name or your band's name. If you want your own domain name, you need to register it and pay a fee. It used to be that all domain names were purchased through Internic (now Network Solutions), but now you can get a domain name in a lot of places.

To find a place to buy and register your domain name, search for *domain registration* in your favorite Internet search engine. You'll end up with a ton of matches to get you started.

After you choose an ISP and register a domain name — if you choose to go that route — it's just a matter of putting up your site and making sure that it works. Your ISP may either give you detailed instructions on how to do this or do it for you.

Getting noticed

If you set up your own Web site, make sure that you submit it to as many search engines as you can; otherwise, people may not be able to find you. You can do this one of the following ways:

✔ **Submit your Web site information to each search-engine site by hand.** This means going to each site, such as Yahoo, and filling out the submission form.

✔ **Hire a submission service to do this for you.** These services enter your Web site information on hundreds (sometimes thousands) of sites for you. These businesses charge a fee that ranges from about $40 to $150, depending on the services and other benefits they offer. The range of services offered by these companies includes one-time submissions to repeated submissions, sometimes as often as every 48 hours.

✔ **Buy software to automatically submit your Web site information for you.** The software can cost more than the submission service does, but with this software, you can submit your information more than once and be sure that your submission goes through. Some software even tracks your ranking in the various search engines.

The major search engines used to include any site for free. All you had to do was complete a submission form describing your Web site and you were set. This has changed dramatically over the last year or so. Now, for larger search engines, such as Yahoo, you need to pay a fee if you're a commercial site — that is, if you intend to sell anything. These fees can be quite high ($299 on Yahoo, for instance).

If your site isn't a commercial site, you can still list for free, but completing the submission form may not get you into a search engine's system. You may have to submit more than once. Also, keep in mind that it can take a month or more for your site to show up after you've placed your submission.

Providing Your Music Online

If you have a Web site, you probably want your visitors to be able to hear your music. You can make your music available for listening online in two ways: by download or by streaming audio. Music downloads are files that your visitors can download to their hard drives and listen to anytime that they want. Streaming audio, in contrast, is a file that your visitor connects to that plays without being copied to your visitor's hard drive. Each of these options has its advantages, which I outline in the following sections.

Offering downloads

Online promotion of your music almost requires you to make downloads available to your potential fans. You can talk about your music all you want, but what people want is to *hear* your music. The purpose of the download is to get your listener to buy your CD or to come see your show.

Put only a few of your best songs on your site (or any site for that matter). If you make your entire CD available, visitors have no incentive to buy the CD.

Streaming audio

Streaming audio is basically an audio file that begins playing before the entire file is downloaded. The advantage is that it greatly reduces the amount of time your listener has to wait to hear your music. The downside is that the quality of the audio can be lower.

You always want to make the process of navigating your site and listening to your music as fast as possible. This provides a much better experience than having to wait. The less time a person has to wait, the more likely he or she is to return. The more repeat visitors that you get, the better the chance you have for selling CDs.

You can create streaming audio in a number of ways, but the two most common are: a RealAudio file (a file format developed by Real Networks) or an MP3 file. The process is the same with either method, except that your filenames are going to be different. Note that you need an encoder that can create a RealAudio file if you want to go that route.

The following steps walk you through the process of getting your MP3 file to stream on your site:

1. **Create an MP3 file using a bit rate from 20 to 32 Kbps — a good range for streaming audio when used over dialup modems.**

2. **Save the MP3 file so that you can identify it.**

   The easiest way to do this is to save your file as *songname*24.mp3 (the 24 stands for 24 Kbps).

3. **Create a pointer file and name it** *songname*24.m3u.

   A *pointer file* is a file that directs your visitor's audio player to the song so that it plays without waiting for the entire song to download. This file contains directions to your MP3 file. For example, your file would contain the following text: http://www.*YourWebSiteAddress*/*songname*24.mp3.

   Keep in mind that if your visitor doesn't have an audio player, he can't listen to your music. It's a good idea to put a link on your site to another site where your listener can download an audio player.

4. **Create a hyperlink on your Web page to the** *songname*24.m3u **file.**

   For example, you can put the hyperlink in some text, like this: Check out our new song, *songname*; then link the text to the file. Or, you can place the hyperlink in a picture or graphic (or both).

5. **Upload your MP3 file, your pointer file, and the new page with your hyperlink to your Web site.**

6. **Go to your Web site and see whether it works.**

Make sure that your site-hosting service has its MIME types configured for MP3. Otherwise, your audio files won't work. (Don't worry. The people who work for your hosting service will know what you're talking about when you mention MIME types. That's their job.)

If all this sounds like too much work, you can just create a link to the streaming files on your MP3 host site. This way, people can still hear your music, even if it isn't available on your site.

Selling Your CDs

Regardless of whether you have your own site, you can always sell your CDs on the Internet through other outlets. An advantage to selling your music through other online stores is that you can capitalize on the traffic that the store generates. A number of online retailers are out there, but the following list gives you the lowdown on some of the major players:

- **CD Baby** (www.cdbaby.com): CD Baby is an online music store that specializes in independent artists. It puts your CD on its site for a small setup fee ($35). For this, you get a Web page (which the people at CD Baby design) with pictures, bios, MP3s, and streaming audio. The site sells your CD for any price you set, takes 9 percent from the sale, and gives you the rest. You even receive an e-mail whenever someone buys one of your CDs. Signing up is easy; just direct your browser to www.cdbaby.com and click the Sell Your CD icon. The instructions are clear, and a lot of helpful articles on the site can help you to, well, sell your CD.

- **GarageBand.com** (www.garageband.com/musicians): GarageBand.com works in partnership with CD Baby. You just set up a membership with CD Baby and list your music on GarageBand.com. This gives you more exposure with no extra expense. GarageBand.com also has some great information to help you sell more of your music and get gigs.

- **Amazon.com** (www.amazon.com): Yes, you can get your music on Amazon.com, boasted as the world's largest online retailer. Amazon.com has an Advantage program that allows you to put your CD on its site and compete with the major-label artists. All you need is a professional CD (retail-ready) package with a UPC code on it. To join, point your browser to www.amazon.com and click the Join Advantage link at the bottom of the page. Follow the directions, and you'll have your music on the most prominent online retailer in no time.

Because the Internet is constantly changing and growing, you may find other sites that allow you to sell your music online. Use your favorite search engine to search for the phrase *sell your CD*. This gives you a ton of other places to consider selling your CD online.

Making the Most of the Web

The whole point of making CDs and putting MP3s of your music on the Internet is to promote and sell your music. To do this, you need exposure. Like any promotion technique, there are no rules except to use your imagination. Experience will be your guide, but here are some ideas to get you started:

✔ **Start an e-mail newsletter.** An e-mail newsletter is an inexpensive way to keep your music on people's minds. Try to be somewhat consistent in sending it out, but don't just send out the same message on a regular basis. Give your subscribers something. Provide new information in your e-mail, such as a press release about where you're playing next or a link to a new song that you've just uploaded. *Note:* Don't send your newsletter to anyone who hasn't asked to receive it. This is called *spamming,* and it's not nice. To build a subscriber list, encourage people to fill in your mailing list sign-up forms at your gigs and on your Web site. Always provide a way for them to unsubscribe to your list and make it easy to do so.

✔ **Put your Web site address on everything.** People can't come to you if they don't know that you exist. So print your Web site address on all your promotional materials, including the CD itself. Also, include your Web site address on all e-mails and Internet correspondence that you send (for example, as a signature on Internet forums).

✔ **Network.** Check out as many independent musician sites as you can. You not only find out a lot about marketing your music, but you also have an opportunity to spread the word about your music. Check out GarageBand.com (www.garageband.com), Getsigned.com (www.get signed.com), and indiecentre.com (www.indiecentre.com) for starters.

✔ **Stay up to date.** Keep track of where you put your music, and check back often to make sure that everything is working properly. Web sites change and go out of business often. Unless you check the site occasionally, you may not know whether your music has disappeared. Also, routinely search for new places to put your music.

✔ **Get linked.** Try to get folks to link from their sites to your own. Likewise, share the wealth and link to other sites that you like. Cross promotion can be a good thing and allow you to pool your fan base with another band. This doesn't take away from your sales (after all, you listen to more than one band's CDs, right?). Visitors to your site will appreciate the link and will probably check back to see whether you have added new links.

Part VI
The Part of Tens

The 5th Wave
By Rich Tennant

"No, I don't want my CDs browned or toasted – I want them _burned_."

In this part . . .

The Part of Tens is a staple of every *For Dummies* book. This Part of Tens contains some information and resources that you can use every day. Chapter 18 contains ten great home recording resources as you continue your search for recording excellence. Chapter 19 provides ten tips that you can use in your studio to improve the quality of your recordings.

Chapter 18

Ten Home Recording Resources

As you can probably figure out from this book, audio recording is a complex subject and one that you can spend a lifetime exploring. Given that, and given that this book can only contain so much information, I've included this chapter so that you can further your pursuit of audio perfection.

In this chapter, you find ten categories for recording resources that can help you further your audio-recording knowledge (not to mention your desire for more gear — a dangerous thing, I know). I introduce you to magazines, Internet resources, and recording resources in your own backyard, among other things.

E-Mail Newsletters

Granted, e-mail newsletters are generally sponsored by music retailers or magazine publishers who want you to go to their sites and hopefully buy something. As transparent as newsletters are as a means of trying to get you to shell out some money, many of the articles included in them are nevertheless well written and informative. Dozens of e-mail newsletters on recording are being published, and more are showing up every month. Here are a few to get you started:

```
www.digitalprosound.com
www.prorec.com
www.soundonsound.com
www.taxi.com/transmitter/0504/
```

Friends

Your friends can be invaluable in helping you discover how to make great recordings. If you have friends who are musicians, you can often talk them into playing on your songs or even get them to collaborate with you on some music. Or, you can record your friends' music to help you find out more about recording. After all, the experience you gain from recording other people can translate into better-sounding music of your own.

Even if your friends aren't musicians, you can often find out a lot about your music by letting your friends listen to what you've recorded. Getting honest and encouraging feedback from a nonmusician may help you see your music more clearly. On the other hand, you sometimes need to be careful about letting nonmusicians comment on your work if they are unable to offer helpful criticism.

Internet User Groups

A *user group* is a place where people who are interested in a particular product (like the Roland V-Studios, for example) can go to discuss problems they may be having with their systems and to share tricks and tips on how to use the product. A user group exists for almost every audio-recording product made. On the Internet, you can find user groups by typing the product name and *user group* into your favorite search engine or go to groups.google.com. You may also find a link to a product's user group on the manufacturer's Web site.

User groups can be helpful not only if you own the product and want to share information about it but also if you want to know whether a particular product is a good choice for you to buy. You can generally find out all about a product's issues, both good and bad, on these sites.

Internet Forums

Dozens of great Internet forums (message boards) cover audio recording, both home recording and pro audio recording. You can find many of them by doing an Internet search for *recording forum* or *home recording forum,* but here are a few great sites to get you started:

```
www.musicplayer.com
www.audioforums.com
www.vsplanet.com
www.homerecording.com
recordingwebsite.com
www.recording.org
```

Local Commercial Studios

Sitting in on a recording session run by an experienced engineer who has the patience to share his or her techniques can save you hundreds of hours of trying to figure out things, such as gain staging, mic placement, mixing, and effects usage. Often the owners or engineers of local recording studios let you sit in on a session (usually for a fee) and may show you some of the techniques that they use.

You can find these studios by looking in your local yellow pages (under *recording studios*), or you can ask around at your local music store for commercial studios in your area.

Local Music and Pro Audio Stores

Your local music or pro audio store can be a great place to meet other people who are interested in recording. Some stores even have user groups where you can meet and discuss recording without using the Internet forums. You can find listings for these stores in your local yellow pages under *musical instrument retailers* or *audio recording sales and service*. Also, many manufacturers tour these stores and often offer free clinics on how to use their products.

Magazines

Magazines can not only keep you informed about recording tips and techniques, but can also let you know about new products and product upgrades. Even if you don't read the articles, the ads are enough to provide you with lots of gear lust. (I apologize in advance for any discomfort this may cause you.) Several recording magazines are on the market, and the most common are as follows:

- *Home Recording: Home Recording* magazine is published nine times per year. You can find out more about it by calling 800-937-0420 or by going to www.homerecordingmag.com.

- *Recording:* Published monthly, *Recording* magazine can be reached by calling 800-582-8326 or by sending an e-mail to info@recordingmag.com.

- *EQ: EQ* is a monthly publication with the addition of a yearly buyer's guide issue. You can contact *EQ* by calling 212-378-0449, by sending an e-mail to circulation@uemedia.com, or by visiting its Web site (www.eqmag.com).

- *Electronic Musician: Electronic Musician* is published monthly. You can reach the magazine on the Internet at www.emusician.com or by calling 800-245-2737.

- *Pro Audio Review: Pro Audio Review* is published monthly. You can subscribe by calling 703-998-7600.

- *Mix: Mix* magazine is published monthly and can be reached at www.mixmag.com or by calling 800-843-4086.

Online Articles

You can find articles on the Internet about everything from MIDI to miking and mixing to effects. You can even sign up for full-length online audio engineering courses. Heck, you can find an article on just about any part of audio recording on the Internet — often for free.

Finding these articles can be challenging, but here are a few ways you can start:

- Join one of the Internet forums and post a topic asking other members where they find online articles.

- Go to the home page of the Internet forum or e-mail newsletter. You'll often find a few articles worth reading.

- Check out online musical instrument retailers. Many of them post articles online.

Other People's Music

You can find out a lot by listening to other people's music. Good or bad, any music that you hear is going to show you something about recording, playing an instrument, or songwriting. Listen to as much music as you can.

Recording Schools

Quite a few professional recording schools operate around the country. The courses that they offer range from intensive two-week courses on basic engineering skills to a full-blown degree program designed to qualify you for a job in a commercial studio. If you're interested in a recording school, you can do a search on the Internet or try these places:

- ✔ **Berklee College of Music:** Boston, MA. You can find out about the program at www.berklee.edu or by calling 800-421-0084.

- ✔ **The Institute of Audio Research:** New York, NY. This school can be contacted by calling 212-777-8550 or by visiting its Web site at www.audioschool.com.

- ✔ **Recording Institute of Technology:** Los Angeles, CA. You can contact this school at www.mi.edu or by calling 323-462-1384.

- ✔ **SAE Institute:** New York, NY, and Nashville, TN. Online, go to www.sae.edu. You can also call the school at 212-944-9121 (NY) and 615-244-5848 (TN).

- ✔ **Los Angeles Recording Workshop:** Los Angeles, CA. You can reach this school by calling 818-763-7400 or by going to www.recordingcareer.com.

- ✔ **The Recording Workshop:** Chillicothe, OH. You can find out about the Recording Workshop at www.recordingworkshop.com or by calling 800-848-9900.

- ✔ **Music Tech/College of Contemporary Music and Recording Arts:** Minneapolis, MN. The school's Internet address is www.musictech.com, and its phone number is 612-338-0175.

Ask around about the benefit of going to a recording school and you'll find some strong opinions. Some people believe that having a certificate from one of these schools can help you land a job, and others will tell you that you're wasting your money. The truth is that the recording industry is changing and jobs aren't as plentiful as they used to be (and they weren't that plentiful back in the heyday of big-budget recording). So if finding stable and steady employment in the audio industry is your goal, I recommend that you get a four-year bachelor's degree in audio engineering, electrical engineering, or even business administration over getting an associate's degree from a trade school. Even with such a four-year degree, you may end up having to find work in a related field at some point in your career.

Chapter 19

Ten Invaluable Recording Tips

Throughout this book, I suggest things that you can do to make your recordings as good as possible. In this chapter, I present you with more simple and effective tricks that you can use to improve the quality of your recordings. You find ways to add more of that sought-after analog sound to your music, fatten up your tracks (add more depth), and increase the overall feel (artistic interpretation) of your performances. You also discover a couple of tips to help you improve the sound of your room, make the editing process easier and quicker, and double-check your mix before you call your song finished.

Using an Analog Tape Deck

If you have a digital recorder and yearn for that analog sound, you can run the tracks out of your recorder, into an analog tape deck, and back into the digital recorder. You can do this for drum tracks or even the final two-track mix. By blending the tape-saturated tracks back in with the original ones, you can add as much or as little of the distorted analog sound into your clean digital tracks as you want and reverse anything that you've done later.

This procedure is really simple. Just bus (route) the outputs of your recorder to the inputs of your analog tape deck, and run cords from the outputs of your tape deck back into two empty tracks in your digital recorder. You can then mix these two new tracks with your originals.

A slight time delay (a few milliseconds) occurs between the original tracks and the returned ones. If you have a graphical editor, you can eliminate this time delay by following these steps:

1. **Choose a single snare drum or bass drum stroke on both sets of tracks.**

2. **Enter the waveform graphical mode and compare the two waveforms to see where they differ; you can use your cursor to determine the distance between the two beats.**

   See Chapter 13 to find out more on editing.

3. **Cut that distance from the front of the tape-returned tracks.**

4. **Double-check your work by listening to both sets of tracks.**

   If both beats play at exactly the same time, you're done. If not, just click the Undo button and try again.

If you don't have a waveform editor, you eliminate the time delay by listening. You can start by picking a time, 20 ms for instance, and deleting it from the front of the tape deck–enhanced tracks. Listen and make any adjustments from there. With a little experimenting and a dose of patience, you can find the right amount to cut. Make a note of this amount because this number will be the same the next time you do this procedure.

Layering Your Drum Beats

If you use a drum machine or an electronic drum set to play your drum rhythms, you can make these rhythms much fatter by layering one sound on top of another. Likewise, you can use this technique to add sampled drum sounds to your acoustic drum tracks to fatten them as well.

If you recorded your drums using MIDI, just duplicate the drum tracks that you want to add to, select the drum that you want to duplicate, and change its patch number to match a sound that you want to add. Depending on your drum machine's polyphony, you may need to record the original tracks to audio before you play the second set of drum sounds. (You can find out more about using MIDI in Chapter 5.)

If your original tracks are from an acoustic drum set, you have to trigger the sound from the drum machine by hand (press the trigger pads in time to the music), or if your audio software has the capabilities (Logic Audio, for example), you can create a MIDI file from the audio track. Then just choose the instruments that you want to have triggered from the new MIDI track.

Decorating Your Room

When you set up your studio, think about the types of materials you use for furniture, floor, and wall treatments. You can improve the sound of your room simply by using materials and furniture to absorb or reflect sound. For example, you can use a couch to catch some of the room's reflections or a bookcase placed on the wall behind you to deflect some sound waves. Carpet on the floor or curtains over your windows absorb sound. In contrast, wood floors and bare walls add reflections and give your room a more live sound.

If you think about how the furniture and decorations in your studio affect sound, you can save time and money when you optimize your room for recording.

Setting a Tempo Map

Before you start to record, set a tempo map of the song within your system. You do this by entering the number of measures (on some systems), the time signature, and the tempo for each section of the song in the Tempo Map or Metronome dialog box in your system. Then, when you record, play to this metronome.

When it's time to do your editing, just choose the section(s) of your song that you want to edit by cueing the measure and beat that you want to work with. This enables you to choose edit points much faster and more accurately and makes quick work of producing loops or assembling a song from parts.

Listening to Your Mix in Mono

After all the effort that you put into getting each instrument to sit exactly where you want it in the stereo field, the last thing you probably want to do is to listen to the song in mono. Doing so, however, enables you to see your mix differently and to hear whether any of your instruments are crowding out the others. Even if you like to have stuff moving in the mix, listening to your song in mono can help you to find problems in the arrangement.

If it sounds good in mono, it generally sounds great in stereo.

Doubling and Tripling Your Tracks

If a track sounds thin to you in the mix, just make a copy of it onto an empty track (if you have one) and use both of them in the mix. Doubling or tripling a track is called *multing* and is especially useful for vocals, particularly backup vocals.

If you don't have the tracks to spare, make a copy of the track you want to mult onto a separate virtual track and then combine those two tracks by using a bounce procedure, which I explain in Chapter 11. You can do this as many times as you want with digital recorders because you don't lose sound quality in the process. If you want, you can mult dozens of times and end up with really thick tracks (don't overdo it though — lots of thick tracks added together can create a muddy mix).

Tapping the Input of Your Mixer

Tapping the input of your mixer means eliminating the mixer's circuitry from the signal. Depending on your mixer, this may provide you with a better sound going to disk. If you have an analog mixer, you may be able to tap the inputs when you record. Tapping the inputs involves using a Y cable. The TRS plug of the Y cable connects to the mixer's input jack, one of the TS plugs goes to your preamp, and the other TS plug goes to your recorder. Check your owner's manual to see whether you can tap the input of your mixer.

The downside to tapping the inserts on your mixer is that your EQ or fader doesn't affect the signal, so make sure that you get the best sound you can from your instrument and get the levels going into the mixer exactly how you want them going to tape.

Overdubbing Live Drums

If you're like most home recordists, you record most of your drum tracks with a drum machine or electronic drum set. You may find them thin-sounding or a bit stiff. A good remedy for both the thinness and stiffness can be overdubbing (adding separate tracks) some real drums or cymbals to add to the electronic ones.

For example, you can add real hi-hats to a rock song. Eliminate the drum machine hi-hats, keep the electronic kick and snare, and play the hi-hat part to the other drums. In many cases, the variable nature of the hi-hats is what creates the feel of the drumming. I discuss overdubbing in detail in Chapter 11.

Pressing Record, Even During a Rehearsal

Get your instruments, mics, and levels set before you start to rehearse your part. Then when you start to practice, press the Record button. You may be surprised when you catch the perfect performance before you plan to record a serious take.

Leaving the Humanity in Your Tracks

Along the same lines of recording your rehearsals, don't be so hooked on getting every note just right that you miss the feel of a performance. Listen to some of the greatest records ever made and you can hear little mistakes. In fact, it's those little mistakes that often make those records so great. So before you go autotuning and editing the life out of your music, give it a good listen and see whether that note you want to fix is what gives the part its character.

Index